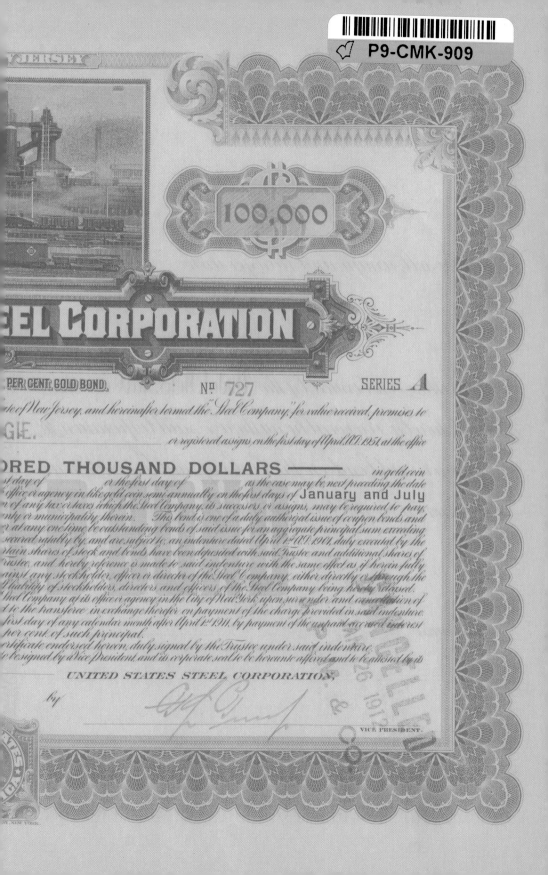

...Y JERSEY

100,000

...EEL CORPORATION

... PER CENT. GOLD BOND. N⁰ 727 SERIES A

...te of New Jersey, and hereinafter termed the "Steel Company," for value received, promises to

...GIE.

...or registered assigns on the first day of April, A.D. 1951, at the office

...DRED THOUSAND DOLLARS —————— in gold coin

...st day of ... or the first day of ... as the case may be, next preceding the date ...office or agency in like gold coin semi-annually on the first days of January and July ...n of any tax or taxes which the Steel Company, its successors or assigns, may be required to pay, ...nty or municipality therein. This bond is one of a duly authorized issue of coupon bonds and ...r at any one time be outstanding bonds of said issue for an aggregate principal sum exceeding ...secured ratably by, and are subject to, an indenture dated April 1st A.D. 1901, duly executed by the ...tain shares of stock and bonds have been deposited with said Trustee and additional shares of ...rustee, and hereby reference is made to said indenture with the same effect as if herein fully ...inst any stockholder, officer or director of the Steel Company, either directly or through the ...l liability of stockholders, directors and officers of the Steel Company being hereby released. ...Steel Company at its office or agency in the City of New York upon surrender and cancellation of ...d to the transferee in exchange therefor on payment of the charge provided in said indenture. ...first day of any calendar month after April 1st 1911, by payment of the unpaid accrued interest ...per cent. of such principal. ...certificate endorsed hereon, duly signed by the Trustee under said indenture. ...designed by a Vice President, and its corporate seal to be hereunto affixed and to be attested by its

UNITED STATES STEEL CORPORATION,

by

VICE PRESIDENT.

# MEET YOU IN HELL

### ANDREW CARNEGIE, HENRY CLAY FRICK, AND THE BITTER PARTNERSHIP THAT TRANSFORMED AMERICA

## LES STANDIFORD

CROWN PUBLISHERS
NEW YORK

Published in the United States by Crown Publishers, an imprint of the
Crown Publishing Group, a division of Random House, Inc., New York.
www.crownpublishing.com

Crown is a trademark and the Crown colophon is a registered trademark
of Random House, Inc.

Library of Congress Cataloging-in-Publication Data

Standiford, Les.
Meet you in hell : Andrew Carnegie, Henry Clay Frick, and the bitter partnership
that transformed America / Les Standiford.—1st ed.
Includes bibliographical references and index.
1. Carnegie Steel Company—History.   2. Steel industry and trade—United
States—History.   3. Homestead Strike, Homestead, Pa., 1892.   4. Carnegie,
Andrew, 1835–1919.   5. Frick, Henry Clay, 1849–1919.   6. Industrialists—
United States—Biography.   7. Capitalists and financiers—United States—
Biography.   I. Title.
HD9519.C2S83 2005
338.7'669142'092273—dc22      2004030947

ISBN 1-4000-4767-6

Printed in the United States of America

*Design by Leonard Henderson*

10 9 8 7 6 5 4 3 2 1

First Edition

To the extended Patterson and Standiford clans
of southeastern Ohio and western Pennsylvania,
so many of them miners, millworkers, and farmers—
decent, hardworking men and women every one.

And to Jeremy, Hannah, and
Alexander, who join the line.

# CONTENTS

# ACKNOWLEDGMENTS

———◆———

I OWE A GREAT DEBT TO A NUMBER of people who have helped me on my way with this book, not least among them Scott Waxman and Emily Loose, who encouraged me to undertake this project to begin with. Very special thanks are due to Michael J. Dabrishus, archivist for the University of Pittsburgh Library, and to Julie Ludwig, assistant archivist for the Frick Art Reference Library in New York, as well as to Donald Swanson, chief of preservation for that same institution.

I would also like to thank Dan Fales, former director of the Frick Art and Historical Center in Pittsburgh; Ron Baraff, director of Museum Collections & Archives for the Rivers of Steel National Heritage Area; John Blades, director of the Henry Morrison Flagler Museum; Gerald Costanzo, director of the Carnegie Mellon University Press; Gil Pietrzak, photo archivist at the Carnegie Library of Pittsburgh; Faye Haun, rights and reproductions associate, Museum of the City of New York; and Millicent S. Monks, David Demarest, Kristin Kovacic, Kimberly Witherspoon, Mitchell Kaplan, Joseph Kaplan, James W. Hall, Rhoda Kurzweil, and William Beesting for their guidance and their invaluable help along the way. I would also like to extend a special note of thanks to Rachel Klayman at Crown for her careful eye, for her innumerable helpful suggestions, and for her unfailing support.

And finally, my deepest appreciation to my wife, Kimberly, who reminds me every day that books are written one word at a time.

# NOTE FROM THE AUTHOR

———◆———

G IVEN THE HISTORICAL SIGNIFICANCE of the United
States' steel industry and the storied exploits of its leaders,
there exists a vast archival record concerning the events and
individuals taken up in this book. In addition, the past century has
seen the publication of several biographies of Andrew Carnegie and
Henry Clay Frick as well as any number of treatises on iron and steel,
many of them exhaustive. I am not sure there is a single salient fact
concerning any of these subjects that has escaped the attention of
some previous writer, somewhere. And yet, my purpose is not—to
paraphrase the noted Texas historian J. Frank Dobie—to unearth
and rebury the same old bones of history. Instead, I have turned my
focus upon the thread of a relationship and have restricted my attention for the most part to matters pertaining thereto. Readers who desire a more extensive examination of any single aspect of this story
will find a selected bibliography at the end of the text. The books
cited there have been invaluable sources. In the instances where I
refer to information unique to any single publication, I have endeav-
ored to provide a citation in the text.

A word is also in order regarding the worth of Carnegie's holdings in today's dollars. If the present value of Carnegie's haul from the
sale of his companies in 1901 were computed based on changes in the
Consumer Price Index it would be about $8 billion, making him a rel-

ative piker compared to modern-day tycoons. However, according to a formula devised by Michael Klepper and Robert Gunther in their 1996 book *The Wealthy 100*, the value of a personal fortune is better understood in relation to the total gross national product of an individual's era. By that measure, Carnegie was worth $112 billion in his day, far ahead of Bill Gates ($85 billion), Sam Walton ($42 billion), or Warren Buffett ($31 billion). Carnegie was to remain the world's wealthiest individual for more than a decade, and he is number two on the all-time list, behind only John D. Rockefeller, whose forced liquidation of Standard Oil in 1913 netted him $212 billion in today's dollars. Readers wishing to convert the dollar figures in this volume may wish to use the 200x factor as a rough indicator of modern equivalencies.

# MEET
# YOU
# IN HELL

If I have not been able to avoid the reputation of being rich during my life, death will at last free me from this stain.

—JOHN CALVIN

Success consecrates the most offensive crimes.

—SENECA

# PRELUDE

## EYE OF THE NEEDLE

———•———

W HEN I UNDERTOOK THIS RETRACING of the intertwined and singular lives of Andrew Carnegie and Henry
Clay Frick, two of the most influential men to emerge
from a remarkable historical period that spawned so many earth-
roaming titans, I was well aware of the conflicted feelings I held
toward my subjects.

After all, I grew up in the 1950s in the hills of southeastern Ohio,
the child of working-class parents in a mining and manufacturing
center. For many years I had watched as my mother and father and
my many aunts and uncles rose early (or late, depending on the shifts
they worked), packed their lunches into bags or tins, and made their
way to the mines or the factories where they fought the machines and
tended the lines for eight largely uninterrupted hours, earning the
wages that kept us going from paycheck to paycheck.

Though Carnegie and Frick were long gone, their legacies were
largely intact and robust. School field trips often took me and my
classmates to the nearby metropolis of Pittsburgh, where the smoke
from the mighty blast furnaces of U.S. Steel and Jones and Laughlin
and so many others turned every Monongahela Valley day into dusk.
The United States was the undisputed leader of the industrialized
world, and the proof, in Pittsburgh, was everywhere we looked.

And if my parents and my aunts and uncles were awe-inspiring
in their ability to rise each day and repeat the same tasks over and
over and over again, without complaint, then those men we saw in

Pittsburgh tending the giant furnaces, dodging railcars, stirring cauldrons of molten steel, breathing air that stunted oak trees into bonsai and dusted faces black, exuded a strength and endurance that seemed superhuman.

How could anyone do such work? I wondered. I knew that I could not.

I had seen that famous television episode from *I Love Lucy* where Lucy and Ethel are ordered to the assembly line in a candy factory, charged with boxing up the endless flow of bonbons to their stations. In short order, the belt speeds up and the rate of arriving chocolates outstrips the ability of our heroines to pack them up. Those who see this episode often find themselves weeping with laughter as Lucy jams chocolates into her apron, stuffs them in her cheeks, tosses the damned things anywhere and everywhere in a doomed attempt to keep up. When I see the episode repeated, I laugh, too, but always with a note of dismay, for I can never forget how the scene struck me the first time I saw it. To my ten-year-old sensibilities, it was as tragic as it was comic.

If you couldn't meet the demands of the assembly line, I knew, you were no more useful than any other piece of dysfunctional machinery. You'd be replaced. And where would the groceries come from then?

Sure, I was smart enough to get the joke, but I also knew that Lucy's bug-eyed panic was a way of making a hard truth a little more bearable.

At the same time, my parents and my aunts and uncles were quick to tell me how fortunate they were to have the opportunity to work. Furthermore, they pointed out, I was doing well in school, so well in fact that I might even entertain the notion of going to college, something that no one in our extended clan had ever done. With this education, I could transform myself and my prospects, and indeed I have often described my life as one long, unbroken effort to stay off the assembly line.

The upside of my family's story was reflected in the books of Horatio Alger Jr., copies of which I pulled from my grandmother's shelves and devoured, along with other rags-to-riches tales, many of them slender, orange, cloth-bound biographies of famous Americans who had risen from nothing.

"We have neither kings nor princes here," one of my teachers often said. "You young men and women can become anything you want. That is the blessing of living in America."

He was right, of course. I have in fact managed to stay off the assembly line. William Jefferson Clinton rose from a broken, abusive home to become president. Andrew Carnegie rose from a penniless wretch to become the richest man in the world, just as every week someone, somewhere, wins the lottery. And if the cynics among us might liken it all to a giant pyramid scheme, at least it can be argued that the few top spots are open to all.

This contradiction at the heart of capitalist enterprise has not escaped the attention of theologians, philosophers, and politicians, of course. On the one hand, we have the famous adjuration from the Gospels that "it is easier for a camel to go through the eye of a needle than for a rich man to enter into the kingdom of God," while the reformer John Calvin argues that the acquisition of wealth is a sign of God's preordained favor. In his groundbreaking work *The Protestant Ethic and the Spirit of Capitalism,* the sociologist Max Weber suggests that Calvin's ideas led to such a sea change among churchmen and their followers that by the beginning of the twentieth century, "doing the Lord's work" and "turning a profit" had become indistinguishable virtues.

In his often-anthologized short story "In the Heart of the Heart of the Country," William H. Gass speaks of the vast numbers of Midwestern farmers and working people who have for decades voted "squarely against their interests," presumably due to some emotionally laden issue dear to the conservative heart—but it is just as likely that these are quite logical individuals eager to support a system in which a son or a daughter might someday, somehow, manage to climb a rung or two or twenty up the economic ladder.

One thing is clear: Carnegie and Frick represent the American ethos of limitless possibility more forcefully than any fictional overachieving shoeshine boy or chimney sweep. Both men were born to poverty, and both became wealthy and powerful beyond imagining. Yet the circumstances that led to their extraordinarily successful partnership seem, in retrospect, as inevitable as the plot turns in a Dickens novel.

The impact of their steelmaking enterprise on the economy at the end of the nineteenth century was as profound as the impact of the American Revolution had been on this country's politics and philosophy a century before. The business practices of Carnegie and Frick and the principles they embodied not only made them the industrial potentates of their time, but continue to influence boardroom and labor relations practices to this day. And the rupture of their once "perfect partnership" illuminates the contradictions embodied in those two hallowed pillars of our thinking: capitalism and the Protestant ethic.

Carnegie and Frick were not the first to wrestle with those contradictions and they were most assuredly not the last. But the making and unraveling of their relationship became, for me, an often-troubling exploration of America's promise to us all—a reminder that monumental achievement comes at monumental cost. Their story offers a vivid illustration of a young nation's steadfast belief in progress and in man's ability to affect his own destiny. As the ancients observed, such thinking may be fine for gods; but when mortals attempt to operate on the same plane—even mortals of heroic proportions—tragedy ensues.

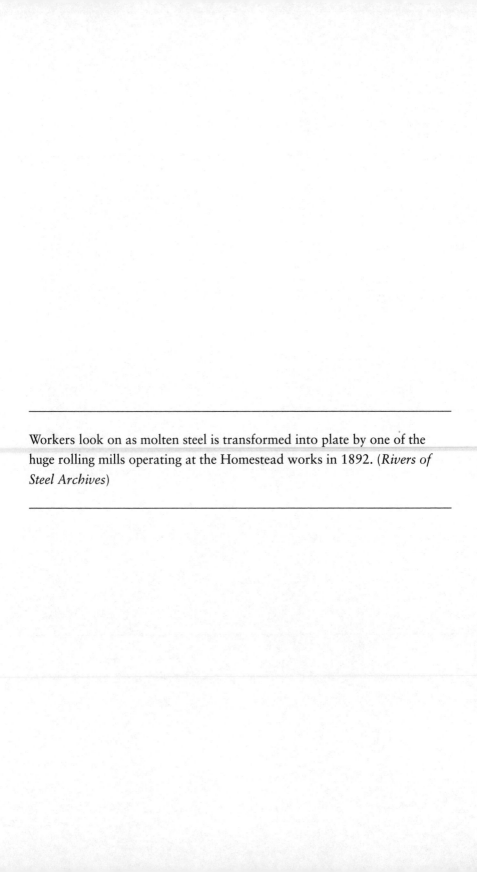

Workers look on as molten steel is transformed into plate by one of the huge rolling mills operating at the Homestead works in 1892. (*Rivers of Steel Archives*)

# PART ONE

# GRAND DESIGN

128" Mill

# 1

## GAUNTLET

———◄-◆-►———

On a late spring day in 1919, so the story goes, only weeks before the Treaty of Versailles put an end to a war that had threatened the very fabric of civilization, one of America's wealthiest men—his holdings valued at more than $100 billion in today's dollars—sat up in his sickbed in his Manhattan home and called to one of his caregivers for a pen and paper.

Andrew Carnegie, eighty-three, once the mightiest industrialist in all the world, now a wizened and influenza-ravaged man who for nearly two years had been under doctors' care in his block-long, six-level mansion on Gotham's Millionaires' Row, took up the instruments brought to him and began to write as if possessed. When he was finished, he summoned to his chambers his longtime personal secretary James Bridge, the man who had helped him write *Triumphant Democracy,* one of the most persuasive tracts ever written in the cause of fair treatment of labor, all the more compelling for its author's position as a titan of industry.

"Take this to Frick," Carnegie said as he handed the letter to his old confidant.

It would have been enough to snap Bridge upright. Surprise

*11*

enough to hear Carnegie mention that name, much less hand over a letter to that person. True, Henry Clay Frick was a fellow giant of industry—recently dubbed one of America's leading financiers by the *New York Times*—and he and Andrew Carnegie had been partners once. Frick had been the man Carnegie trusted above all others to manage the affairs of Carnegie Steel, a manufacturing combine so vast that its output surpassed that of the entire British Empire.

But, so far as anyone knew, the two men had not exchanged a word in nearly twenty years—not since Carnegie drove Frick out of the business and Frick successfully pressed a monumental lawsuit against his former partner, the first in a long string of vengeful acts.

Had Carnegie divulged the contents of the letter, the secretary's expression would have likely turned to outright astonishment. As it was, Bridge left Carnegie and made his way down Fifth Avenue from the awe-inspiring, sixty-four-room mansion across from Central Park at 91st Street to an even more imposing structure some twenty blocks south.

It was Bridge's good fortune that Carnegie had selected him to be the bearer of this missive, proof positive that he had managed his way back into Carnegie's good graces. For it was true that Bridge had authored his own acts of treason against Carnegie. In the early 1900s, while he was working on a revision of *Triumphant Democracy* that would have brought him a renewed flood of royalties, Bridge got word that Carnegie, still stinging from a series of rebukes from labor, would not permit a reissue of the book.

As a result, Bridge did the unthinkable: with information fed to him by Frick and others on the outs with Carnegie, he went to work on a book titled *The Inside History of the Carnegie Steel Company*, an account that reassessed any number of myths concerning Carnegie, including his role in one of the most violent labor strikes in United States history, 1892's infamous Battle of Homestead, where many were killed and injured on both sides. It was an event that had long dogged the thin-skinned Carnegie.

Bridge was fortunate, however; time and circumstance had changed Carnegie's perspective, not only upon the actions of others, but upon a number of his own as well. By most accounts, the last years of Andrew Carnegie were marked by great swings in the mood of "the world's richest man." Carnegie, who acquired that sobriquet in 1901, when he sold his Pennsylvania steel empire to rival J. P. Morgan for the then-unimaginable sum of $480 million, had spent many of the intervening years giving away his fortune.

In addition to the funding of some 2,800 public libraries across the United States and as far away as Fiji and New Zealand, he had endowed the Carnegie Institute of Technology in his adopted hometown of Pittsburgh, Pennsylvania, the Carnegie Research Institution in Washington, D.C., and the Carnegie Educational Foundation in New York City, as well as the Endowment for International Peace. This last endowment was, in the final decade of his life, the cornerstone of his attempts to sway the nations of the world from their fixation upon war as a solution to political problems.

Carnegie's efforts to secure world peace would cost nearly $25 million ($5.5 billion today), but that was a pittance compared to all his giving. According to Carnegie biographer Peter Krass, Carnegie was fond of turning to an assistant during his later years to ask, "How much did you say I had given away, Poynton?" To which the answer was an inevitable "$324,657,399." To this day he is often credited with having established the precedent of corporate philanthropy; as one commentator observed, when Bill Gates makes a gift of some of his hard-earned millions, it is probably the ghost of Andrew Carnegie that guides his outstretched hand.

And yet Carnegie, for all his largesse, remained a troubled man. In 1914, speaking at the anniversary celebration of one of the libraries he had founded in western Pennsylvania, the white-bearded, slightly built benefactor, bearing an odd resemblance to Edmund Gwenn's Santa Claus in *Miracle on 34th Street,* said, "I'm willing to put this library and institution against any other form of benevolence. . . .

And all's well since it is growing better and when I go for a trial for the things done on earth, I think I'll get a verdict of 'not guilty' through my efforts to make the earth a little better than I found it."

Beneath his self-confidence and optimism, the defensive undertone was clear: speaking scant miles from the site of that bloody Battle of Homestead, where steelworkers still lived in bleak houses and lacked the power to organize in any meaningful way, Carnegie knew full well that many a man in Homestead would dispute his claim that all was well and growing better.

And in the five years since 1914, little had changed in the mill towns of Pittsburgh. A massive, nationwide strike to protest wages and working conditions in the steel industry loomed in late 1919, and Homestead still stood as the symbol of labor's difficult struggle. How much guilt Carnegie truly harbored is a secret he would carry to his grave, but the fact that he had sent an eleventh-hour communiqué to the man to whom he'd entrusted the defense of the Homestead plant on the fateful night of July 5, 1892, spoke volumes.

By the time Bridge arrived at the Frick mansion, a modern-day palace that its owner had vowed would make Carnegie's place look like a hovel, Bridge would have been beside himself, not only wondering as to the contents of the message he carried, but fearing the response of the man to whom it was addressed.

Though Frick, like Carnegie, stood at only five feet three inches (at a time when the average man was five feet seven), and was white-bearded by now as well, he would never be mistaken for Santa Claus. Photographs of the era reveal his features as handsome, but Frick's countenance was intimidating, and that had been no hindrance in his dealings with business rivals and union organizers. "You see that his head is there, placed on that body, for his triumph and your defeat," one of his contemporaries observed. Thus, while Carnegie had gone to great pains to portray himself as a benevolent friend to his workers, he had delegated the job of holding the line on wages and other demands to Frick—a Patton to Carnegie's FDR, as it were.

Bridge knew Frick's legendary toughness well—this was one executive as willing to use his fists as his voice to deal with an enemy or a rival—and he could have been forgiven his apprehension as Frick tore open the envelope and scanned its contents.

Frick glanced up at Bridge accusingly, as if the messenger knew full well what was in the letter. "So Carnegie wants to meet me, does he?"

Bridge could only stare back, dumbfounded.

But a meeting was precisely what Carnegie had called for. In his careful script, Carnegie had reasoned that both he and Frick were growing old, and that past grievances were beneath their dignity. In truth, they were first among equals. Surely it was time to meet and patch up the wounds they had inflicted upon each other. Time to make amends and prepare to meet their Maker.

The words might have touched a chord in almost any other man, but Henry Clay Frick, still the ranking board member of U.S. Steel, showed no sign of gratitude or relief.

By this time Bridge might have been edging for the door. Frick's ire was, after all, legendary. He'd gone toe-to-toe with strikers, assassins, and even Carnegie himself, and had rarely met a grudge he could not hold. Long before Frick had constructed the mansion that would dwarf Carnegie's "Highlands" up the street, he had gone out of his way to purchase a tract of land in downtown Pittsburgh, then built a skyscraper tall enough to cast Carnegie's own office building next door in perpetual shadow.

"Yes, you can tell Carnegie I'll meet him," Frick said finally, wadding the letter and tossing it back at Bridge. "Tell him I'll see him in Hell, where we both are going."

# 2

## THE STAGE IS SET

———➤◆◄———

HENRY FRICK'S REACTION ON THAT New York spring day in 1919 can be traced back to the events of a fateful summer in Pittsburgh, Pennsylvania, some thirty years before, when a tragedy unfolded whose reverberations can still be felt. Of course, as is always the case when tracing history, there is no stopping anywhere, truly, for seeking out first causes is something like following the warp and weft of an enormous knitted sweater. Pulling on one string always bunches up another, and smoothing that only leads to the knot in the next, and so it is with the story of Carnegie and Frick.

Still, Independence Day of 1892 will do as a starting point. As that anniversary of the nation's founding approached, most citizens of the United States were aware that their world was changing at a rapid pace—technologically and otherwise—though they could not have understood just how pivotal the era in which they lived would be judged by future historians.

By anyone's lights, material progress was mind-boggling. Though not in widespread use, the device known as the telephone had come into being in 1876, and the electric lightbulb had followed three years later. People everywhere could now dream, at least, of someday having such magical devices at their beck and call.

On the other hand, men were still buttoning up their trousers in 1892, and women needed help with the backs of their full-skirted dresses, for it would be another year before the zipper made its debut. It would be three more years before the movie projector made its first appearance, while the player piano (1894), refrigerated air-conditioning (1902), and the radio station (1920) were still the stuff of dreams and whimsy.

The country, just over a century old, comprised only forty-four states, with Wyoming having joined the fold on July 10, 1890. Still to come were Utah (1896), Oklahoma (1907), and New Mexico and Arizona (1912). As for Alaska and Hawaii, no mention need be made. Battles with Indians were still the stuff of major news: Custer had been dead only sixteen years, and the Battle of Wounded Knee had taken place just before the dawn of the New Year of 1891.

The population of the republic stood at barely 61 million when the results of the official census were announced on June 1, 1890. Some five and a quarter million of them lived in Pennsylvania, second in numbers only to New York's six million. Though Philadelphia was the largest city in the Keystone State, in the far western section lay the important industrial city of Pittsburgh. Its 250,000 residents, living in and about the confluence of the Allegheny and Monongahela Rivers (with ready access to the nearby Ohio), made it—at a time when most substantial commerce still relied on water for the transport of heavy goods—the thirteenth-largest city in the nation.

One day Pittsburgh would be the home of the first radio station (KDKA), and in 1958 Dr. Jonas Salk would, at the University of Pittsburgh, develop the vaccine that would virtually wipe out the disease commonly referred to as "infantile paralysis."

In 1892, however, few Pittsburgh residents would have dreamed of radio stations or miraculous cures, or known, even, of the work of the Duryea brothers, who were about to unveil the first gasoline-powered vehicle. Nor would there have been many streets in the hilly city on which their puny, one-cylinder contraption would have been drivable.

Many more would have been familiar with the phenomenon of the rise of the popular music industry, though no one would have referred to it that way. They might simply have hummed a few bars of "After the Ball," the 1892 creation of a promoter named Charles K. Harris, who wrote and published the song in an unabashed attempt to prove that a popular tune could be marketed as a "million seller."

Harris did not let the absence of a radio network or payola-ready disc jockeys or jukeboxes, which had yet to be invented, deter him. He finagled the inclusion of the song into a highly popular traveling variety show, and would eventually persuade John Philip Sousa to play it daily for visitors to the Chicago World's Fair of 1893. Harris's creation was soon selling as many as five thousand copies of sheet music a day, and would ultimately sell not one million but five million copies. This was a "sky's the limit" country.

The more leisured or literate of the Pittsburgh population might have been familiar with a book titled *Looking Backward: 2000–1887,* a clumsily written but engaging piece of utopian fiction that had become the most popular American novel since *Uncle Tom's Cabin.* Edward Bellamy's novel imagined a future America with no class distinctions, a wholly nationalized industrial establishment, and an equal distribution of wealth. Bellamy's book sparked the formation of many clubs and discussion groups, and was a favorite of socialist-leaning organizations such as Eugene Debs's Populist Party, an organization not unknown in what was rapidly becoming the steel capital of the world.

There was much talk in 1892 Pittsburgh about the upcoming presidential election, in which Democrat Grover Cleveland was waging a spirited campaign against the incumbent Republican, Benjamin Harrison. Cleveland had actually received nearly 100,000 more popular votes when the two had opposed each other in the previous election of 1888 (5,540,000 to 5,447,000), but the tally from the Electoral College had delivered the victory to Harrison, 233 to 168.

In Pittsburgh, a workingman's town, the opinion of the citizenry was divided: many favored the Democrat Cleveland out of general principle; others were prepared to vote for the Republican Harrison, who championed stiff tariffs that protected American-made industrial goods against foreign competition. The tariffs were the brainchildren and the darlings of the steel industry's owners, but laborers, who feared losing jobs because of cheaper foreign imports, supported them, too.

The contest between Cleveland and Harrison was a matter of partisan politics for many, then, but it also symbolized deeper currents in a country still raw and ingenuous. A fierce national pride still united a rebellious populace, among whom a few were old enough to have personal memories of British invaders actually sacking the nation's capital and burning the White House in the early part of the century; and only a quarter of a century previously, a huge civil war had riven the nation over issues of self-governance, territorial integrity, and questions of liberty and justice for all. It was a country that had been forged upon not only the concept of equality, but the practice of it.

And while the finer points of liberty—including universal suffrage and equal rights—remained nettlesome, the expanding Western frontier had for at least a century provided Americans with the illusion of—if not the literal opportunity for—material advancement open to all. This was the land of the gold rush and the land rush and the homestead allotment, and all it might take to advance one's life significantly was the willingness to overcome fear, hitch up the team, and venture toward the unknown.

This grand optimism and expansionist spirit was fueled not only by the advancements in technology that had marked the years since the Civil War, but also by the tremendous growth in industry that supported and grew out of scientific development. The discovery of oil in northwestern Pennsylvania in 1859 touched off one such momentous development, though that industry's initial contribution to American society came in the form of kerosene, an inexpensive fuel for lamps. Suddenly, nighttime illumination was no longer the indulgence of the very few who could afford the cost of whale oil, of which there was a dwindling supply. With John D. Rockefeller and Henry Flagler at the forefront of the Standard Oil combine, production of oil in the United States would grow from two thousand barrels in 1859 to more than 64 million barrels at the end of the century.

Another major development was the vast expansion of the nation's rail system. As the Civil War began, there were fewer than 30,000 miles of track in all the United States, and much of that was in varying gauges and states of repair. Owing to the enterprise of such men as Cornelius Vanderbilt, who had earlier developed the nation's steamship freight and travel network, J. Edgar Thomson, longtime head of the Pennsylvania Railroad, and J. P. Morgan, who threw much of the weight of his family's banking enterprise into rail investment, the 1890s saw the width of railroad tracks standardized and nearly 163,000 miles of roadway put into use.

To build this vast network of track and bridges, no supporting industry was more important than iron and steel. Most of those early 30,000 miles of railway had been made of iron, an industry initially banned in the British colonies but accounting for 835,000 tons of product by 1860. The technological advancements that allowed for the mass production of steel and the vast expansion of the rail system proceeded hand in hand to the end of the nineteenth century, when the United States was turning out 10 million tons of steel, more than Great Britain, France, and Germany combined.

In less than half a century the United States had been transformed—from a largely agrarian and underdeveloped federation of competing interests, to a relatively cohesive economic juggernaut promoting a jackpot mentality in anyone willing to work hard and take the occasional chance.

Perhaps no single individual was more influential in spreading the gospel of upward mobility than Horatio Alger Jr. (1832–1899), whose series of novels featuring the exploits of penniless but morally upright urchins (Tattered Tom, Ragged Dick, et al.) reaping fortune's rewards through decency, hard work, and courage would sell more than twenty million copies. At the other end of the fictional spectrum lay the work of Mark Twain, whose 1873 novel *The Gilded Age* satirized the unbridled greed and political shenanigans indulged in by the politicians and get-rich-quick schemers of the day.

While Twain saw nothing to approve of in the actions of his characters or the real-life manipulators, such as the Tweed Gang, who served as his inspiration, the novel's title would in time come to evoke almost the opposite of what he had intended. The phrase "Gilded Age" is now understood as the largely grand and stirring period in American history stretching from the post–Civil War years through the turn of the century, a time during which the United States would undergo a revolution as significant as the grand political experiment that had forged it in the first place.

During this period, with its political foundations firmly established, the United States would set the stage to become not only moral exemplar to the world, but also its leading economic power. The age of the Founding Fathers was over. The Age of the Titans had begun.

◆　　◆　　◆

IT WAS A TRANSFORMATION that was not without pain or detractors. Writers such as Bellamy and Twain and Hamlin Garland and Stephen Crane (who would initially publish his *Maggie: A Girl of the Streets* in 1893 at his own expense) powerfully portrayed those cast aside or ground beneath the wheels of Manifest Destiny. Eugene Debs tossed aside practical considerations and, as the champion of a rising American labor movement, campaigned fervently if unsuccessfully for the presidency in five elections, espousing what would become the slogan of the Social Democratic Party: "While there is a soul in prison, I am not free."

At the same time, the German sociologist Max Weber was developing the concepts that would form the foundation of *The Protestant Ethic and the Spirit of Capitalism* (1904–1905), in which he sought to explain the profound changes that had taken place in traditional Western culture as a result of the rise of "institutionalized" capitalism.

Weber, a jurist by trade, was no ideologue, and no call for revolution accompanied his analysis. He was quick to point out that capitalist enterprise had been practiced virtually from the beginning of civilization, by emperors, warlords, rug merchants, and buccaneers alike. According to Weber, however, never before had capitalism become so inextricably woven into the ethos of a nation, and the consequences were not all good.

Weber argued that the elevation of capitalism to the status of Protestantism had come as a result of the teachings of a number of post-Reformation followers of Calvin, whose doctrines profoundly altered traditional precepts of their faith. With its emphasis on the concept of predestination, Calvinism placed a premium on the ability of man to judge his place in the hereafter, and material accumulation was put forward as one infallible measure of God's favor.

In time, Weber argued, the concept of working in order to live was reversed. In an industrialized society, man now lived in order to work. And the surest indication of "good" work was the amassing of wealth. Certain elements of traditional iconography—Christ driving the money changers from the temple, the selfless vow of poverty, and the Golden Rule—were turned on their ear. In the new "rational" Protestantism, the single-minded pursuit of profit was not only justified, but became a virtual commandment.

Inevitably, bigger became better, and there were moral arguments to prove it. One of the inescapable corollaries of such thinking, Weber argued, was what he called the "rational capitalistic organization of labor." Workers were no longer individuals but "hands," and the manipulation of the "work force" to provide the maximum profit for an enterprise was not only defensible, but likely to ensure a factory owner a future place among the heavenly host.

While Weber's work remains for many the most influential and provocative in Western social thought, it held little sway among those on the front lines of getting and spending as the nineteenth century neared its close. Balanced against such notions were those of men who had enjoyed the fruits of capitalism, or yearned to do so, no matter what the odds.

If Irish and German immigrants had served their time in the mills and mines of a developing industrial nation and were now threatening business as usual by demanding a say in their working conditions and pay scales, there were also tens of thousands arriving from Eastern Europe to whom even the worst circumstances in the American workplace seemed a godsend. Call a desperate Hungarian just off the boat a scab or a strikebreaker as some might, but it is easy to understand why, with a starving family to feed, he would not listen or even comprehend.

And beyond the promise of mere subsistence in America shone the myth of streets paved in gold that had persisted since the arrival of the first conquistadors. If it had only required of an early settler that he go west, preferably at a young age, to remake himself, then clearly a citizen of the 1890s, with an Alger-like glint in his eye, could point to newly minted real-world models to fuel his most fantastic dreams. One such role model was Henry Flagler, who had left the upstate New York home of his Presbyterian minister father in the early 1850s as an unschooled teenager with twelve cents in his pocket. Forty years later he'd made one $100 million fortune as the co-founder of Standard Oil, and was on his way to making a second as a railroad baron in the untrammeled wilderness of Florida.

The citizens of Pittsburgh could point to their own boys of the streets who had made fabulously good, among them the Scottish immigrant Andrew Carnegie and his rags-to-riches Swiss-German partner, Henry Clay Frick, now steel barons and multimillionaires both. Not only had Carnegie and Frick started with nothing and worked their way to the top, they were local heroes whose accomplishments had provided a livelihood for thousands in the Monongahela Valley and its environs.

If penniless upstarts like Flagler, Carnegie, and Frick could do it, then why couldn't anyone? And if some of their fellow dreamers tumbled beneath the wheels in the attempt, wasn't that just the way of the world?

Furthermore, the unglamorous stuff produced in such vast quantities by the foundries and factories of Carnegie and Frick was itself inspiring. For if the backbone of the first American Revolution had been moral, the spine of the new revolution was forged of steel, and that was a great source of pride in the city of Pittsburgh.

◆　　◆　　◆

THERE HAD BEEN AN IRON INDUSTRY in the New World from the earliest days, with a blast furnace established near what is now Saugus, Michigan, in 1645. The smelting of iron and the production of iron implements such as stove castings, pots and pans, nails, ship plating, and farming tools had continued in the colonies and states ever since, but it remained a cottage industry throughout the seventeenth and eighteenth centuries, with smelting furnaces fueled exclusively by charcoal and their location dictated by proximity to plentiful sources of wood.

In the 1830s, however, things began to change. Anthracite coal, a substance so dense it is classified as rock by geologists, began to supplant charcoal as a source of fuel, and vast deposits of coal had been discovered in western Pennsylvania, leading to the establishment of a number of smelting furnaces in the area. Although England had until then been the undisputed leader in iron production, that, too, was about to change.

Cast iron had formed the backbone of the Industrial Revolution from the earliest days of the eighteenth century, when William Darby introduced in his native England the first large-quantity processes for smelting, casting, and forging quality iron. Iron had its limitations, however: Lower-grade ores contained significant impurities, and products made of it could be brittle, limiting the size and application of finished goods.

Steel, a far superior alloy of iron, had a precise carbon content of between 0.15 and 0.25 percent and was much stronger, more resilient and ductile. First produced in small quantities in Central Asia in the fifteenth century, steel had become more widely available in the mid-eighteenth century, when a Swedish metallurgist, Torbern Bergman, and a British manufacturer, Benjamin Huntsman, developed a process to ensure a more consistent product. "Swedish Steel," however, remained prohibitively expensive, and even one hundred years later, in 1850, total steel production in England, far and away the world leader, was barely 60,000 tons.

In 1855, however, Henry Bessemer received the British patent for a process that would change the world. By forcing a blast of air through a mass of molten iron held inside his "Bessemer" converter, excess carbon and other impurities could be removed and additives reintroduced later. The process allowed for the production of steel at a rate as rapid as one ton per minute, and made it as cheap to produce as iron.

Within five years another method for mass-producing steel—the "open hearth"—was introduced, resulting in even greater efficiency. By the end of the nineteenth century, world production of steel was approaching 30 million tons, some five hundred times what it had been barely a half-century before, and almost totally supplanting the production of iron, which had slipped to 16 percent of the volume of its new cousin.

This prized new substance took the form of rails, ships, I-beams for skyscrapers, endless miles of cable and piping, machinery, armaments, and tin plate for cans, providing the medium with which and upon which the modern world was reshaping itself. Rails already spanned the American continent, extending the possibility of significant commerce to nearly every nook and cranny of the land. True, the automobile industry had not yet been born, and no one could yet imagine the voracious appetites that would be stoked by it. Still, it was clear that steel would lead the way into the new millennium.

If the amount of steel being produced had reached staggering levels, the shift in its locus of production was no less profound. Although the discovery of the western Pennsylvania coalfields had spurred the development of the iron industry in that area, U.S. production of iron before the Civil War remained insignificant, and U.S.-made steel was virtually nonexistent.

However, an American steelmaker named William Kelly had received his own patent for a Bessemer-like "blast" furnace in 1857, spurring new interest in an industry previously fragmented and marginalized in the United States. In addition, the development of the coalfields in Western Pennsylvania had created a plentiful source of "coke," or baked bituminous coal, a substance that could provide the fuel necessary for the economical production of steel in significant quantities.

Less than a decade following the end of the Civil War, the production of iron in the United States had reached 41 percent of that of England, and by 1892 the balance was about to tip in favor of the former colonies for the first time in history. At the same time, Pittsburgh was on its way to its own position of dominance. By 1875, one-quarter of all the iron rolled in the United States came from the city. By the turn of the century Pittsburgh would account for more than half of all the iron and steel made in the United States, and twice as much as was then being made in all of England.

Thus was a single American city on the verge of outstripping all Britannia in the production of the most important ingredient of an industrialized age as Independence Day of 1892 drew near. From a city of fewer than fifty thousand in 1850, Pittsburgh had more than quin-tupled in size, and served as the home of such giants of industry and banking as George Westinghouse, Alfred Hunt and Charles Hall (Alcoa), and Andrew Mellon. None was more important to the "Iron City" than Andrew Carnegie and Henry Clay Frick, whose opera-tions in the city had more than quadrupled their output in the previ-ous decade and were now producing more than a million tons of steel each year.

The facilities of Carnegie, steel plenipotentiary, and his chief exec-utive officer, Henry "King of Coke" Frick, constituted the single most important employer in and around Allegheny County, with nearly four thousand working at their signature mill installation in nearby Homestead, just east of Pittsburgh on the banks of the Monongahela. The Homestead Mill had been built in 1881, when the surrounding village numbered fewer than six hundred. By 1892 the plant had ex-panded to house four new open-hearth furnaces and was by itself the nation's leading producer of rolled steel. The surrounding town of Homestead was now home to nearly eight thousand residents, the wel-fare of virtually every one of them tied to the fortunes of Carnegie Steel.

Since the profits of the company had totaled nearly $5 million in 1890 and steel production at Carnegie was up, totaling more than 20 percent of the entire country's output, the mood in Pittsburgh should have been jovial as the nation's birthday approached.

Instead, a pall had descended, for a strike loomed at Homestead, the premier facility of the Carnegie operations. It was more than a strike, in fact, for the plant's gargantuan operations had been halted summarily by Carnegie and Frick, and a massive new fence topped by guard towers now encircled its perimeter, the entire facility trans-formed to such an extent that the men who had formerly worked there called it "Fort Frick."

Here, in this village on the banks of the Monongahela, at the very time when prospects for the nation and its most vital industry had never been better, loomed the prospect of open warfare. What would transpire there would become known as the Battle of Homestead, the deadliest clash between workers and owners in American labor history, one that would forever tarnish the image of the country's richest man and drive a wedge of acrimony between him and his former partner and right-hand man that would endure to the grave.

"How could we have come to such a pass?" was the question on the lips of more than one resident of Pittsburgh in 1892. It is a question that more than one of its citizens repeats to this very day.

# 3

## BY THE BOOTSTRAPS

———◆•◆———

NDREW CARNEGIE'S ASSOCIATION WITH Pittsburgh dated back some forty-four years, to the summer of 1848, when he arrived as a penniless Scottish immigrant of twelve, along with his father, Will, his mother, Margaret, and his younger brother, Tom (his sister, Anna, had died in 1841). Carnegie's father had been a master weaver in the city of Dunfermline, but in the wake of Ireland's Great Potato Famine he could no longer find work.

As a result, the family sold everything and came, as so many of their fellow Scotsmen did, to America. In the case of Carnegie's family, their journey would end in Allegheny City, a suburb of Pittsburgh, to which Margaret's sister and brother-in-law had immigrated in 1840.

The Pittsburgh that the Carnegies found was a rough-about-the edges manufacturing town of nearly fifty thousand, ideally situated for riverborne commerce. Chockablock with tanneries, cotton mills, and iron smelters, it offered unfettered opportunity for those willing to endure the harsh conditions of factory work. Further schooling, beyond the few years he had received in a rudimentary Scottish classroom, was out of the question for young Andrew, whose mission now was to help his family survive. His first employment was as a bobbin boy in a weaving mill, a six-days-a-week, twelve-hours-per-day occupation for which he was paid $1.20 a week.

Carnegie was diligent and hardworking, however, and what scant schooling he had received in Scotland stuck with him. He found a clerk's position in another mill, and then happened into a position as a delivery boy for a telegraph company in downtown Pittsburgh for what must have seemed the princely sum of $2.50 a week. Before long, Carnegie had picked up telegrapher's skills, including the ability to translate the clicks and clacks of Morse code directly into text or speech. His skill and self-confidence attracted the notice of a number of influential customers, including Thomas Scott, who was then an assistant superintendent for the western division of the Pennsylvania Railroad.

Scott had recently made the decision to string his own telegraph lines for the railroad, and had it in the back of his mind to hire an assistant who would serve as his personal telegraph operator. In February 1853, Andrew Carnegie, not yet eighteen, accepted Scott's offer of the job for thirty-five dollars a month, the first step along his path to greatness.

Working as an assistant for a railroad executive was a vastly less taxing and far more remunerative occupation than that of factory worker or telegraph clerk, of course, but the real benefit to Carnegie was the practical business education that he received from his association with Scott, who also introduced him to the concept of investment. When, in 1856, Scott took him aside to deliver an insider's tip on Adams Express, a delivery company about to sign a favorable contract with the railroad, Carnegie made a fateful decision.

While he lacked the five hundred dollars he needed to invest— "Five hundred cents was nearer my capital," Carnegie wrote in his autobiography—the young telegrapher persuaded Scott to advance him the money, then scurried about to various friends for help in repaying the loan. (Until the day he died, Carnegie perpetuated the myth that his mother mortgaged the family home so that the investment could be made, but biographer Joseph Frazier Wall points to a promissory note in Carnegie's papers that suggests otherwise.)

Whatever the source of funds, the risk paid off. One day not long after he bought the stock, he arrived at work to find an envelope on his desk. Inside was a check for ten dollars from the cashier of the Adams Express Company. These dividends provided the first income "I had not worked for with the sweat of my brow," as Carnegie later wrote in his autobiography. " 'Eureka,' I cried. 'Here's the goose that lays the golden eggs.' "

Not long afterward, more inside information led to Carnegie's investment in the Central Transportation Company, a firm that would soon begin the production of sleeping cars for the railroad, based on patents for seats and convertible couches secured by inventor T. T. Woodruff. By 1863, Carnegie's one-eighth interest in the new company, for which he had originally borrowed about $200, was producing annual dividends of more than $5,000. "Blessed be the man who invented sleep," Carnegie would write.

Meanwhile, by 1859, Scott had become vice-president of the Pennsylvania Railroad, and promoted Carnegie to the post of superintendent of the Western Division, at the offices based in Pittsburgh. Carnegie, then just twenty-four, had officially become an executive, with an annual salary of $1,500.

With his newfound wealth, Carnegie was able to move his family to the suburb of Homewood, only ten miles east of the smoky central city where he had grown up, but light-years away in terms of culture and sophistication. For the first time he mingled on a regular basis with individuals whose educational and social stores were vastly beyond his own. Now the neighbor and regular houseguest of former secretary of war and foreign diplomat William Wilkins, Carnegie resolved to better himself in a fashion that Horatio Alger might have charted for one of his protagonists. He took French lessons, read the classics, refined his table manners, and studied the likes and dislikes of the American leisure class until he felt at ease among his new neighbors.

Meanwhile, with the outbreak of the Civil War, Carnegie's old boss Thomas Scott was summoned to Washington, where he was appointed assistant secretary of war. To help with the charge of moving men and matériel expeditiously across the North's network of rail lines, Scott summoned Carnegie, whose brief but vivid experiences in a panicked Washington convinced him that private enterprise was far more capably organized and directed than government. His disdain for government may have insulated him from guilt regarding later charges that the Pennsylvania Railroad, among others, had gouged the United States for transportation costs of matériel and was thereby profiting from the war.

Although those charges, which ultimately led to a congressional investigation, were indisputably true, the results of the inquiry proved fruitless. In any case the scandal derived from policies put into effect by men much higher in the railroad's hierarchy than Carnegie. For his part, Carnegie had already pledged his allegiance to the railroad and charted his course: He simply turned a blind eye to the matter.

Besides, other matters distracted him from what he considered a stain solely upon his employer's record. In the fall of 1861, shortly after his return from Washington, Carnegie was approached by a group of businessmen (including one of his new Homewood neighbors, iron manufacturer William Coleman) who persuaded him to visit a region north of Pittsburgh where a new substance known as oil had been discovered in quantities so plentiful it was bubbling to the surface of the earth and running freely down the surface of the area's streams. Until then, oil had been of little practical use except as a nostrum believed to cure a wide array of vague ailments, from the vapors to ague. When its by-product, kerosene, proved useful as a substitute for whale's oil in lamps, however, the rush to tie up the rights to oil lands was on.

Carnegie took one look at the mad scene in Pennsylvania's new oil country and made his decision. Parlaying his interest in the sleeping-car company, he was able to raise the necessary cash and join a group of investors to found the Columbia Oil Company. It was another in a series of timely decisions: by 1863 he was receiving nearly $18,000 in yearly dividends from "black gold." In addition, the new company also recapitalized, and shares for which Carnegie had originally paid ten dollars were suddenly worth fifty dollars.

It was a lesson that Carnegie would not forget. When another such venture presented itself in 1862, he did not hesitate. The incidence of sabotage on the North's rail lines had greatly increased with the advent of the Civil War, with wooden trestles and bridges being particularly vulnerable to arson, and Carnegie's old mentor Scott approached him with the notion that he might take advantage of his contacts in and around the Pittsburgh iron mills and railyards to assemble a group that could make bridges of a substance far more difficult to burn.

The new company, Scott explained, would enjoy a virtual lock on new bridge-building operations for the Pennsylvania Railroad, a privilege that might require the submission of judiciously calculated bids, but one certain to yield generous profits. Carnegie was eager to act on yet another gilt-edged tip. The Piper and Shiffler Company (which would later become the Keystone Bridge Company) was formed early in 1862, and to Carnegie it was the investment that turned out to be "the parent of all other works."

By 1863 Carnegie was earning more than $45,000 a year from this and all his other investments, compared with a mere $2,400 from his railroad salary. Yet he understood that it was the contacts he made and the information he derived from his association with the railroad that made everything else possible. While Carnegie had by this time developed a desire to break clean of working for anyone else, he was uncertain about severing his ties with a community of interests that had served him so well. It may have been the one time in his life when indecision was a boon.

In 1864, after dabbling in one Allegheny City ironmaking concern with his younger brother, Tom, Carnegie joined with his bridge-building partners, Piper and Shiffler, and other associates, to form the Cyclops Iron Company, which would allow them to secure the raw materials for their projects without recourse to a middleman. The foundation for his success had now been laid.

Despite these momentous steps toward a grand future, it was a period of significant personal difficulty. When he found himself called up by the Union to fight in the Civil War in mid-1864, a stunned Carnegie pondered the alternatives, then spent $850 to hire a substitute to undertake his service for him. It was an option that was legal and often exercised by young men of means at the time, and one that Carnegie defended as a patriotic gesture. After all, he reasoned, the draft law of 1863 gave him the choice of paying the government a mere $300 to avoid service altogether. In Carnegie's eyes, he had expended $550 that he didn't have to, and, instead of evading service, had seen to it that another body had been added to the fray.

Shortly thereafter, word reached Carnegie of another potential complication, this time life-altering rather than life-threatening: he was about to be offered a promotion to Tom Scott's old job of superintendent by the board of the Pennsylvania Railroad. It was a difficult choice for a man who had risen to his present lofty station through his association with the company, but Carnegie saw himself as guided by his conscience. Determined to make a fortune and certain that he could never do so as a salaried man ("I saw no means of doing this honestly, at any salary the railroad company could afford to give"), he tendered his resignation to the Pennsylvania Railroad and turned his energies to iron.

Since neither Carnegie nor his new partners in Cyclops Iron knew much about the manufacturing business, the newly formed company experienced considerable difficulty in gearing up for actual production. As a result, the ever-pragmatic Carnegie turned to the principals of the competing firm, in which his brother Tom still maintained an interest, and brokered a merger, despite considerable rancor between several parties on opposing sides. While the exercise cost Carnegie the intimacy of his old friend Tom Miller, the newly formed Union Iron Works was a great success, providing him with an additional income of $20,000 in 1867.

Had he known what was to come, Carnegie might well have redoubled his efforts in iron, but he had climbed to where he was via telegraph and railroads, and perhaps that accounts for his temporary retreat to more comfortable haunts.

The telegraph business was dominated in the 1860s by Western Union, guided by the able and tough-minded William Orton, a former commissioner of the Internal Revenue Service. Orton's determination to dominate the telegraph business led to the demise of many a lesser competitor, but also to creative responses from those in danger of being gobbled up. Carnegie hoped to join the ranks of a number of lesser players who had begun to organize smaller, regional telegraph companies with no real intention of doing significant, long-term business of their own. The idea was to organize sufficiently to present one's firm as an up-and-comer, a potential competitor, and then accept a handsome buyout from Orton.

Following this tack, Carnegie first formed his own company, Keystone Telegraph, and then secured a contract with the Pennsylvania Railroad to run lines along the company tracks from Pittsburgh to Philadelphia. Before he could even approach Western Union, however, an intermediary firm, the Pacific and Atlantic Telegraph Company, came courting. In the resulting merger and stock swap, Carnegie tripled the value of his telegraph holdings without having strung a single mile of wire.

Using his new position as a major stockholder in the P&A, Carnegie engineered the appointment of a good friend as its general superintendent. Then, in the final step, he went behind the backs of all his new partners to engineer a secret deal for a merger with Western Union and profited further by snatching up shares of the P&A from unwary stockholders in advance. Though what he did was legal at the time, when word leaked out, there was a stampede by stock-holders to cash in, not only putting an end to Carnegie's scheme but painting him in the eyes of critics as a Machiavellian figure, profiting at the expense of fellow stockholders. It was the first time that Carnegie felt the sting of negative public opinion, and for what he considered normal business practice. He reacted in what would become typical Carnegie fashion, blaming a change in Western Union management for cutting off the buyout before all his friends could be taken care of.

At nearly the same time, a second investment pitted him against another legendary businessman. George Pullman, as owner of the sleeping-car company that bore his name, had blithely lifted any number of patented features from those designed by T. T. Woodruff for Carnegie's Central Transportation Company (CTC), enhancing them to create the luxurious Pullman car, a fixture on many Western rail lines. Pullman, however, was intent on seeing his new and improved cars roll on rail lines coast to coast. Because of Carnegie's influence, Pullman's prospects of bypassing the influence of the Chicago-based CTC seemed dim until Carnegie learned that Union Pacific officials were considering adopting Pullman's cars for use on their fast-growing network.

Instead of drawing a battle line, Carnegie deployed his skills as a backroom negotiator. He approached Pullman one evening after a round of negotiations with Union Pacific in New York City and made a proposal that startled the sleeping-car magnate: he should simply stop all this going-it-alone and join forces with Carnegie. Pullman had only to agree to merge with Central Transportation, creating a new company; the newly melded group could then strike a far better deal with the Union Pacific than they could while battling each other for the coveted contracts. The only hitch was that Pullman would have to agree to pay $20,000 to aggrieved officials of the CTC, who were ready to sue Pullman for patent infringement.

Taken with Carnegie's brazenness, Pullman agreed to the plan, though he never did pay the agreed-upon fees. Instead, Carnegie would have to broker another deal that finally ended the impasse. In an elegantly devised scenario, Pullman's newly formed company agreed to lease all the equipment and patents owned by CTC for 99 years, at $264,000 a year, a sum $14,000 greater than the company's net earnings for 1869. Why go to the bother of running a company, then, when you could earn more for sitting on your hands, reasoned CTC officials—and thus yet another Carnegie deal was struck.

In the meantime, Carnegie had made another significant decision: he had left his adopted hometown of Pittsburgh, taking up residence in New York City at the opulent St. Nicholas Hotel, the very place where he had first met with Pullman during the railroad talks. His mother, Margaret, was installed in an adjoining apartment, while his brother, Tom, stayed behind to tend to Carnegie business interests in Pittsburgh.

Carnegie had been drawn to New York by the same charms that had lured other tycoons of the day, including the Vanderbilts and the Rockefellers. He had also decided that if he aspired to join the ranks of society's greats, he should have a presence among them. The fact was that, at the tender age of thirty-three, he listed personal assets of some $400,000 and, at a time when an average wage earner might bring home about $300, Carnegie enjoyed an annual income of more than $50,000 (equivalent to about $10 million in current dollars). The canny Scotsman was no longer a workingman, but a bona fide capitalist who had borrowed less than a thousand dollars to end up with everything he had.

With railroad building at an all-time high and westward expansion in full swing, Carnegie's imagination was fired by the prospects inherent in his Keystone Bridge holdings. A number of bridges had been proposed for rail lines crossing the Mississippi River, and the thought of such feats of engineering appealed to the adventurer as well as the investor in Carnegie. He joined forces with a Midwestern contractor, the Keokuk and Hamilton Bridge Company, to win one

2,300-foot Mississippi-crossing contract, then landed the contract for the more formidable St. Louis Bridge, a project with an estimated cost of more than $5 million.

In order to finance the latter, the directors of the St. Louis and Illinois Bridge Company decided to sell bonds (which would be retired by the profits from leases sold to railway companies using the bridge). Carnegie, who was already in line to profit from proceeds to Keystone as builder of the bridge, as well as from the inevitable increase in the St. Louis and Illinois stock he would take as partial payment for his work, struck next upon a third stream of revenue from the same project.

Aware of the growing interest among European investors in the booming economy of the post–Civil War United States, Carnegie proposed to the St. Louis and Illinois executives that he travel to London carrying the right to sell $4 million in bonds to build the St. Louis Bridge. If successful, Carnegie would receive $50,000 in St. Louis and Illinois stock—stock that would of course increase dramatically in value once the offering had been completed.

The board agreed, and Carnegie was off to sell his bonds. In London, he met with Junius Morgan, an American banker who specialized in selling United States securities to the British market. Though leery at first, Morgan was impressed with Carnegie's assurances that the new bridge was the gateway to westward expansion and a portal that would enjoy a virtual stranglehold on American rail commerce. In the end, Morgan agreed to buy a substantial portion of the bonds at 85 percent of their face value. Carnegie had not only fattened his bank account but had added "bond salesman" to his résumé.

Though he was drawn to the easy profits to be made in bond sales and enjoyed great success initially due to his business reputation and influential friends, bond sales would also give Carnegie his first true tastes of failure and deceit. When a Davenport-to-St.-Paul railroad project for which he had sold the bonds collapsed because of mismanagement, Carnegie's commission was withheld; then there came an involvement with the Union Pacific Railroad and a brief but troubled stay on its board during the scandal-ridden days of 1872, when it was discovered that other UP officials had bribed members of Congress to overlook questionable financing tactics during the race to complete the construction of the transcontinental railroad.

At the same time, Carnegie and some of his old associates, including George Pullman and Tom Scott, had been selling off significant amounts of their newly acquired stock in the UP, taking advantage of the boost in prices their appointment to the board had spurred. Compared with the actions that earned Martha Stewart a few months in a "cupcake" facility, such baldfaced manipulations might today garner their perpetrators twenty years at hard labor. Even in the relatively unregulated business climate of 1872 (the Sherman Anti-Trust Act would not become a reality for another eighteen years), moral indignation was high. The resulting scandal forced Carnegie and his friends out of the Union Pacific and engendered a round of finger-pointing as to whose idea the sell-off had been.

Although he would escape any legal consequences, it was a bitter lesson for the Calvinist-born Carnegie, and provides a glimpse of the internal contradictions that would bedevil him throughout his life. Carnegie's upbringing had predisposed him toward honesty and a high regard for the opinion of others. But those attributes sometimes collided with his overwhelming ambition.

Four years earlier, in fact, he had penned himself a letter in which he stated, "Man must have an idol—The amassing of wealth is one of the worst species of idolatry. No idol more debasing than the worship of money. . . . To continue much longer overwhelmed by business cares and with most of my thought wholly upon the way to make more money in the shortest time, must degrade me beyond hope. . . . I will resign business at Thirty five." It was a noble pledge, but one he was too ambitious to honor.

In a move that foreshadowed his rupture with Frick, Carnegie sought to resolve the matter by shifting the blame for the 1872 scandal to the Union Pacific founders. And he would later write self-servingly of his disappointment in his autobiography. "I saw that I was still young and still had a good deal to learn," he concluded. "Many men can be trusted, but a few need watching."

Whatever the truth of the matter, Carnegie found himself in 1872 driven from the board of what had become one of the country's most notorious corporations, and denied payment from the vaunted Keokuk Bridge project, which collapsed, never to be built. He was not only two years past his own imposed deadline for retirement, but was wallowing in the very moral quagmire he had warned himself against.

He could scarcely forget that his own father had been ground down by "progress," his hard-won skills as a weaver made obsolete by the emergence of machine-made goods. In addition, his maternal grandfather, Thomas Morrison, had been a radical-minded Dunfermline politician and publisher early in the century, whose passionate calls for land reform and equality—"Each shall possess; all shall enjoy. . . . Every man a lord; every woman a lady; and every child an heir"—would echo not only in Carnegie's father's consciousness but in his own.

It was that very concept of equal opportunity which had given young Andrew Carnegie the sense that he could outstrip his humble origins, and that formed the basis of his eternal gratitude for the "land of opportunity" that allowed him his meteoric rise. So while Carnegie could be ruthless in his pursuit of material success, he could be equally passionate in his defense of justice for the common man.

While still working as a telegrapher's assistant in Pittsburgh, for instance, he was incensed to discover that the Mechanics' and Apprentices' Library, where he spent his few leisure hours in pursuit of knowledge, had changed its policies to require a subscription fee from all but formally apprenticed young workers. Carnegie wrote an outraged letter to the editor of the *Pittsburgh Dispatch* that persuaded the library board to rescind its edict.

And while his steadfast desire to "improve himself" despite his scanty formal education might be viewed only as an effort to gain entrance to circles of influence from which he would otherwise be excluded, the record suggests otherwise. According to biographer Wall, it was an enduring disappointment for Carnegie, whose expectations had been colored by the example of his widely read father and uncles, to discover that so many of the successful men with whom he now hobnobbed were so limited culturally. He complained that he had only met one railroad executive capable of quoting a line from Burns or Shakespeare.

Long after his arrival in New York, Carnegie continued his pursuit of knowledge for its own sake. Having heard of Anne Lynch Botta, a devotee of the arts, at whose home Edgar Allan Poe had delivered the first public reading of "The Raven," Carnegie made it a point to meet and befriend her, a connection that would prove momentous.

In earlier days, Botta's regular guests had included William Cullen Bryant, Daniel Webster, and Ralph Waldo Emerson. By the time she and Carnegie met, her guest list included the likes of Julia Ward Howe, Matthew Arnold, Henry Ward Beecher, and another well-to-do progressive thinker, Courtland Palmer. Palmer introduced Carnegie to a discussion group of his own making, and soon Carnegie was a regular at the monthly meetings of the Nineteenth Century Club, a forward-leaning assemblage that included a young man named Theodore Roosevelt, and where the writings of the British philosopher Herbert Spencer held considerable influence. Spencer's provocative arguments applied the still-startling principles of biological evolution laid out by Darwin in his *Origin of Species* (1859) to social development.

In Spencer's view, social change was driven not, as philosophers of the Enlightenment would have it, by a benign and invisible hand, but by the ceaseless struggle for survival between individuals. Spencer argued that this ongoing contest had produced the laissez-faire industrial society, which was proof, in his eyes, of the ever-improving nature of the process.

To Carnegie, who had been able to pull himself up by his boot-straps, Spencer's notions were more than compelling. They seemed, from his vantage point, to be irrefutable truths, inextricable from the fact of his own being. If Carnegie had succeeded, then anyone could succeed, and those who fell by the wayside did society a favor. The central tenets of Social Darwinism appeared to Carnegie to explain the mysteries of existence itself; he would evermore fasten upon the principles of just reward when he found them convenient, and just as conveniently ignore the implications for the less fortunate.

As he would write in his autobiography, "I had found the truth of evolution. 'All is well since all grows better' became my motto, my true source of comfort. Man was not created with an instinct for his own degradation, but from the lower he had risen to the higher forms. Nor is there any conceivable end to his march to perfection." Carnegie would return to these notions time and again, both as foundation for his own writings and as justification for his most momentous actions, some of which history would applaud, many of which it would condemn.

# 4

# CONVERGENCE OF THE TWAIN

---◆---

**B**OLSTERED BY THE NOTION THAT HIS rise in the business arena would pay dividends for society as a whole, and conditioned by years of operating at full throttle, Carnegie began to rethink his earlier determination to quit the field of battle at an early age. If what was good for Andrew Carnegie led inevitably to the betterment of the world around him, then perhaps it made more sense to end the scattershot approach to accumulating wealth and "put all good eggs in one basket and then watch that basket," as he wrote.

The question was, which eggs and which basket? He had already soured on bond sales, and the disappointment and scandal that he had narrowly avoided in railroad building put him off that direction as well. He still had his holdings in oil, but the rough-and-tumble of that still-unproven business where John D. Rockefeller and Henry Flagler were quickly gaining a stranglehold in northern Pennsylvania held little attraction for him. In the end, Carnegie's interests turned back to the field he had entered almost by accident more than a decade before: iron and steel.

One of the men with whom he had met on his foray to England to sell rail bonds in 1872 was the inventor Henry Bessemer. As a result of the process for transforming iron to steel that bore his name, a quantity of steel that might formerly have taken as long as two weeks to produce could now be made in fifteen minutes. Though Bessemer had based his work upon the earlier experiments of a bankrupt Kentucky steelmaker named William Kelly, who had received his first patent in 1856, it had taken considerable time to transform the process into one that was consistent and economically feasible. As Carnegie had seen firsthand when the Pennsylvania Railroad experimented with steel-capped rails in the mid-1860s, the quality of the finished product varied widely, and the costs, when compared to iron, were still prohibitive.

Nonetheless, Carnegie understood the industry's vast potential appetite for an improved form of iron. Not only did everything in the business move on iron rails, but the cars and the engines were built of iron, as was the machinery that loaded and serviced them, and as were the new bridges that spanned the rivers and chasms of the American West. If there were a cheaper and more durable substance than iron, it would lead to a revolution in the business, not to mention a fortune for those who got in on the ground floor.

In the post–Civil War United States, where growth seemed to have no bounds, it was also understood that the apparently limitless expansion of commerce would naturally be served by railroads. Though Carnegie had been burned by railroad building itself, he understood that an occasional failure could not hold back the expansion of the nation's rail system into every part of the country where business might be conducted. And if one were to gain a favorable position feeding the appetite for expansion of a good portion of this industry, while assuming none of the accompanying risks . . . well, then, why would one not think of placing steel eggs in steel baskets?

When his talks with Henry Bessemer convinced him that sources of impurity-free iron ore had recently been discovered that would allow the British to begin production of high-grade steel rails for export to the United States, Carnegie made up his mind. He returned to

Pittsburgh intent upon building his own steel mill and beating the British to the punch.

He rounded up his brother, Tom, and six other business associates as partners in the new venture, and persuaded Edgar Thomson, the first president of the Pennsylvania Railroad, to lend his name to the new mill. The Edgar Thomson works would be built on Braddock Field, a former battleground of the French and Indian War, conveniently located some twelve miles east of Pittsburgh and adjoining the Monongahela River, as well as a line of the Pennsylvania and Baltimore & Ohio railroads. Carnegie would contribute $250,000 of his own to the new enterprise, with the others rounding out the total capitalization of $700,000. Given that most mills at the time had been launched with one-quarter to one-third as much capital, Carnegie's announcement caused a major stir in Pittsburgh.

As it turned out, however, he could not have chosen a worse time to begin. A financial panic had begun in Europe in early 1873, causing the collapse of the Vienna stock market and sweeping on through the rest of the major markets on the Continent, until ruin finally swept all the way to London. On September 18, the tide reached the United States, when the banking firm of Jay Cooke, heavily extended in rail construction loans, was forced to close its doors in bankruptcy. The consequences led to panic and sent the United States into its first great depression.

Railroad building, which employed numbers of workers second only to agriculture, had seemed impregnable until that time. More than 35,000 miles of new track had been laid since the end of the Civil War, and the "golden spike" had been driven at Promontory, Utah, in 1869, joining the East and West Coasts by rail at last, igniting the imagination of expansionists and investors everywhere. As a result, Cooke's firm had funded plans for the building of a second transcontinental railroad, the Northern Pacific, and was heavily invested in several other new lines.

But with the flow of speculators' funds from Europe abruptly cut off and domestic investors suddenly wary, the bubble of optimism burst. The New York Stock Exchange would close its doors for the first time in history, remaining shuttered for ten days. Of the more than 360 railroad companies in the United States, fully one-quarter declared bankruptcy. Nearly twenty thousand businesses of all types failed, and one-sixth of the nation's workforce found itself out of work.

The collapse of railroad projects in which Carnegie was involved led his old mentor Thomas Scott to beg his former protégé for loans that would shore him up. Carnegie, however, stood resolute. He had sunk what he had into the construction of the Edgar Thomson Mill, and his loyalty and his capital would reside there. Carnegie would write that spurning Scott's pleas "gave me more pain than all the financial trials to which I had been subjected up to that time," but his course was set. The Edgar Thomson Mill was his first priority and its stacks would rise, no matter what.

Despite the fact that Carnegie's assets were in danger from various suits brought by investors in railway projects that were failing all about him, he was able to convince local bankers in Pittsburgh that he was solvent, and thereby avoided foreclosure on construction loans for the mill. And when high winds caused the collapse of a portion of the Edgar Thomson roof as it was being maneuvered into place, Carnegie managed to secure yet another loan to make up the cost.

The depression actually played into his hands; as he pointed out in an 1877 letter to the plant's first general manager, William Shinn, the decreased demand for materials and labor caused by the economic downturn resulted in a nearly 25-percent savings over the costs Carnegie had projected. For Carnegie, it was another invaluable business lesson: the best time to expand was when no one else dared to take the risks.

On September 1, 1875, the first steel rails rolled off the line at the Edgar Thomson Mill in Braddock, Pennsylvania, an event overseen by the man Carnegie had chosen as his plant superintendent, Captain Bill Jones, a Civil War hero and legendary steelmaker who had overseen the installation of one of Bessemer's converters at the rival Cambria Iron works in Johnstown, Pennsylvania, sixty miles to the east. The hiring of General Manager Shinn and Superintendent Jones typified the personnel decisions of Carnegie, who was fond of saying, "There is no labor so cheap as the dearest in the mechanical field."

For key positions, he hired the best and paid top dollar, though he held all who worked for him strictly accountable, demanding no less dedication and effort from others than from himself. He also preferred to compensate his chief executives with an interest in the company that would supplement a modest salary. For one thing, he had discovered for himself that ownership rather than salary provided the true path to riches. He also understood that making a man a partner bound him to the firm far more effectively than did a handsome salary, which could easily be outbid by a rival concern. While Carnegie may not have pioneered the practice, his widespread use of the technique is much emulated today, though Carnegie would surely be ambivalent about modern schemes to share profits with rank-and-file workers.

In addition to the maintenance of a loyal and fiercely hardworking chain of command, Carnegie's success can be attributed to another lesson he had learned on the way up: the value of meticulous cost accounting. This was likely the most valuable legacy from his days working under Edgar Thomson at the Pennsylvania Railroad. After forming the Cyclops/Union Iron Works, Carnegie revolutionized that industry's practice by applying the same standards he had learned in freight hauling to the foundry's production line.

As a result, when Union Iron or Keystone Bridge submitted a bid on a project, there was no guesswork involved. If Carnegie chose to undercut a rival's figure, he did so with absolute confidence that he could deliver what he promised *and* make a profit, for his was the only firm in the field with near-fanatical devotion to cost accounting.

As Charles Schwab would later put it, "Carnegie never wanted to know the profits. He always wanted to know the costs."

His insistence on careful recordkeeping extended beyond data on material in versus product out. To a degree that had never been practiced before, Carnegie demanded a log be kept comparing the productivity of individual workmen, supervisors, and even entire shifts. Those who excelled could expect to advance, and even to become partners in a Carnegie enterprise. "If he can win the race, he is our racehorse," as Carnegie put it. "If not he goes to the cart."

Even his key employees were not spared Carnegie's heavy-handed management style. To almost every positive report out of Edgar Thomson, Carnegie's response was "Good, but let us do better." Despite the storied efficiency at the Thomson works, Captain Jones was the recipient of an endless series of Carnegie memoranda urging him to find ways to cut labor costs until Jones was moved to write an angry reply: "I must earnestly say let us leave good enough alone. Don't think of any further reductions. . . . Our labor is the cheapest in the country."

Carnegie's approach may seem ruthless, but the idea of treating the complex process of manufacturing like a giant machine with component parts that must be constantly retooled seemed to him completely natural. It was an approach that reflected his faith in Spencer's doctrine of ever-evolving struggle, and one that holds in most industry to this day.

Efficiency, however, was the least of Carnegie's worries as he began his career as a steelmaker. The more important goal was to find customers for his product. By 1876, nearly half of all United States railroads had filed for, or were nearing, bankruptcy, and the price for finished rails had dropped nearly in half. Furthermore, his chief intended customer at the Pennsylvania Railroad, Edgar Thomson, after whom the new mill had been named, had died, and his relations with Thomas Scott, his other contact from the railroad days, had been cut.

Still, Carnegie persevered. While other manufacturers were charging seventy dollars a ton for their rails, Carnegie offered his for sixty-five dollars, following another of his well-known dictums: "Cut the prices, scoop the market . . . watch the costs and the profits will take care of themselves." Also, the depression once again proved to be a boon to Carnegie. The price of raw materials fell so precipitously that Carnegie would write to Junius Morgan in the summer of 1876 boasting that he was able to produce his rails for less than fifty dollars.

Still, the effects of the depression lingered, and business opportunities, especially in the railroad industry, were limited. As a result, the ever-resourceful Carnegie, who served as principal salesman for his iron and steel interests, pursued a wide variety of projects. In 1876 he landed a contract for Keystone Bridge and Union Mills with the Philadelphia Centennial Exposition, which agreed to construct half of its facilities out of iron and steel; and in 1878 he signed a contract to supply all the steel for the building of the Brooklyn Bridge. Not long after, he reached an agreement to supply the steel used in the building of the New York City elevated railway.

All along, Carnegie had been resistant to forming cost-fixing alliances with other manufacturers as a way out of his difficulties—not because he was above such manipulation, but because he was confident that he could make his rails more cheaply than anyone else. Invited in 1877 to join such a "pool" by the owners of the other leading area firms, including Pennsylvania Steel, Jones & Laughlin, Scranton Iron & Steel, Bethlehem Steel, and Cambria Iron, Carnegie balked when he deemed his proposed share to be too small. Were they actually offering him 9 percent of the total pie when he could make steel more efficiently than any of them, he asked in disbelief, pounding the table around which his fellow titans sat. Preposterous! What did he need with them? With that, he drew up his five-foot-three-inch frame in indignation, and walked out of the meeting.

Indignation aside, however, Carnegie was a pragmatist. So it was not long after he had stormed out of that meeting that he approached his peers at both Cambria and Bethlehem Steel to form such alliances, albeit at terms more favorable to himself.

In any case, and despite the difficulties he encountered, Carnegie's new enterprise proved a success. The Edgar Thomson works turned a profit of $11,000 in its very first month of operation, a feat that Carnegie was proud of pointing to as unique in the annals of modern manufacturing. If anyone had ever done better, in fact, they were apparently keeping it to themselves; by 1878, profits at Edgar Thomson had risen to more than $400,000, against the company's $1.25 million total capitalization.

"Where is there such a business!" Carnegie crowed to Shinn, and to others he expressed the confidence that he had truly arrived. His iron and steel interests were so solidly established, he said, that he could easily take a leave of months with no fear of ill effects. And with that in mind, he set out on an eight-month voyage around the world. The trip took Carnegie and his mother to Japan, China, Ceylon, India, and Egypt, among other exotic locales, and inspired him to undertake his first significant literary project, a traveler's memoir that blended his experiences with philosophical reflections prompted by the trip. It was more than closet scribbling; Scribner's agreed to publish the volume in 1884, under the title *Round the World*.

As to the nature of the philosophical ruminations, Carnegie had found during his travels nothing but support for his conviction that survival of the fittest was not only the operating principle upon which the world order depended, but that Darwinism justified every action he would take in his own business life. The measuring stick was calibrated in dollars, and every tick that Carnegie marked off was a sign of progress toward the greater good.

Of course, Carnegie did not find it easy to impute an equal capacity for fostering such growth to others, certainly not to his competitors or even to his own employees. Shinn, for one, had cabled Carnegie during his absence, seeking a raise as well as a change in title, from general manager to chairman, this in recognition of what most would see as a four-year, remarkably successful stewardship of a major manufacturing enterprise. For Carnegie, favor was to be bestowed, not sought, and he was always wary of any seeming power grab by a subordinate. When he stalled, Shinn began negotiations with a competing steelmaking firm in St. Louis.

Carnegie exploded when he discovered what Shinn was up to. He demanded his manager's resignation on the spot, and Shinn complied. Carnegie appointed his brother, Tom, as chairman of the company and, in order to secure the loyalty of his remaining linchpin employee, raised the salary of Captain Jones (a down-to-earth sort who had always steadfastly refused any offer of partnership in the company) to $25,000 a year, pointing out that the figure was the same as that of the President of the United States. It was a staggering sum for a "working man," to be sure, but Carnegie had it to spend: profits at Edgar Thomson had risen to $512,000 in 1879 and to $1,550,000 by 1880.

With profits soaring, his brother as chairman, and Jones's loyalty effectively purchased, Carnegie settled into the pursuit of a long-cherished goal, that of besting the steel production of his most despised rivals, Cambria, Pennsylvania Steel, and Bethlehem Steel. Since labor costs had already been cut to the bone and efficiency was at the apparent maximum, prospects for Carnegie's desire seemed dim, until Captain Jones hit upon a solution that would have a profound effect, not only on Edgar Thomson, but on United States manufacturing practices in general.

Until that time, men at Edgar Thomson, as elsewhere, worked one of two twelve-hour shifts. Jones, however, had watched closely as the efficiency measures put into place reached a point of diminishing returns. After months of cajoling and pushing, Jones, a hands-on manager, determined that it was simply impossible for human beings to expend maximum effort for so long a period, and came up with a suggestion. They could simply divide the workday into three shifts rather than two.

Men could maintain almost any pace for eight hours, Jones reasoned, and after sixteen hours of rest they would return refreshed, ready for more of anything. The company would thereby gain a greatly increased output while expending the very same amount on wages. Jones's elegant notion was not only wildly popular with the men, it proved to be as effective in practice as it seemed on paper, and the eight-hour workday was born to steel.

At the same time, Carnegie continued his quest to cut costs, focusing now on the raw materials demanded by the steelmaking process. After iron ore, the next indispensable substance for the production of steel was coke, a substance derived from baking bituminous coal in conical-shaped ovens resembling beehives, to drive off impurities and yield a hot-burning, nearly smokeless cake (the term is a derivation of "coal cake") of almost pure carbon. When mixed with iron ore and heated, the coke combined with impurities in the ore to form "slag," and leave behind a pure molten iron. It required nearly one ton of coke in order to smelt an equal amount of iron, though the purer the coke, the more efficient the process.

A steady supply of high-grade coke at a consistent price was thus essential to the efficient production of iron and steel and had led Carnegie to buy his own coke ovens in the nearby Connellsville coal region in the early 1870s. He had also brought his cousin George "Dod" Lauder, a trained coaling engineer, across from Dunfermline to manage them. By the early 1880s, however, the demands of Carnegie's mills had far outstripped the capacity of his coke ovens, and besides, their limited capacity meant that Carnegie could actually buy cheaper coke from competing operators.

As a result, Carnegie decided to sell his own ovens and buy all his coke on the open market. To that end, he dispatched his brother, Tom, to the Connellsville coal region, about forty miles southeast of Pittsburgh, to meet with the principal manufacturer of coke in the area, Henry Clay Frick. The object of Tom's trip was to see if Frick might be interested in buying the Carnegie ovens. Although Carnegie's intention was simply to reduce his business expenditures, it was a decision that would one day exact more from his purse and his person than he could possibly have dreamed.

# 5

# THE KING OF COKE

————◆————

THOUGH HE HAD NOT STARTED OUT as a penniless immigrant, Henry Frick was not a stranger to hard times. Born in 1849, he was the second son of John W. Frick, a failed painter and an only slightly more successful farmer, whose forebears had emigrated from Switzerland to the colonies in the early 1700s. The younger Frick, named after the Kentucky senator Henry Clay, who spent much of his late career trying to broker a compromise between North and South on the issue of slavery, grew up on the family farm near Mount Pleasant, just north of Connellsville, often falling prey to one illness or another, including typhoid fever, and working hard just to keep himself fed and clothed.

His maternal grandfather, Abraham Overholt, of German descent, had fared better than the rest of the Frick clan, however, and young Henry would eventually enjoy the benefits. He left home at sixteen to live with an Overholt uncle, who in turn sent him off to college, at Otterbein College, near Columbus, Ohio. There Frick received his first inklings of a wider world, including an exposure to literature and painting, in which he began to dabble himself.

He was an indifferent student, though, and in less than three months he returned to Mount Pleasant to work in his uncle's general store, a step that he saw as the first in pursuit of a career in business. In the fall of 1868 he moved to Pittsburgh, where he worked as a clerk in one of the city's better department stores for seven dollars a week and where he first honed a talent for sales.

It was not long before his aging grandfather Abraham, struck by Frick's industry and determination, offered him a position as a book-keeper in the family distillery business (Old Overholt still survives as a popular brand of rye whiskey) at Broad Ford, Pennsylvania, at the rate of $1,000 per year. Frick readily accepted, but hardly had he returned home than Abraham Overholt died. It was January 1870, and Frick was suddenly in need of another job. It was doubtless a wrenching turn of events for a twenty-year-old who had thought his future secure, but in retrospect fate had done him a favor.

Frick went to work for a cousin, Abraham Tinstman, who had bought several hundred acres of coal-producing land in the area a decade or so before, and was now involved in the manufacture of coke. Tinstman was having a difficult go of it, and was casting about for new partners who might provide an infusion of capital. Sensing an opportunity to cash in on the booming iron and steel activity all about them, young Clay, as he was known, made the rounds of various family members and, aided by his impending inheritance of some $10,000 from his late grandfather's estate, managed to borrow enough to secure a 20-percent interest in the newly organized firm.

One of the first actions of the company was to purchase an additional 123 acres of coal lands and begin the construction of a new coking plant. It was Clay Frick who traveled to Pittsburgh to seek a loan for these activities, and the banker who considered the matter was a flinty man of fifty-seven named Thomas Mellon, whose background as a judge must have enabled him to discern the potential of a slightly built whippersnapper who stood scarcely more than five feet tall and had little to offer as collateral beyond his confidence in the future of coke.

In later years, business associates and rivals would often comment on the power of Frick's gray-eyed gaze when it lit upon you. Perhaps it was the strength he saw in Frick's eyes that convinced Mellon, or perhaps it was his awareness of the Overholt blood that ran in the veins of the quiet but determined young man before him, but in any case he approved the loan.

Before the first new oven had been completed, Frick was back to apply for a loan for a second, though this time one of Mellon's officers heard the petition and recommended the request be denied. Tom Mellon asked a mining engineer for an independent opinion before making the final decision, however, and the report was soon back: "Manager may be a little too enthusiastic about pictures [a reference to Frick's budding interest in art] . . . but knows his business down to the ground." It was enough for Mellon, who approved the loan.

He would approve many more after that. By the end of 1873, Frick and Company, as the firm had become known, owned two hundred coke ovens, selling everything it could produce to the rapidly expanding Bessemer steelmakers in the region.

Then came the economic collapse that nearly destroyed Carnegie and prevented his entrance into the business. As iron and steel declined, so did coke. But Frick (who would later recall it as one of the most grueling times in his life) proved as undaunted in the face of adversity as Carnegie had been. Instead of turning tail, he used the depression and the confidence he had cultivated with Tom Mellon to his advantage, judiciously purchasing the coal lands and coke ovens of his failed and failing competitors. At about the same time, when a local railroad company went under, Frick snapped it up and offered it to the Baltimore & Ohio Railroad in turn. The deal for ten miles of railroad track netted him $50,000.

Again in 1878 he reorganized his business, this time as H. C. Frick and Company, and used the proceeds to lease other idle works and lands. His relentless acquisitions continued until, by 1882, the company owned some three thousand acres of coal lands and operated more than a thousand coke ovens, about a quarter of all those in the area.

At the lowest ebb of the coke business, prices had fallen to ninety cents per ton, about what it cost to produce, even with wages at rock bottom. By 1878, however, prices had begun to recover: first to two dollars, then to three dollars, and finally to five dollars per ton, at which point profits were three dollars of the total. By the end of 1879, at age thirty (and some three years sooner than Carnegie), Frick reckoned himself a millionaire and was fielding more demand for his coke than he could possibly handle.

Though prices in coke typically waxed and waned, the size of Frick's operation insulated him through the lean times. In the early 1880s, he would produce and sell almost a million tons of coke in a year, netting nearly $400,000 annually in the process.

Frick had also devised another way of bolstering profits: because the mines and the ovens in which his laborers worked were often located far from towns where food and other necessities could be easily purchased, the company began to open and stock its own stores. Workers could not use cash in the company stores and were often required to "charge" a certain percentage of their wages as a condition of employment, or take some of their pay in company scrip that could only be redeemed in a Frick store, where prices were generally inflated.

Though company officials would defend the practice as an expensive amenity maintained for the convenience of their labor force, the bottom line suggested otherwise. Profits in store sales (for the same period that earned Frick nearly $400,000 in coke) netted the company another $33,000, at a profit margin of nearly 17 percent. Suggest to the owner of a contemporary supermarket (where a profit margin of 2 to 3 percent is considered generous) that he could do as well, and he would likely explode in laughter.

For Frick, as for Carnegie, labor had become an impersonal aspect of the business equation, not an assembly of flesh-and-blood individuals furthering a common enterprise. Through the lens of Darwin's social relativism, the owner who failed to squeeze the last wasted dollar out of labor costs was as wasteful and negligent as the one who spent too much on grease or whale oil. Survival as a businessman was determined in the same way as was survival among all species—compete successfully or die.

It was an attitude that Frick would take to new heights in the coke industry and a trait that Carnegie would eventually try to exploit to his own advantage. For now, however, he wanted only to interest the "King of Coke" in taking the Carnegie coke ovens off his hands, a matter that he surmised would take little effort, given Frick's well-known interest in acquisition.

It also seemed that Carnegie had done his homework on Frick and was impressed with what he found. In his autobiography, Carnegie wrote that Frick's company not only owned the best coal lands in the Connellsville area and produced the best coke from it, but also "had in Mr. Frick himself a man with a positive genius for its management. He had proved his ability by starting as a poor railway clerk and succeeding."

Although Carnegie had gotten some of the particulars wrong, Frick's rise from humble beginnings was obviously intriguing to him. If nothing else, it would have signaled to Carnegie that Frick was another of the fellow "fittest," and those were the individuals with whom Carnegie sought to align himself, especially when seeking business advantage.

In any case, Tom Carnegie followed through on his brother's charge, sending word to Frick in November 1881 that they would like to sell him their Monastery Coke Works near Latrobe, or at least seek some arrangement by which Frick would take over the purchase and sales of the coke from the hundred or so ovens located there.

Because the works were located some thirty miles to the northwest, on the fringes of the prime Connellsville vein, Frick wrote back that he would have to have a firsthand look at their operations before he could respond. There were other reasons why Frick delayed immediate action. In June of that year he had attended a society function in Pittsburgh, along with Andrew Mellon, the son of Thomas, with whom Frick had struck up a friendship. At the party, Frick's eye had fallen upon a dark-haired young beauty he judged to be the most attractive woman in the room. Mellon, who had once courted her himself, told Frick that she was Adelaide Childs, the daughter of a well-to-do Pittsburgh shoe manufacturer, Asa P. Childs.

As Frick's great-granddaughter and biographer, Martha Frick Symington Sanger, tells the story in *Henry Clay Frick: An Intimate Portrait,* Frick begged Mellon for an introduction. Mellon, in turn, began searching the room for an older intermediary to perform such duties, as etiquette required. Frick, however, was no time-waster. While Mellon dithered, Frick approached Adelaide on his own and struck up a conversation. In short order, Frick had secured permission to call upon Adelaide, then twenty-five, and three months later they were engaged.

At the time that Tom Carnegie approached Frick on the sale of the coke works, Frick was in the midst of plans for his wedding, which was to take place on December 15. Business would simply have to wait.

It did not have to wait long, however. Since their six-week honeymoon began in New York City, Andrew Carnegie invited Frick and his bride to have lunch with him and his mother, Margaret, at his hotel, at which he hoped to consummate the proposed partnership.

Frick, as it turned out, was not uninterested in an arrangement with Carnegie, for he had run up considerable debt in his relentless pursuit of competitors' holdings as well as in his involvement with a venture known as the South Fork Fishing and Hunting Club, a private resort he'd formed with partners on a former canal reservoir in the mountains northwest of Pittsburgh. While accounts vary as to whose idea it was, Carnegie's or Frick's, the result that was toasted at the meeting produced benefits for both. The H. C. Frick Coke Company was to become the exclusive supplier of coke for all of Carnegie's iron and steel works. Frick would take a half-interest in the Carnegie coke works at Monastery, and though Carnegie would brag to competitors that he now controlled half of the King of Coke's holdings, he would actually receive little more than a 10-percent interest in Frick's company.

While it was reported that the meeting of the Fricks and the Carnegies was lengthy and voluble (though Carnegie would have been the one to carry the conversation without much help from the more taciturn Frick), the most memorable line was delivered by Margaret Carnegie. After listening to her son toast the formation of the new partnership, it is reported, she responded in classical Scots fashion, "Ah, Andra, that's a verra good thing for Mr. Freek, but what do we get out of it?"

Doubtless Carnegie explained to her later what they got out of it: the assurance of a steady supply of coke at a price that would be influenced, if not controlled, by their new association with Frick. The price to be paid would be settled on by Tom Carnegie and Frick each January 1, and would remain in effect for the year that followed.

From Carnegie's point of view the partnership seemed a success for other reasons as well. In December 1882, Carnegie wrote to Frick to express his delight at how well their partnership was working: "I am much pleased with the statement sent me—I think we can live in any kind of weather," he concluded. And in April 1883, Frick sent a report to Tom Carnegie showing that over the previous fourteen months, H. C. Frick had sold almost 950,000 tons of coke at a profit of $378,000, a net return of nearly 23 percent.

Frick followed up on this good news by urging Carnegie to invest in the acquisition of more land and ovens in the Connellsville area. When Carnegie wavered, Frick wrote him a testy letter that acknowledged Carnegie's genius in general, but reasserted Frick's confidence in his own judgment when it came to matters of coke and coal.

"I have great admiration for your acknowledged abilities and your general good judgment, and would much prefer to defer to your views," Frick wrote Carnegie in August 1883, "[but] in the matter of the values of the properties in question and the propriety of increasing our stock, I shall have to differ from you and I think the future will bear me out." Whatever Carnegie may have thought of this obstreperousness, he gave his approval, and the capacity of Frick Coke was doubled.

Frick continued to pursue acquisitions vigorously, bankrolling some of his purchases with sales of his stock to Carnegie. In addition, the Carnegies also set about buying up the stock of H. C. Frick owned by partners with whom Frick had been involved with early on. The process continued until the fall of 1883, by which time Carnegie's original boast had proven true.

He now owned 50 percent of the H. C. Frick Coke Company, with original Frick associates holding 33 percent, and Frick holding the remaining 16 percent. The company still bore Frick's name, and he was still regarded as the leading figure in the world of coal and coke, but as a monarch, he was decidedly less powerful. Furthermore, the benefits to Carnegie's iron and steel works were considerable. On the average, his plants paid about eighteen cents less per ton for their coke than did competitors. The result was a savings of some $50,000 for a year's operations ending in 1885, about 4 percent of net profits. By 1888, dividends from H. C. Frick operations would total almost $2 million, which were slightly higher than the total of those from the Carnegie iron and steel works themselves.

The situation was not always comfortable for Frick. During the inevitable periods of slack demand for coke, he was invariably called upon to lend his support to various coalitions of coke manufacturers formed in order to avert price wars as well as the outright collapse of coke interests. On one such occasion in 1884, recounted by Kenneth Warren in *Triumphant Capitalism,* at a time when nearly half the coke ovens in the Connellsville area sat idle, a group of producers known as the "Coke Syndicate" met and agreed to fix the price of coke at $1.50 per ton.

Having got wind of this, Carnegie sent an emissary, John Walker, to the coke producers' meeting to inquire what the price would be for him. Without hesitation, Frick told Walker, "A dollar-fifty a ton."

Walker shook his head. Whatever price Frick and his fellow coke makers might be able to squeeze out of his other customers was of little consequence: Carnegie would pay H. C. Frick $1.15 per ton and there would be no further discussion of the matter.

Frick was stunned, but he also realized how the power had shifted. "Gentlemen," he said to his fellow coke producers, "you have just heard what the worthy representative of the majority stockholders in the H. C. Frick Coke Company said." In the next breath, he resigned his position in the Coke Syndicate, then left the room to embark upon a voyage to Europe, returning only when Carnegie cabled an apology through a mutual friend.

It might have been a warning to Carnegie that Frick was not easily "managed," but when his old friend and partner Henry Phipps reminded Carnegie of the public blow that Frick's pride had taken, Carnegie set the matter aside, for by and large the association between Frick and Carnegie worked to the benefit of both.

Frick's talent for spotting acquisitions at a bargain was as infallible as his knack for managing his properties efficiently. And Carnegie, while recognizing the need to be more discreet in revealing the details of his arrangements with Frick, enjoyed increased profits from his iron and steel operations as well as a significant return of dividends from his investments in coke. By 1889, Carnegie's company had received over $500,000 in dividends from H. C. Frick Coke, and he himself had received nearly $500,000 more.

In addition, Frick had proven himself quite useful to Carnegie in other ways. In one instance he was able to intercede on behalf of Carnegie, who was involved in a dispute with the Philadelphia Company over the price of natural gas. When an impasse loomed, it was Frick who suggested that the case be arbitrated by the son of the eminent former Pennsylvania jurist, none other than Andrew Mellon.

On another occasion he helped Carnegie obtain favorable freight rates from the Pennsylvania Railroad.

There were other, less tangible advantages to the association with Frick as well. Some found the generally reserved Swiss-German the possessor of a more refined temperament than Carnegie, who sometimes seemed to try too hard to project the enthusiasm and bonhomie he deemed essential to business relations. James Bridge, the Englishman who would become Carnegie's literary assistant, later wrote in *Millionaires and Grub Street* that for all his legendary toughness, Frick normally maintained an "extremely courteous, almost deferential manner. . . . He seemed more polished, more refined than the Carnegie brothers, who . . . had the rough friendliness of Western men who do big things."

For his part, Frick not only relished the access to Carnegie's capital but saw in their continued association an avenue to his own extravagant dreams. Coke was important, yes, but ultimately it was a secondary element in a much grander scheme. From the first days of his association with Carnegie, what Henry Clay Frick longed for was an entry into steel.

# 6

## GOOD FOR THE GOOSE . . .

———➤◆◄———

Though Frick was justifiably proud of his accomplishments, and continued his energetic stewardship of H. C. Frick Coke through the first half of the 1880s as zealously as if he were still a sole proprietor, it took no particular genius for an ambitious man to see where the future lay. Andrew Carnegie had become immensely successful as one of the leaders of the emerging steel industry, and Frick was determined to grow beyond his role as mere purveyor to the mighty, no matter how lucrative and secure that post might be. Furthermore, he was willing to divest himself almost completely of his holdings in coal and coke if that was what it would take to accomplish his goal.

By the end of 1885 he had formulated a plan to buy into the Carnegie interests, a move that he intended to finance by selling off most of his remaining stock in H. C. Frick Coke. Though it would leave him with a mere 4 percent of the company that bore his name, Frick was as resolute about his entry into steel as Carnegie had been some fifteen years earlier.

Henry Phipps, a childhood friend of the Carnegies' and a partner since the days of Cyclops Iron, encouraged Frick, but the Carnegies were more resistant. When he heard of Frick's plans, Tom Carnegie wrote back a less than enthusiastic note: "In the matter of your prospective interest with CB [Carnegie Brothers] and Co. I cannot help but think that you should become a manager. . . . I wish you to reconsider and submit the matter to AC—good bye—I'm off to Florida—nothing can trouble me further for months, Yours TMC."

"AC" was even more pointed in his response. In late February 1886 he composed a lengthy letter to Frick that began by saying, "[I]n my opinion you propose what would be the mistake of your life. Your career must be identified with the Frick Coke Co. You never could become the Creator of CB and Co. Twenty years from now you might be a large owner in it, perhaps be the principal, still the concern would not be your work and you could not be proud of it."

Carnegie carried on at some length in this scolding tone: "I cannot imagine how your pride permitted you to think for one moment of sinking to an insignificant holder of 4 percent in your own Creation. To think that you could ever be influential in its councils with such a petty interest is absurd. You would merely be the agent of the real men in the concern. . . . The idea is suicidal."

He urged Frick to set his sights instead on reacquiring control of his own company and concluded with a reprise of his own advice to himself from the eggs-and-basket days: "I believe you will make more millions by concentrating than by scattering. . . . I never could advise you to divide your thoughts and time between concerns when your own field was fully open before you. Go and possess it or sink into merited insignificance."

It was hardly the response that Frick had hoped for, and the prospect of being dictated to by "real men" whose virility was measured by the size of their holdings must have stung. But whether as a result of dispassionate calculation or pure intuition or some combination of both, Frick was determined to find a way into steel.

There is, it should be noted, a school of thought among historians which posits that the notion of genius is misguided, that the emergence of a Vanderbilt or a Carnegie or a Rockefeller onto the world stage is a kind of accident. In 1950, the historian Thomas C. Cochran published a paper urging the adoption of a new form of "entrepreneurial history" that would focus not on the anecdotal and unique qualities of individual business leaders, but upon the cultural and social structures that produced such men.

In this view, had Rockefeller inadvertently stepped into the path of a train as he scurried about northern Pennsylvania tying up oil leases, forces greater than the will of any single individual would have given rise to a replacement, with the result that skaters might today circle endlessly about an ice rink in Someotherperson Center. Similarly, had the Black Death in Europe claimed the right (or wrong) ancestor, the world might be celebrating the plays of Smithy rather than Shakespeare.

Part of Cochran's aim was to discredit the nineteenth-century myth of rags-to-riches achievement. In truth, the vast majority of men who rose to prominence in the iron and steel industry were white, Anglo-Saxon Protestants whose parents were of the upper class or the upper middle class, whose families had lived in the United States since well before the Civil War, and whose fathers and grandfathers had been involved directly or indirectly in the iron business from its earliest days. According to a study undertaken by industry historian John N. Ingham *(The Iron Barons: A Social Analysis of an American Urban Elite)*, only 12 percent of iron and steel manufacturers were born outside the United States. According to Ingham, all of 1 percent of manufacturers had fathers who had been unskilled workmen in the iron and steel trades before them.

The figures are interesting to the modern eye, of course, and Cochran's is an intriguing notion, inviting any number of fanciful scenarios. But such thinking undervalues individual brilliance and achievement, and the statistics actually make the accomplishment of such men as Frick and Flagler and Carnegie all the more impressive. As the late cable TV programming pioneer Peter Barton put it in his memoir, *Not Fade Away*, "Ninety-nine percent of people in business just move preexisting pieces around the board. Entrepreneurs create. If they are very good at what they do . . . they may leave behind something that will continue after they're gone."

In his *Giants of Enterprise* (2002), Harvard Business School professor Richard S. Tedlow expands on this view. There was nothing inevitable about the accomplishments of men such as Carnegie, Tedlow says. "No theory of institutions which does not take account of the talent, genius, idiosyncrasy, and, at times, idiocy of the individual leader can explain how American came to do best what it does best."

Tedlow argues that had men such as Carnegie and Frick been born in Italy at a certain time in history, they might have become composers. Had they been Russians, they might have been novelists. If born Portuguese, they might have become navigators. But, born in a country that has excelled in the production of entrepreneurs, that was what they became.

For whatever reason, Henry Clay Frick made it his business to make steel his business, and not even such stinging rebukes as those he received from one of the most powerful tycoons of the day could dissuade him. For the moment, however, there was little he could do but bide his time.

No one who lived in the 1880s could be deceived concerning the frailty of human existence, not even those who enjoyed the fullest bounty of a "Gilded Age." Fully 215 of every thousand children born did not survive the first year of life. At the turn of the twenty-first century, in contrast, the infant mortality rate was 7.7 per thousand. A person born in 1880 might have expected to live all of forty years. Today the average life expectancy stands at seventy-six.

Actuarial statistics of the Frick and Carnegie era dictated that one in four children would not survive to celebrate an eighteenth birthday, and deadly epidemics of cholera, yellow fever, typhoid fever, and influenza were a part of everyday life. As recently as 1866, a cholera outbreak claimed the lives of nearly 1,200 New York City residents, and physicians of the 1880s were divided on the question of whether the still highly suspect "germ theory" explained the transmission of disease, or whether those who succumbed were simply genetically, psychologically, or spiritually predisposed to fall ill and die.

In any case, most cities still lacked piped water, processes of chlorination, and sanitary sewers; and the development of sulfa drugs, penicillin, and antibiotics was still a half-century away. Even as the United States prepared to take command of the industrialized world, the prospect of serious illness and death was a constant threat to the rich as well as the poor.

Henry Frick had himself contracted scarlet fever as a boy and later suffered an attack of rheumatic fever. The effects of the diseases would haunt him all his life, making him prone to stress-related flare-ups of rheumatoid arthritis that rendered him helpless for days or weeks at a time.

Nor were the Carnegies immune to ill health. In the fall of 1886, Andrew Carnegie fell ill with typhoid. As he lay gravely ill at his Cresson, Pennsylvania, summer home, where it was hoped that the cool, clean air of the Alleghenies would assist his recovery, his brother, Tom, hard at work in Pittsburgh, was stricken with pneumonia.

An alarmed Henry Phipps contacted fellow partner John Walker to express his fears that both would die. Walker, the no-nonsense emissary who had once dictated terms to Henry Frick, observed that while the notoriously hard-drinking Tom Carnegie might have a tough go of it, it would take more than typhoid to finish off the abstemious and iron-willed Andrew, even if the older brother was over fifty at the time.

Walker's prophecy proved correct on both counts. Andrew Carnegie would survive. But his beloved brother Tom died, on October 19, just five days after he fell ill.

While Henry Phipps was pressed into service as chairman of

Carnegie Brothers, everyone understood that it was a stopgap arrangement. Phipps was a lifelong and loyal friend to the Carnegies and was the possessor of a keen financial mind. But he had neither the will nor the temperament of a leader.

Managers within the ranks were already consulting Henry Frick on pressing issues of purchasing, and on November 1, 1886, a still-grieving Andrew Carnegie offered Frick the opportunity he had coveted for so long, and at terms Frick could scarcely have hoped for: Frick would receive $100,000 of Carnegie Brothers stock for the sum of $184,000, all of it payable upon receipt of future dividends.

While the death of his brother (and principal firm manager) had been a severe blow, Carnegie saw advantages in promoting Frick to fill the void at Carnegie Brothers. Tom had always exhibited a ready grasp of the complexities of the steelmaking business, and he had been a well-respected manager. But to hard-charging Andrew Carnegie, his brother had sometimes proven to be a bit reluctant and risk-averse as a competitor and entrepreneur. There would be no such timidity with Frick, of that much Carnegie was certain, and if it meant allowing Frick his wish to buy into the company, it was a small price to pay. It had taken the death of Tom Carnegie to accomplish it, but Henry Frick was now a partner in steel.

# 7

# A ROCK AND A HARD PLACE

———◆———

THE SERIOUS ILLNESS THAT HAD BEFALLEN Andrew Carnegie and the death of his friend Tom Carnegie had not only saddened but jolted principal partner and company chairman Henry Phipps. To ensure that the company would never again face the prospect of collapse or takeover owing to the death of its founder, Phipps convinced Carnegie that they should prepare the first of what became known as the "Iron Clad Agreements."

As Phipps pointed out, though Tom Carnegie's holdings in the company were sizable (about 17 percent), Andrew had the where-withal to absorb most of his brother's interests and reach a settlement with his brother's widow to pay for them over time. But had it been Andrew Carnegie who died, his majority interests in the Carnegie companies would have required immediate liquidation of the entire enterprise, thereby ensuring bankruptcy for the company.

The Iron Clad Agreement that Phipps devised functioned as a safety net, ensuring that the company had ample time to arrange for the purchase of a deceased partner's shares, at book value. The period varied according to the size of the interest held, from four months to acquire holdings of 4 percent or less to fifteen years in the case of Carnegie's vast holdings.

It sounded reasonable, especially in the light of recent events. But a closer look at the terms of the agreement revealed that Phipps and Carnegie had taken advantage of the situation to leverage greater control over the company's fortunes. The agreement included a provision that required any partner, dead or living, to sell his interest upon a vote of three-quarters of the other parties and interests in the firm. As a result, though he himself would never be subject to such provisions, Carnegie could easily marshal the forces necessary to squeeze out any partner who became troublesome.

It is doubtful that either Phipps or Carnegie was prompted to draft the clause by the entrance of Frick into the firm, though one day it would seem so. Moreover, there is no record of Frick objecting to the terms; like the other partners, he signed the agreement, thus indissolubly wedding his fortunes to Carnegie's.

If Carnegie had envisioned a long and blissful honeymoon with the new partner he had hailed as a management genius, his hopes were soon dashed. Over the course of the 1880s, steel had become increasingly important within the allied metals industry, and the demand for coke had risen to unprecedented levels. The situation was good for coke producers, obviously, but it placed a strain on steel manufacturers to maintain a steady supply of coke at a reasonable price. The situation also emboldened laborers in the coke fields, who began to sense the increasing leverage they held in demanding a fair wage.

In addition, railroading had returned from the recession of the late 1870s with a vengeance. The year 1886 would prove to be a record setter, with rail production reaching 120 percent of any previous year's output. At the same time, men who saw owners profiting at record levels were being forced to work in the coke regions at rates agreed upon in 1884. Old grievances concerning the mandated use of company stores and traditional accusations that the company was shorting men on the weights of coal and coke they produced also resurfaced.

Nor were Carnegie's works safe from labor agitation. In late 1885, recognizing that his own workers would become restless once they learned of the record $3 million in profits accrued by his firm, Carnegie sought to forestall trouble by issuing a blanket 10-percent raise. But for the more skilled and experienced workers it was not enough. They were also restless for a return to the eight-hour shifts that had been rescinded during a business downturn.

When the furnace men began to organize, Captain Jones, with his employer's blessing, launched a preemptive move of his own, dismissing seven hundred skilled operators and calling in strikebreakers or "scabs" to replace them. The actions so outraged the rank and file that a general walkout began, bringing a complete halt to production. By April, Jones and Carnegie were forced to give in to the demands of the striking workers, and the men went back to their jobs, the eight-hour shifts restored.

Labor unrest was not confined to the arena of steel. Everywhere new immigrants were gaining perspective on their place in the scheme of things and demanding a say in their working conditions as well as a share in the soaring profits enjoyed by owners. In March 1886, New York City horse-car drivers and conductors went on strike to demand, among other things, that their workday be reduced from sixteen to twelve hours. When scabs were brought in to replace them, riots broke out, bringing transport within the city to a halt.

On May 4, a rally in support of the growing call for a nationally mandated eight-hour work shift was called in Chicago's Haymarket Square, galvanized by an ongoing strike by workers at the nearby McCormick Harvesting Machine Company. On the previous day, police had fired into a group of protesting strikers, killing four. The May 4 rally was one of several organized by labor and anarchist groups in Chicago, and elsewhere, to protest the killings.

Though about thirteen hundred showed up at Haymarket Square, many left when it began to rain. Only three hundred or so die-hards remained when a squadron of two hundred or so policemen descended on the square, demanding that the assembly disperse. As angry shouts flew back and forth and nightsticks began to flail, a bomb exploded in the midst of a knot of policemen. One died instantly, and seven more would succumb to their wounds. Panicked officers began to fire indiscriminately at anyone who moved. Eight people in the crowd were killed, and another hundred were wounded, as many of them officers as protestors.

The Haymarket Riot spurred a nationwide wave of fear, much of it directed at recent immigrants, who formed the majority of unskilled labor's rank and file. Though the person who'd thrown the bomb was never identified, eight anarchists were charged, and seven received death sentences, further inflaming passions on both sides of the issues.

When unrest threatened to spill over to the immigrant-heavy workforce in the coal and coke fields of Pennsylvania, Carnegie, whose own unskilled labor force included a sizable contingent of the newly arrived, dashed off an overheated note to Frick: "I agree that these foreigners must learn they can't quit work and riot in this free country."

It was quite an about-face for a man who, in response to the growing labor difficulties of the day, had just published a pair of hotly debated articles in *Forum,* the recently minted New York "magazine of controversy." In the first, published in April 1886, Carnegie traced what he called the "triumphal march" of labor's three-hundred-year struggle against capital, and observed that a contempo-  rary laborer stood on equal terms with his employer and enjoyed the "dignity of an independent contractor."

He concluded with a statement that infuriated any number of his fellow capitalists: "The right of the working-men to combine and to form trades-unions is no less sacred than the right of the manufacturer to enter into associations and conferences with his fellows."

Those who had witnessed Carnegie's unsuccessful efforts to lock out his furnace tenders at the Edgar Thomson works in 1885 must have wondered if the author of the *Forum* article was truly the same man. If he saw the contradiction, however, Carnegie did not let it deter him. After all, this was the same year that would see the publication of his most popular volume (he would publish eight books in all), *Triumphant Democracy*.

With the help of James Bridge, who polished and extended Carnegie's pithy if sometimes overly telegraphic prose, Carnegie had delivered to Charles Scribner's Sons a five-hundred-plus-page paean to the superiority of the American system, where, in his eyes, democracy and capitalist enterprise were entwined in a fashion far more productive than—as well as morally superior to—the workings of the British and European monarchies. He boasted that America's workingmen were of a much more refined class than their British counterparts, living a lifestyle where "wife-beating is scarcely ever heard of, and drunkenness is quite rare."

And in an equally ingenuous tone, he proclaimed that his adopted nation maintained no imperialist armies, but "spends her money for better ends and has nothing worthy to rank as a ship of war." If he had any notion that within a few months he would approve the building of a specialty mill within the Homestead works devoted to the production of ships' armor, Carnegie was not admitting to it in *Triumphant Democracy*. Whatever its factual and logical shortcomings, the book's unfailing optimism proved popular both at home and abroad. Even workingmen found the book easy to come by, for a number of labor organizations underwrote sizable purchases of the volume for distribution among the ranks.

For the most part, conservatives and fellow boosters of the capitalist enterprise praised Carnegie's sentiments, while liberal thinkers were more apt to take issue. On the heels of the book's publication, Herbert Spencer wrote Carnegie to argue that unbridled ambition was a curse for the average American. In a country where the concept of advancement was foreign, Spencer wrote, "each has to be content with the hum-drum career in which circumstances have placed him, and . . . is led to make the best of what satisfaction in life fall to his share."

In its review, *The Dial*, a self-proclaimed "socially humanitarian" magazine once edited by Ralph Waldo Emerson, questioned whether or not the statistics trotted out by Carnegie on productivity and railroad expansion were the true gauge of a country's merit. "It wouldn't hurt if we had less bragging and more books," *The Dial* concluded.

Despite such cavils, *Triumphant Democracy* went through four printings in the United States and racked up even greater sales in Europe—likely aided by its quasi-scandalous scolding of the monarchy. Indeed, a mass-market paperback edition sold more than forty thousand copies in Britain, a sizable figure even by today's standards.

Undeterred by the critics who found his logic specious or by his many peers who feared he was encouraging the critics of big business, Carnegie published a second, equally confounding article in the wake of the Haymarket debacle, this in the August 1886 issue of *Forum*. In it he downplayed the fear that the nation was on the verge of a workingman's insurrection, and went so far as to defend workers who sometimes turned to violence: "To expect that one dependent on his daily wage for the necessities of life will stand by peaceably and see a new man employed in his stead, is to expect too much."

As if these sentiments did not seem dangerous enough to his fellow industrialists, he then made the declaration that opponents on both sides of the issue would use against him ever after: "There is an unwritten law among the best workmen," Carnegie penned, in near-biblical tones. "Thou shalt not take thy neighbor's job."

Historians have labored long to explain the contradictions between Carnegie's public statements and his zealous anti-union practices. Some point to the influence of his impoverished childhood and his awareness of his forebears' democratic leanings. Had Carnegie been challenged, he would surely have defended himself vigorously as the possessor of a special understanding of the laborer, having himself been "one of the downtrodden." And he would always on some sentimental level identify with the less fortunate. But for all his noble sentiments, he had long ago ceased to be a workingman, and whatever the tenor of his public statements, his energies were now devoted to preserving his new status as an accumulator.

Nevertheless, Carnegie continued to make noble statements about the workingman to the very end of his life, seemingly untroubled by those who criticized his business and labor practices. As to *why* he might have done so, the most cursory examination of the history of American business shows that Carnegie is scarcely the only man of prominence who wanted very much to be liked.

◆　　◆　　◆

WHATEVER THE SINCERITY OF Carnegie's feelings for the workingman, he would soon encounter more trouble from that quarter. Tensions in Frick's coke works finally reached the breaking point in late 1886, when workers there, many of them recent immigrants from Hungary and other Eastern European countries, who were indiscriminately referred to as "Huns" or "Hunkies," organized with the help of the Knights of Labor and the Amalgamated Association of Mine Laborers, demanding wage increases of up to 20 percent.

Carnegie suggested that Frick turn the matter over to an arbitrator, and Frick reluctantly complied. The result was the offer of a 10-percent increase. The unions refused the offer, however, and went on strike at the end of the first week of May 1887.

Frick soon found himself in a difficult position. Steelmakers besides Carnegie whom he supplied were condemning him for his inability to deal fairly with his own workers (and thereby ensure an uninterrupted delivery of the coke that was the lifeblood of their businesses). On the other hand, his fellow coke manufacturers were warning him not to give in to the workers' demands and grant wage concessions that would ultimately have to be matched elsewhere and thus cut into the profits of the entire industry. One, Colonel James M.

Schoonmaker, wrote to Frick, warning that Frick's association with Carnegie made him a seeming pawn of the steelmaking interests.

"There never was and probably never will be a better opportunity than now for you either to be the President of the H. C. Frick Coke Company for all time in the future or merely a representative of other interests in the sacrifice of your own," Schoonmaker said. A former Civil War hero, Schoonmaker continued with an appeal to Frick's virility. "You are bound by all the ties of honor to stand by those whose interests are identical with yours," he said. "We are bound to come out all right if you stay with us and I never have doubted your nerve or manhood in any issue past or present."

On the other side of such entreaty was Carnegie, who, despite being on vacation in Scotland, fired off a cable to Frick demanding that he settle with his men so that production could proceed without interruption at Edgar Thomson, Union Mills, and the newly acquired Bessemer Steel Company at Homestead. Carnegie was accustomed to obedience from his subordinates, but if he expected unquestioned subservience from Henry Frick, he had gravely miscalculated.

The truth was that Frick had, from the beginning of his career, been a hard-liner on labor issues, incensed by the interference of labor organizers in what he considered a process properly left to the discretion of owners. The Molly Maguires, a secret society for the protection of laborers formed in Ireland, had found its way to the coalfields of Pennsylvania as early as the 1840s, and during a miners' strike in the mid-1870s had been blamed for the murder of several local law enforcement officers, elected officials, and mining personnel. It was not lost on Frick that one of his fellow owners had stamped out the threat by importing a number of Pinkerton detectives from Philadelphia to infiltrate the group. Information provided by the undercover agents led to the hanging of at least twenty men suspected of involvement in the killings.

Frick himself had succeeded in quashing strikes in his coke fields, and a story related by Martha Frick Sanger illustrates his penchant for summary action. During an 1877 railroad strike that disrupted the shipment of coal and coke in the Connellsville area, Frick accompanied a sheriff's deputy to help evict a striker who lived in a shack on the property Frick had sold at a handsome profit to the Baltimore & Ohio Railroad. Told that he would have to leave, the striker refused. Frick, who weighed all of 130 pounds, glanced at the deputy and an unspoken message passed between them. In the next moment they grabbed the obstinate striker by the hands and feet and flung him off the embankment where they'd been arguing, and into a nearby creek. As the striker struggled to his feet, he found his belongings flying after him, including his mattress, bedclothes, and razor.

When it came time to make a decision regarding the strikers in his own backyard, then, Frick reverted to form. He might have been goaded by Colonel Schoonmaker's jabs at his manhood, or he could just as well have been remembering Carnegie's threats that he would one day find himself in a diminished position on his own turf. As the *Illustrated Weekly,* a popular New York–based publication, once put it, "Mr. Frick is of a forceful, self-reliant nature, and in previous conflicts with labor organizations has shown a determination to carry his point at all hazards."

Whatever the reasons, Frick responded in rather startling fashion to Carnegie's demands that he settle with the strikers. In a letter delivered to Henry Phipps and John Walker, Frick got quickly to the point: "As you hold a majority of the stock and are entitled to control in the Frick Coke Company, and in viewing what has passed between us on the subject, I feel compelled to vacate my position as its President. I therefore enclose, herewith, my resignation."

He went on to argue that giving in to the present set of demands would set an unfortunate precedent for future strikers, and complained that he was being unfairly squeezed by Phipps and Carnegie. "I object to so manifest a prostitution of the Coke Company's interests in order to promote your steel interests," he wrote, as if unaware that Carnegie's dire predictions concerning the loss of control of one's destiny had finally come true. "Whilst a majority of the stock entitles you to control, I deny that it confers the right to manage."

He might have declined to recognize this truth, but such denial did not change it. A terse cable from Carnegie followed: "Please don't mislead me second time remember suffered enough last time make no mistake no stoppage tolerated. Reply."

Frick's reply came in the form of a confirmation of his resignation, which took effect in early June 1887. And in July, while Henry Phipps struggled to replace him at the reins of a business he scarcely understood, Frick went on an extended European vacation. If Phipps and Carnegie were intent on running the coke business, then have at it, his actions seemed to say.

The local press had a field day with the story. CARNEGIE THUNDERS FROM HIS CASTLE IN THE SCOTTISH HIGHLANDS—HIS BOLT WRECKS THE SYNDICATE—FRICK OVERPOWERED RESIGNS—HUNGARIANS DANCE WITH GLEE, read one headline, enough to send anyone on vacation.

Frick took his time touring Germany, Switzerland, Austria, and France, but on his way back to the United States, a cable from Carnegie reached him, one that he had doubtless been expecting. "Come and spend a week with us," Carnegie wrote. "It's superb— Come and see what one gets in Scotland these summer days."

The cable had originated at Kilgraston House, a rented estate where Carnegie, at age fifty-two, was honeymooning with his new wife, the former Louise Whitfield, daughter of a New York City merchant. Carnegie had met Louise in the mid-1870s and from then on had courted her steadily, if surreptitiously, owing to his mother's skepticism that any woman could be good enough for her Andra.

Though Margaret Carnegie was a tireless champion of her first-born son, she was wary of female interlopers. As illustration of the hold she exerted, Carnegie biographer Joseph Frazier Wall relates a story from Carnegie's bobbin-boy days. When he returned home from work one evening to find his mother weeping in despair, the twelve-year-old Carnegie hurried to her side and begged her not to cry. "Some day," he swore, "I'll be rich, and we'll ride in a fine coach driven by four horses." Margaret stopped crying long enough to retort, "That will do no good over here, if no one in Dunfermline can see us." As the tale goes, Carnegie was not put off. He amended his declaration then and there: one day they would return to Dunfermline itself in their own coach and four, and the whole town would know about it.

As it happened, the two did make that triumphant return, in 1881, when Carnegie's mother was invited by city fathers to lay the cornerstone for one of his public libraries. It was exactly as Carnegie must have dreamed it would be, some thirty-four years previously, with one exception: another woman had entered the picture. That woman was Louise Whitfield, and Carnegie wanted her to come along. As a first step, Carnegie had managed to persuade his mother to visit Louise's mother to assure her that all would proceed with the proper decorum.

Though other young friends of Miss Whitfield's were scheduled to make the trip, Margaret Carnegie was not fooled. As Wall tells it, she made her visit to the Whitfield home, all right, and even proposed that Louise be permitted to make the journey. But when Mrs. Whitfield politely responded by asking Margaret what she thought of it all, Mother Margaret saw her opening. "Well," she said, drawing herself up, "if she were a daughter of mine, she wouldna go."

The trip to Dunfermline proceeded, but without Louise, as Carnegie, despite his power in the business arena, remained cowed by his mother. He also remained smitten by Louise Whitfield, who was twenty-two years his junior, and in 1883 became secretly engaged to her.

As long as Margaret was alive, however, they would not marry. It was not until late in 1886 that the matter was resolved. On November 10, less than a month after the death of his brother, and while Carnegie himself drifted in and out of his typhoid-induced delirium, an enfeebled Margaret Carnegie finally died. So fearful was his physician that his mother's death would send Carnegie into a tailspin, he arranged for her coffin to be lowered from her bedroom window rather than risk having Carnegie see it carried past his bedroom door.

The deaths in close succession of his brother and mother did have a profound effect on Carnegie, who wrote in his autobiography, "My life as a happy careless young man, with every want looked after, was over. I was left alone in the world."

If his childhood was over at the ripe old age of fifty-one, Carnegie was not left alone for too long. With his mother gone, he and Louise were free to plan their long-postponed nuptials—and on April 22, 1887, less than six months after his mother's burial, the two were married in a private ceremony at the Whitfield home. Less than an hour after the wedding, they embarked on a cruise to London and from there traveled to Scotland, where they settled in at Kilgraston, near the town of Perth, and where Carnegie would invite Frick for a conciliatory visit. (Some family members have questioned Carnegie's storybook devotion to Louise, by the way. As it is told by one of his nieces, Carnegie had long been smitten by Tom's wife, Lucy, and in fact proposed marriage to her shortly after his brother's death. According to Nancy Carnegie, only when Lucy dismissed his advances out of hand did Carnegie turn back to Louise.)

As Frick had toured Europe in the weeks following his resignation, Phipps had given in to workers' demands and production had resumed at H. C. Frick Coke. This "return to normalcy" had, however, come at considerable cost. Carnegie might have been relieved to see his furnaces fired up again and steel rolling out the doors, but it troubled him greatly to realize that he was paying twelve and a half percent more than his competitors for his coke. Perhaps Frick had been right.

As a result, Frick had received any number of entreaties from Carnegie, Phipps, Walker, and other members of the board of the H. C. Frick Coke Company, all holding out the olive branch and suggesting overtly or subtly that he reconsider his decision to resign. It had not escaped them that while profits from the firm's sales of coke still rolled in, they might have been twelve and a half percent greater if Frick had remained at the helm.

Finally, Frick decided that he had let Carnegie stew long enough. In September, during a stopover in London, he left his son Childs, then four, and his daughter Martha, two, with a governess while he and his wife Adelaide traveled to Kilgraston to meet with Carnegie. Though Carnegie never publicly disclosed what passed between them, and Frick wrote only that he and Carnegie had taken a long stroll during which Carnegie "brought up the coke matter which we discussed pleasantly and then dropped it without going into the future," the message must somehow have been delivered.

Upon his return to the United States, at the meeting of the H. C. Frick Coke Company on November 5, 1887, Henry Phipps resigned as president and Frick accepted immediate reelection to the position.

If all seemed well and getting better, the incident had taught both partners important lessons about each other. Carnegie saw that Frick was no puppet, but rather a man willing to take considerable risks in defense of his principles. If Frick's actions made clear that he was less pliable than others in Carnegie's circle, they also indicated a strength of will that might be useful if applied to others.

On the other hand, Frick's admiration and awe of Carnegie were tempered by the realization that Carnegie's self-interest reigned supreme. Given Frick's diminished interest in H. C. Frick Coke, it was more important than ever to carve out an enhanced position in the steel concern. It was a matter of self-preservation.

Carnegie was wise enough to grasp Frick's point of view, given that he was the one who had pointed out to Frick the inevitability of this very lesson. And because he had also seen in Frick a managerial capacity second to none, he was willing to overlook Frick's resignation as the understandable act of a proud man. If Frick had been a competitor, he might well have been consigned "to the cart," but as a partner with valuable skills, he deserved a second opportunity.

Carnegie determined to put Frick's managerial talents directly to work within the steel companies, and to ensure Frick's loyalty Carnegie offered him an increased share of the company.

Carnegie's decision might have taken longer to put into practice if it were not for Henry Phipps's decision to retire. In an October 1888 letter to the Carnegie Brothers board, Phipps explained that at age forty-nine, with twenty-eight years in the iron and steel business behind him, and a comfortable estate amassed, he was ready for a respite. He would remain a partner in the firm and a trusted adviser to Carnegie, but his role in the day-to-day affairs of the company was at an end.

The board accepted Phipps's resignation as chairman and appointed David Stewart, a Carnegie business associate and partner from the days of his move to Homewood, as a successor. But almost immediately Stewart died. Clearly the time for Frick had arrived, and on January 14, 1889, Henry Clay Frick was named chairman of Carnegie Brothers and Company, his interest in the company having been increased from 2 to 11 percent.

Carnegie wrote Frick a glowing letter of congratulations that ended with him "expressing my thankfulness that I have found THE MAN, I am always yours, A.C." Frick responded in like manner, seeming to embrace his position at the feet of the throne: "Please advise me a day or two before you arrive in Pittsburgh. Don't want to be away on your arrival as I have many things to ask you about."

The stage seemed set for a long and harmonious relationship between owner and manager, between the nation's most accomplished investor and the man he deemed a genius at making one's investments pay. Even the cautious Henry Phipps had joined the bandwagon, penning a note to Carnegie from a stop on a long-postponed European vacation: "With Mr. Frick at the head, I have no fear. . . ."

Had such unalloyed sentiments been expressed in a novel, experienced readers would have known to expect the worst. This being real life, however, the players in this drama forged blithely ahead.

# 8

## FIRM HAND AT THE WHEEL

———➤◆◄———

S URELY THERE WERE OTHER men in the Carnegie organization who might have been tapped to succeed Phipps and Stewart, men who might have managed well enough at the head of
what had become a vast and diverse business empire propelled on-
ward by the force of its own internal energies. As one modern American president confided during a singularly candid television
interview, "You come to Washington with these grand ideas, but the
truth is that government is so massive and so complex that it is almost impossible for any individual to make a huge difference. It's like
being the captain of an enormous ocean liner. It is going to keep on
going no matter who is at the wheel."

Phipps had done well enough at the wheel of Carnegie Brothers,
of course, and Stewart would likely have done as well, if he had lived.
But to Carnegie, Frick represented something special. Not only had
Frick risen up from nothing, as Carnegie had, and not only had he
proven himself the master of an allied industry—an essential subsidiary to that of steel—Frick had an ambition, a singleness of purpose, and a lack of self-doubt that even Carnegie envied.

Not only did Frick share Carnegie's formulaic view of the

manufacturing enterprise, he exhibited no compunction whatsoever about putting theory into practice. For Frick, there were no paeans to his former brethren among the ranks and no convoluted justifications as to just how and why the rights of workers might somehow be maintained without interfering with a steady flow of profit. Men worked in Frick's plants under the conditions dictated by a competitive marketplace. You either liked it or you went flying down an embankment with your worldly goods hurtling right after you. To operate otherwise was, in Frick's view, financial suicide.

Had Freud's theories taken hold by that time, outsiders might have seen in Frick the embodiment of Carnegie's unfettered id: the perfect profit-driven creature, untroubled by any pusillanimous ego. As it was, most of the others on the Carnegie Brothers board surveyed the complex web that their enterprise had become, and they nodded in agreement when Carnegie decreed that Henry Frick's time had come.

◆　　◆　　◆

OVER THE YEARS, Carnegie's holdings had steadily diversified. To ensure that his Union Mills had a steady supply of "pig" iron, the most basic form of the substance that is molded into usable products, Carnegie had in 1870 formed a separate company to build a huge blast furnace in Pittsburgh dubbed, following the custom of the time, "Lucy," after Tom Carnegie's wife. Though the giant furnace was soon producing 300 tons of iron per day (100 tons had previously been considered a phenomenal output), even that was not enough to satisfy the appetite of Union Mills and Edgar Thomson.

A second furnace went up at Lucy in 1877, and two more were soon installed on the grounds of Braddock's Edgar Thomson works. Much of the pig iron produced by these operations was sent along to other Carnegie works, but at times of slack demand, iron was sold to competitors, and the effort required in maintaining this separate enterprise was formidable.

Additionally, in October 1883, Carnegie had acquired the holdings of one of his nearby rivals, the Pittsburgh Bessemer Steel Company at Homestead, just two and a half miles west of Edgar Thomson, on the south side of the Monongahela River. Pittsburgh Bessemer, built in 1881 on a site where farms had once sprawled, featured two of the most modern and efficient versions of the converters that gave the company its name. Because of a downturn in demand for rails and chronic labor problems, however, the plant was struggling in 1883.

Also key to the plant's struggles was the fact that most of the skilled workers at Pittsburgh Bessemer were members of the Amalgamated Association of Iron and Steel Workers, one of the more powerful national organizations of its type. The AAISW had been formed in the mid-1870s, not as a radical, strike-prone group, but as one dedicated to achieving its goals through negotiation and persuasion. As its own literature proclaimed, "[I]ts history proves it to have been conducted on the theory that the labor organization which secures to its members their rights with the least friction is the one that recommends itself most highly to workmen, to employers and to the public."

Moderate sentiments, perhaps, but to William Clark, the general superintendent of the original Homestead operation, any union was a bad union. Within four months of Pittsburgh Bessemer's opening, Clark called on his skilled workers to resign from the AAISW. When they refused, Clark locked the doors and announced that even those men who agreed to his demands would have to return to work at reduced wages. At that, the entire workforce walked out and a ten-week impasse ensued. Clark finally gave a verbal concession to his workers, who agreed to return, but on the following day he reneged on his agreement and the workers walked out again.

The company's board of directors had had enough by that point, and they sacked Clark and agreed to terms with the union. Hardly had production begun again, however, than rail prices slumped and the firing of a union worker threatened another stoppage. At that point it was the Pittsburgh Bessemer stockholders who rebelled, voting for a sellout of the plant and an end to the headaches of such a business.

Carnegie, who had viewed the struggles of his rival with some interest, and likely with considerable glee, was not surprised when he was approached with an offer. Always ready to snatch up a bargain, and undaunted by a lull in the volatile steel market, Carnegie agreed to buy out Pittsburgh Bessemer's stock at face value, and even offered an exchange of Carnegie Brothers stock for those who preferred it.

As it turned out, nearly everyone took the cash, except for one W. H. Singer, who exchanged his $50,000 stake for Carnegie stock. Singer's choice was a wise one: by 1902 his investment had grown to be worth $8,000,000.

Carnegie also profited, of course. He had paid just about cost for what was generally agreed to be the most modern steel plant in the country, one that could easily be converted from the production of rails to that of steel beams. Carnegie anticipated a leveling-off in the rail business and accurately predicted that the next boom in steel would come from its use as a structural material in building. By 1885, when 70 percent of steel production was still in rails, Carnegie's new Homestead operation was rolling I-beams off the line. (By the early 1900s, rails would constitute only 28 percent of total steel production.)

At the time of Homestead's conversion, however, the management of all these disparate business entities was becoming unwieldy. As a result, in 1886 Carnegie formed a new company—Carnegie, Phipps—merging the operations of the Lucy Furnaces and the Homestead Mill. The structure of the new concern paralleled that of Carnegie Brothers, where he also held a controlling interest.

He might have combined all his operations under one umbrella but for his concerns about the growing "trust-busting" tendencies among politicians. By keeping the two entities distinct, Carnegie could more easily maintain that they were independent, even though he, as majority partner in both, could easily manipulate the flow of materials and services whenever he saw the advantage. Though anti-trust law would one day put an end to such maneuvering, Carnegie reasoned that he was only employing sound business practice.

With Phipps gone from both organizations, Carnegie's need for a management "genius" was genuine, and the eager Frick was the natural choice. The new chairman commenced the exercise of his duties with relish, immediately firing the company's accountant and replacing him with his own man. According to biographer George Harvey, Frick worked from dawn till dusk, taking no holidays and familiarizing himself with every detail of the company's business.

By the middle of the summer, Frick's solicitations of advice from Carnegie had turned into notes suggesting he be left alone: "I cannot stand fault-finding and I must feel that I have the entire confidence of the power that put me where I am." If he sounded a bit paranoid, perhaps the incident of the previous year, when Carnegie had undercut him during the coke strike, was still fresh in Frick's mind.

Carnegie was quick to reassure Frick. "Let me express the relief I feel in knowing that the important departments of our extended business are in the hands of a competent manager," he wrote, adding that "Phipps and I exchanged congratulations on this point." It was apparently enough to assuage Frick's concerns, and the partnership seemed off to a solid start.

Frick would soon prove his worth in matters outside the direct realm of management. In 1888 another competitor, the Allegheny Bessemer Steel Company, had commenced operations five miles or so upriver from Homestead, featuring "direct-rolling," an innovative method of processing steel that eliminated one of the traditional but costly steps of cooling and reheating ingots before they were pressed into rails and the like. Carnegie, distraught when he got the news that a competitor had found a leg up on costs, came up with one of his more imaginative responses.

Knowing he could never match the price of steel produced in this way, he sent a letter to every railroad company in the United States, advising them of the new process known to be in use at Allegheny Bessemer and warning that the elimination of the time-honored second heating of ingots would result in a lack of "homogeneity" in the rails, even implying that this could lead to rail failure and fatalities. There was not one scintilla of evidence for Carnegie's claim, scientific or otherwise; he had simply plucked the "homogeneity" concept out of thin air, and he couched his warning in language vague enough to preclude a legal response.

But if the implications were subtle, the effect was profound and immediate. Orders to Allegheny dried up in an eyeblink. Even the investment partners at the firm began to question their plant managers about the validity of their methods. Intermittent labor disputes slowed production even further, and before long the original partners were desperately seeking a fresh infusion of capital in order to maintain operations. Partners in the enterprise fretted that they would never be able to escape the cloud under which Carnegie's absurd charges had placed them.

And then in stepped Frick to the rescue, offering the major stockholders in Allegheny Bessemer $600,000 for a plant that had cost more than $1 million to build. Frick's initial offer was rejected, but he had expected as much. When he returned with an offer of $1 million, to be paid in the form of bonds issued by Carnegie Brothers (and not to mature for five years), the anxious partners snapped it up.

By the time the bonds matured, operations at the innovative Duquesne mill—their supposedly inferior practices having been put immediately into place at all Carnegie plants—had paid for themselves half a dozen times over. Even given the standards of a far more brawling and far less litigious era, the acquisition would go down as perhaps the most scurrilous episode in the annals of a fiercely competitive industry, and certainly as the greatest bargain in the history of steelmaking.

In his *Inside History of the Carnegie Steel Company*, James Howard Bridge quotes a Carnegie partner of the time who was questioned about whether or not he thought Carnegie's tactics were legitimate. The unidentified partner responded by saying that "under ordinary circumstances he would not have thought it legitimate; but the competition set up by the Duquesne people was also not legitimate, because of their use of this direct rolling process. . . . If they had made rails by our method, we would have recognized them as legitimate competitors."

Whether or not he endorsed such specious logic, Carnegie was ecstatic about the acquisition of Allegheny Bessemer, and his faith in his new manager was validated: "F. is a marvel," he exclaimed to his partners. "Let's get all F's."

WHILE CARNEGIE WAS DELIGHTED to have acquired the holdings of the last of his serious steel-producing rivals in the Monongahela Valley, and clearly assigned credit for the feat to Frick, he was as pleased with having subsumed the methods of production at Duquesne as he was with having acquired the mill itself. What he had purchased in terms of know-how would pay far greater dividends at Carnegie Steel than would ever show up in the balance sheet at Duquesne.

As more than one of Carnegie's managers would recall, the owner was always more interested in what it cost to produce goods than in revenues or profits. Carnegie would repeat the mantra time and again: profits and prices were cyclical, subject to any number of transient forces of the marketplace. Costs, however, could be strictly controlled, and in Carnegie's view, any savings achieved in the cost of goods were permanent. Carnegie rarely balked when his managers suggested improvements to the physical plants of his operations, not if the goal was greater efficiency in production.

During a visit to England in 1885, for example, Carnegie got wind of the fact that his British counterparts were beginning a shift in their methods of steel production, as significant a change as the adoption of the Bessemer converter nearly twenty-five years before. In the late 1870s a young amateur chemist by the name of Sidney Gilchrist-Thomas, a clerk at a London police court, had, in his spare time, concocted a method of steel refining that would allow the use of a much lower grade of iron ore than could be used in the Bessemer converter. Thomas had discovered that applying a heat of about 2,500 degrees Fahrenheit (about 500 degrees hotter than was used in the Bessemer converter) would drive off the high levels of phosphorus found in much of the low-grade ore indigenous to the British Isles. Thomas had developed a new "basic" lining that he claimed would allow retrofitted Bessemer converters to withstand the higher heat.

Carnegie had been interested in the Thomas process from the beginning, but the practical results had been mixed, and ore reserves in the United States were generally of a much higher grade than those available in Europe anyway. What Carnegie learned in 1885, however, reignited his earlier enthusiasm.

Over the past few years the British, too, had discovered that the Thomas process produced uneven results in their Bessemer plants, and had begun to lose faith in it, until new tests revealed a surprising fact: when used in open-hearth furnaces, the Thomas process functioned flawlessly, even with low-grade ore. It was a discovery that would revolutionize the industry.

The open-hearth method, developed by German craftsman Charles Siemens, had been around since the early 1860s, but it had been deemed too expensive for all but a few applications. If Thomas's advancements meant that the far more widespread and vastly cheaper reserves of low-grade iron ore could be used to produce steel, however, then everything changed.

Quite distinct from the Bessemer process, which involved the propulsion of a blast of air upward through a bell-shaped container, the open-hearth method had two fires blazing at either end of an "open" vat of molten iron. When alternating currents of air and gas were forced through the flames and over the iron, impurities were burned off, and the waste gases produced were trapped and used to superheat the next cycle of air and gas, a cycle that continued until the iron had turned to steel of sufficient quality.

Bessemer steelmaking was not for the faint of heart, as Sir Henry Bessemer himself made clear: "The powerful jets of air spring upward through the fluid mass of metal. The air expanding in volume divides itself into globules, or bursts violently upward, carrying with it some hundredweight of fluid metal which again falls into the boiling mass below. Every part of the apparatus trembles under the violent agitation thus produced; a roaring flame rushes from the mouth of the vessel, and as the process advances it changes its violet color to orange, and finally to a voluminous pure white. . . .

"During the process the heat has rapidly risen from the comparatively low temperature of melted pig-iron to one vastly greater than the highest known welding heats; the iron becomes perfectly fluid, and rises so much above the melting-point as to admit of its being poured from the converter into a founder's ladle, and from thence . . . to several successive moulds."

Tending to the Bessemer process was an arduous if spectacular endeavor, often leading to fatalities when converters exploded from heat or overflowed; however, the open-hearth process could be even more dangerous, requiring considerable endurance and physical dexterity from workers as they braved intense heat to dump additives into the enormous open vats of molten metal. More than one worker had tumbled from an overhead catwalk into a pool of red-hot steel, "creating his own mold," as it was said, and countless others were burned and blinded by flying splatters.

Though at the time the open-hearth process was almost unknown within the United States steel industry, Carnegie had learned of Siemens's work early on and had authorized the installation of two open-hearth furnaces at the Edgar Thomson works in 1873. He soon discovered, however, that aside from special orders requiring a final output of the very highest grade of steel, the process was of limited value, and though he kept the furnaces in functional order, he had given them little attention until he came back from Britain in 1885.

Now that his earlier faith in the Thomas process had been reinvigorated and his British counterparts were predicting an end to the use of the time-honored Bessemer converter, Carnegie did not hesitate. He ordered the installation of an open-hearth furnace using the Thomas method at the Homestead plant, and in March 1888 the first run was completed. The results were so heartening that by December Carnegie had become convinced that basic hearth furnaces represented the future of steelmaking.

Although it meant scrapping hundreds of thousands of dollars' worth of Bessemer converters, Carnegie was undeterred. As he wrote to William Abbott, Frick's counterpart at Carnegie, Phipps and Company, "Even if we save half a dollar per ton by the changes, it would justify a large additional expenditure now."

If he had to make a case concerning costs with Abbott, Carnegie had no such difficulty with Frick, for on this issue the two men were of one mind. Frick had made his way in coke by the same reckoning that Carnegie had in rail and then in steel: if you knew your costs down to the penny, you were always on firm ground. Furthermore, Frick had always understood how essential new technologies were in driving costs down. Each man, however, had his own particular province where cost control became nearly an obsession.

Carnegie's fixation was on the freight rates charged by rail carriers—not surprising, given his background. Since he was aware of every shenanigan a railroad might devise in an attempt to extract the maximum from its customers (and had tried most of them himself), he sought to drive a better bargain on behalf of his steel interests. When he discovered that William Vanderbilt was planning to build a line across the state to Pittsburgh that would compete with his old employer, the Pennsylvania Railroad, Carnegie rounded up a group of partners to invest $5 million, giving their group about a one-third interest in the project.

Things looked good for Carnegie, who didn't care whether he ended up doing business with Vanderbilt's new South Pennsylvania Line or with George Roberts, then the president of the Pennsylvania Railroad. With two competitors for his business, he knew he would find a lower rate with one or the other.

Unfortunately for Carnegie, interests even larger than his own took a hand in the matter. Fearful that such impending competition would prove ruinous to both railway interests in which he had placed substantial bond offerings, Wall Street mogul J. P. Morgan, the son of former Carnegie benefactor Junius Morgan, intervened and brokered a compromise between Vanderbilt and Roberts. According to the agreement, Vanderbilt would give up his charter for the South Pennsylvania Line in exchange for the Pennsylvania Railroad's interest in the West Shore, a New York–to–Buffalo line that, when completed, would have gone into competition with Vanderbilt.

Work on the South Pennsylvania Line, which had cost some two thousand lives and many millions of dollars, ceased immediately. The already completed bridge pilings, graded roadbeds, and tunnels blasted through bedrock would remain unused for almost half a century before engineers for the Pennsylvania Turnpike would put them to use in constructing their roadway. When Carnegie discovered what had happened, he was furious, but with a minority control over the project there was little he could do but vow never again to trust the banking house of Morgan.

Carnegie even went so far as to address the Pennsylvania legislature in the spring of 1889, decrying the lack of meaningful rail competition in the state, and calling for the formation of a governmental commission that would oversee the establishment of a fair rate schedule. It was an amazing speech, coming as it did from a champion of the laissez-faire approach to business regulation, but even the considerable clout that Carnegie wielded in western Pennsylvania was no match for the might of the Pennsylvania Railroad. Legislators listened politely to Carnegie's impassioned speech, and some supported his efforts, but in the end no legislation was forthcoming.

Even Frick took a dim view of Carnegie's histrionics over Morgan's tactics, suggesting that he would have been better off keeping his $5 million in his pocket to defray rail costs than going up against the impregnable Pennsylvania Railroad. As Frick pointed out, railroad companies formed a large part of the customer base for the products of Carnegie Brothers, and it seemed better policy to curry good relations with major customers than to go all-out against them. As he wrote to Carnegie in August 1889, "It is very much pleasanter to agree than differ with you and in most things I would and will defer to your judgment . . . but I always hold to the opinion that your attack on P.R.R. was wrong and I should deprecate its renewal."

# 9

## TWO STRIKES . . .

———————▶◆◀———————

THE JUDICIOUS TONE OF FRICK'S note to Carnegie was a clear reflection of how their relationship stood at the time. While Frick did not hesitate to differ with Carnegie, he held his superior in high regard. They were indeed kindred spirits, risen up from the ranks of store clerkdom to become captains of industry and united in their determination to amass great personal wealth. Furthermore, they shared a business philosophy that set them apart from their peers, most of whom were more concerned with net profits and dividends than with the reduction of fixed costs.

There were points of divergence, to be sure. Both Carnegie and Frick agreed on the necessity of containing the costs of labor in the manufacturing process, but each man's approach to the problem, at least as far as the public could see, was distinct.

As a coke operator, Frick had been a hard-nosed opponent of labor organizing; any mine owner who would toss a striking worker into a creek with his mattress flying after him could hardly be classed otherwise. Despite his storied ruthlessness, however, Frick did not altogether lack a sense of humor. Recently restored home movies show him mugging and clowning at Eagle Rock, the family's summer retreat on Boston's North Shore.

And Pat Barnett, a librarian at the Frick Art Reference Library and the granddaughter of a Frick acquaintance, tells of an epic practical joke he played on his friend Andrew Mellon, who often traveled with his wife on a private railcar attached to a regular Pennsylvania Railroad train. On one occasion a conductor entered and demanded their tickets. Mellon explained who they were and that it was *their* car, but the conductor announced, "This is my train and if you don't have tickets, you're not going anywhere." The conductor signaled the engineer to brake at the next stop, and they were summarily ejected onto an empty station platform somewhere in the Pennsylvania hinterlands. The dumbfounded Mellons were at a loss—until another train pulled up, and a familiar figure emerged from the train's stairwell, wreathed in steam. "Andrew!" came the voice of Henry Clay Frick. "Fancy meeting you here!"

Carnegie, on the other hand, had a troublesome need for approval (grandchildren visiting in later years were often bribed by their parents to let "Grandpa Negie" win at cards), a trait that led him to behave in contradictory ways—lauding the efforts of unions even as he sought to undermine them. In fact, it is said that he kept a special file in his desk where any favorable public utterances concerning him were tucked away. In the aftermath of those *Forum* articles, which so troubled his fellow industrialists, the Brotherhood of Locomotive Engineers had named a division after him and appointed him an honorary member of their union, a gesture to which Carnegie often pointed with pride. Next to the certificate designating him a "union man," Carnegie kept a copy of his response to Brotherhood officials: "I feel honored by your adopting my name. It is another strong bond, keeping me to performance of the duties of life worthily, so that I may never do anything of which your society may be ashamed."

One can only imagine Frick's dismay at hearing of such utterances. In practice, however, Carnegie did things that would have won Frick's approval as surely as they would have shamed him in the eyes of the Locomotive Engineers. By 1887, some ten years after Captain

Jones had led the fight for the institution of the three-shift, eight-hour workday at the Edgar Thomson works, the practice had yet to be adopted at any other steel mill in the country. Carnegie, moreover, had seen that it was more expensive to maintain three distinct workforces than two, and ordered that as of January 1, 1888, workers at Edgar Thomson would return to the two-shift, twelve-hour day.

The moment Carnegie's decision was announced, workers at the plant went out on strike. After a conference with Jones, Carnegie announced that the plant would close until the men agreed to return, on his terms, and he held fast for four months, until representatives of the Amalgamated Association of Iron and Steel Workers agreed to negotiate. Carnegie then arranged a meeting of all the workers at Edgar Thomson and invited anyone to stand and air a grievance. According to a Carnegie biography written by Burton Hendrick, one workman stood and began to stammer, "Mr. Carnegie, take my job, for instance . . ."

At which point Carnegie interrupted, delivering one of his most inspired lines: "Mr. Carnegie takes no man's job."

Almost as one, the workers exploded in laughter and, as they stamped their feet, began to chant the now-famous mantra, "Thou shalt not take thy neighbor's job."

After the crowd had calmed, Carnegie went on to describe his proposal for ending the impasse, the implementation of a sliding wage scale tied to the price of steel. Citing a recent downturn in profits, he offered the men a choice: with a full understanding of the difficulties the company faced, they could return to the eight-hour shift at a reduced wage; or they could agree to the twelve-hour shift with the promise of higher wages to come, once steel prices rose. In essence, Carnegie argued, the latter choice would make them partners in a glorious enterprise sure to benefit them all, if not the world as a whole. Buoyed by Carnegie's rhetoric, the men, by secret ballot, overwhelmingly chose the latter option. At essentially no cost to himself, then, Carnegie had found a way to skirt the union demands.

During the following summer of 1889, Carnegie faced a similar problem at his Homestead works, an ominous foretaste of things to come. From the day he had taken over operation of the four-thousand-worker plant, most of the skilled workers at Homestead, about one-quarter of the workforce, had maintained their affiliation with the AAISW. The contract negotiated by the union paid these workers on a flat, per-ton basis, and given that production at Homestead had risen dramatically over the past six years, any change to a sliding scale would have meant significant wage cuts to all these "tonnage" men.

Nonetheless, from a European vacation spot, Carnegie cabled company president William Abbott with orders to issue the announcement: workers would be forced to sign an agreement indicating their acceptance of such a change, if they wanted to continue their employment.

Meanwhile, calamity of a different sort had been brewing in the Carnegie orbit. The spring of 1889 had been an unusually wet one in western Pennsylvania, and the last week of May had seen heavy rainstorms in the area nearly every day. Late on May 30, a pleasant enough Memorial Day was punctuated by yet another torrential downpour.

The members of the South Fork Fishing and Hunting Club, enjoying their sailing and fishing and paddle boating on Lake Conemaugh, the main feature of the exclusive enclave near Johnstown, some sixty miles east of Pittsburgh, hastily took shelter, and the more sagacious of them might have glanced with some concern toward the earthen dam that held back the vast, swollen waters of the lake. At one mile wide by three and a half miles long, and more than seventy feet deep in spots, Lake Conemaugh was said to be the largest artificial body of water in the world at the time, and its many delights had attracted the crème de la crème of Pittsburgh society. But the dam itself had long been a sore spot for the thirty thousand largely working-class citizens of Johnstown who lived fourteen miles—and 450 feet of vertical drop—downstream, along the banks of the flood-prone Little Conemaugh River.

Even before Henry Clay Frick, Benjamin Ruff, and fourteen other prominent Pittsburgh area residents had pooled their resources to buy the old canal reservoir from the Pennsylvania Railroad ten years earlier, engineers had pointed to various defects in the earthen barrier known as the South Fork Dam. The spillway was inadequate and choked by fencing meant to keep expensive stocked fish from escaping the lake, auxiliary discharge pipes had long ago deteriorated and been welded over, and leaks were routinely spotted at the base of the dam, even in the driest of times.

Such observations did not, however, galvanize the club or its membership—which had grown to include Carnegie, Andrew Mellon, Philander C. Knox, and a number of other prominent Pittsburghers—into any meaningful action. In fact, several feet had been shaved off the top of the dam to permit the construction of a road that would allow easier access from the rail station to cottages on the far side of the lake. There had always been complaints about the dam, the reasoning seemed, but the dam had always held.

And so it did, until 4:07 p.m. on the afternoon of May 31, 1889, when, following a night and day of steady rain, a sudden "roar like thunder" reverberated through the canyon below the dam. The sodden earthworks had split like the rind of a rotted melon, and 20 million tons of water exploded down the narrow gorge toward Johnstown.

The wall of water, sixty feet high, tore down the canyon at more than forty miles an hour, obliterating everything in its path. It took out the huge stone viaduct used by the Pennsylvania Railroad to cross the river canyon, then plowed on into Woodvale, the company town maintained by the Cambria Iron Works, one of Carnegie's oldest rivals. In seconds, a population of one thousand was reduced to none. The wave, now a deadly froth of boulders, steel rails, and shattered houses, hit the grounds of the Gautier wire works next, fracturing red-hot furnaces, drowning its workers, and sweeping up miles and miles of newly fabricated barbed wire into the mass.

In less than twenty-five minutes the wave hit Johnstown, sweeping up what structures it did not immediately flatten, then slamming finally to a halt against the mighty stone arches of another Pennsylvania Railroad bridge at the junction of the Little Conemaugh and Stony Creek Rivers. Those still alive, clinging or wrapped by wire to shards of wood and roof, or caught inside bobbing houses, might have thought themselves saved when the rush of waters suddenly stopped.

But it was then that several tanks of oil and fuel uprooted by the flood crashed into the splintered pile at the bridge, causing the entire mass to burst into flame. As anguished bystanders watched from the shore, more than eighty people were burned alive in that ghastly coda to the flood. Ultimately, more than 2,200 lost their lives.

Accusations against the South Fork Fishing and Hunting Club and its construction supervisor, Benjamin Ruff, were swift, with scores of lawsuits threatened and filed. Negotiations with Carnegie's men at Homestead were put on hold as Captain Jones led a contingent of three hundred workers from the Edgar Thomson works to aid the rescue effort.

The Frick and Carnegie companies donated about $15,000 to a relief fund that swelled to nearly $4 million, with contributions coming from around the nation and the world. The South Fork Fishing and Hunting Club donated $3,000, Andrew Mellon another $2,000, and other members contributed as well. However, inconceivable as it may seem to us in our litigious society, no one was ever held responsible for the catastrophe, and not one of the associated lawsuits ever proved successful.

Flood or no, by June 13, Frick seemed impatient to get back to business as usual, writing Carnegie that in light of the Johnstown tragedy, it had been impossible "to do anything with the railroad men . . . but things are beginning to shape themselves." Carnegie, fresh from a visit to the World's Fair in Paris, quickly cabled back, "Glad all is getting back to normal," and urged Abbott to press the men at Homestead to agree to terms or face a shutdown.

Perhaps distance had addled Carnegie's sense of the prevailing mood among his workers, or perhaps the result would have been the same even without the pall cast by the events in Johnstown. In any case, this was one time that the have-nots were in no mood to listen to the dictates of their master. And so it was little surprise that the men refused Carnegie's terms.

Carnegie considered the matter closed, literally. Homestead was not to reopen until the men agreed to work at a figure that he contended would make his steel sufficiently profitable. The strategy had worked before, and he had no doubts that it would work again. Abbott, however, did not prove to be the steadfast general Carnegie had hoped for.

Facing his first strike as a leader of men, Abbott attempted his own means of resolution: he placed ads in local publications offering employment to scab labor. When a group of hopefuls approached the Homestead works, accompanied by a sheriff and 125 deputies, they discovered two thousand striking workers blocking the gates and clearly ready for a fight. In short order, the sheriff and his men and the would-be strikebreakers made a retreat.

Once news of Abbott's tactics spread, workers at nearby Edgar Thomson threatened a sympathy strike. Though Carnegie had anticipated such a move and had told Captain Jones to try to placate the workers until his return, Abbott panicked at the prospect of a Carnegie-wide shutdown. As a result, he agreed to negotiate with the AAISW, and a compromise was reached. The union agreed to work at the sliding scale, but in return, the AAISW was recognized as the sole and rightful bargaining agent at Homestead. The contract was to extend for three years, until July 1, 1892. It meant that no man could be fired or hired at the Homestead works without the union's approval.

Although Carnegie was pleased to have secured the agreement of the men to work for the sliding scale, he was less happy about the entrenchment of the union's position. As he said in a letter to Abbott shortly after, "The great objection to the compromise is of course that it was made under intimidation—our men in other works now know that we will 'confer' with law breakers." Carnegie went on to reaffirm his conviction that the most effective response to a strike was simply to close the plant. "Seems to me a curt refusal to have anything to do with these men would have brought matters right in less time. . . . Whenever we are compelled to make a stand we shall have to shut down and wait as at E.T. [Edgar Thomson] until part of the men vote to work, then it is easy."

Though Carnegie's method was less confrontational, its effect was no less harsh upon the men thrown out of work. Perhaps something in the tactic appealed to Carnegie's complex nature—as if he were saying, "See, I am willing to suffer as well, if you persist in such misguided efforts." But to a man whose family faced eviction and starvation, the degree to which Carnegie "suffered" would have seemed mild indeed.

In any case, hardly had things returned to normal within the Carnegie empire when disaster struck. On the night of September 26, 1890, one of the recently installed basic blast furnaces at the Edgar Thomson works exploded. Captain Jones, who had been standing on a nearby catwalk, was hurled backward by the blast and fell into a red-hot casting pit below. Though his men managed to extract him from the hellish coals, he was terribly burned and had lapsed into a coma. He died two days later, without ever regaining consciousness.

Not only a skilled and beloved manager who had somehow balanced the demands of a taskmaster owner with the rights of his men, Jones was also one of the most innovative technical minds in the industry. In fact, more patents were registered to his name than to any other individual in steel, and those inventions had been an incalculable benefit to Carnegie operations.

Perhaps the most significant of these was the "Jones Mixer," an enormous vat that could hold as much as 250 tons of molten pig iron delivered from various furnaces. The device allowed for the holding and redistribution of molten iron without the need for reheating; given the tremendous amounts of fuel required in heating, the Jones Mixer eliminated one of the most expensive operations in the traditional steelmaking process.

When Henry Phipps began to review the papers left in Jones's files, the magnitude of the company's loss began to sink in. Two days after the Captain's funeral, Carnegie representative George Lauder called on Jones's widow and reached an agreement to purchase all of Jones's patents for $35,000. No one could ever put a dollar figure on the value of those inventions to Carnegie, but as biographer Joseph Frazier Wall put it, the acquisition was more than a bargain, and rivaled the significance of the Duquesne works acquisition the following year.

The tragic death of Jones introduced yet another legend-to-be into Andrew Carnegie's inner circle when, desperate for a replacement, Carnegie appointed to the position one Charles Schwab, the twenty-seven-year-old superintendent of his Homestead works. A former general-store clerk who was uncharacteristically jovial for a budding industrialist, Schwab (no relation to the modern-day stockbroker of the same name) had been hired by Jones personally. The Captain, who patronized the grocery store where the then-seventeen-year-old Schwab worked, was taken by the young man's cheerful manner. When Schwab declared that although he didn't know a thing about steel, he would nonetheless make a fine employee, Jones hired him as a stake driver for E.T. on the spot, and the good-natured Schwab was soon the Captain's personal assistant, carrying messages on a regular basis from Jones to Carnegie, who also found Schwab's lighthearted demeanor a tonic. With a temperament that made him a favorite of his workmen as well as his superiors, and a willingness to accept Carnegie's orders without question, Schwab's lack of technical expertise posed no problem. He would be appointed superintendent at Homestead by the time he was twenty-five.

To Frick, the death of Jones, whom he had always regarded as too sympathetic to labor, provided the impetus for a move he had planned for some time. With Abbott in a weakened position at Carnegie, Phipps, and Jones out of the picture at Edgar Thomson, Frick approached Carnegie with an ambitious proposal: now was the time to reorganize his eggs into one basket, once and for all. Carnegie Brothers and Carnegie, Phipps should become one entity, Frick argued, and the new firm should be recapitalized to more accurately reflect its true worth. The latter move would permit the distribution of a small interest in operations to many of the young managers who were vital to the company's future and thereby ensure their loyalty.

Though Carnegie was hesitant to lose the advantage of one of his companies being able to trade upon the credit of and borrow from the other, Frick pointed out that the Frick Coke Company was still in vigorous existence and could remain so, for such purposes. He went on to argue for the main object of this proposal, his own appointment as chairman of combined operations. As Frick reminded Carnegie, in a single year as head of Carnegie Brothers, he had increased profits from a little less than $2 million to more than $3.5 million. Clearly Carnegie had chosen a management genius. Why not let the genius manage everything?

In Carnegie's mind, there appeared no argument not to, and papers were soon drawn up. The agreement would take effect on July 1, 1892, merging Carnegie, Phipps with Carnegie Brothers and Company to create the Carnegie Steel Company, capitalized at $25 million (two and a half times the combined value of the two previous entities). Andrew Carnegie would hold 55 percent of the new company's stock, worth about $14 million, Frick and Henry Phipps would each hold 11 percent, or about $2,750,000, and nineteen other partners would each hold 1 percent. That left about 4 percent to be held in trust for future distributions to worthy partners-in-waiting, one of whom would be the willing Schwab, who had taken over operations at the Edgar Thomson works after the death of Captain Jones.

Everyone involved was happy. With Frick in charge, Carnegie

could step farther away from day-to-day operations, and the other partners could rest assured that their interests had nowhere to go but up. As for Frick, he had managed to beat the odds and the grim scenario Carnegie had painted upon his entry into the company, rising from the apex of one industry to become the chief operating officer of the largest and most powerful steelmaking company on earth, all in the space of a decade.

There they were, then, the toasts of not only Pittsburgh but the entire industrialized world: Schwab, Carnegie, and Frick, poised for passage to yet another level of accomplishment on July 1, 1892. It was to have been such an auspicious date.

And so it was, but for far different reasons than any of them anticipated.

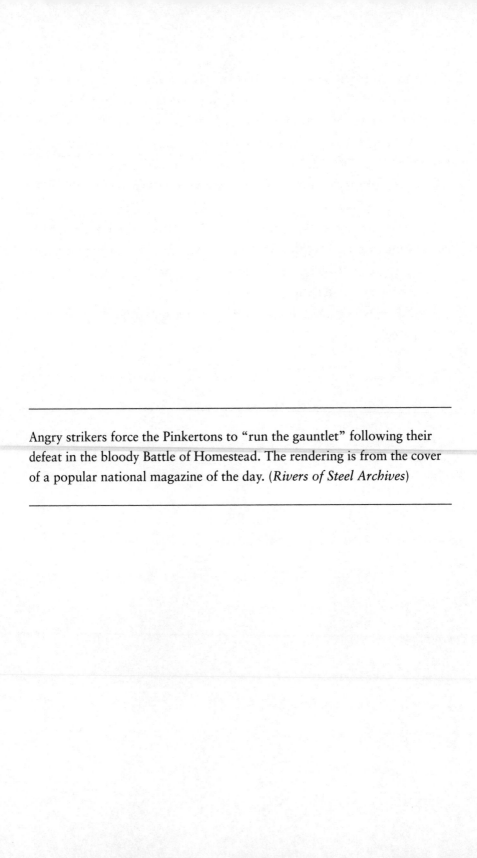

Angry strikers force the Pinkertons to "run the gauntlet" following their defeat in the bloody Battle of Homestead. The rendering is from the cover of a popular national magazine of the day. (*Rivers of Steel Archives*)

# PART TWO

# BLOOD ON THE RIVER

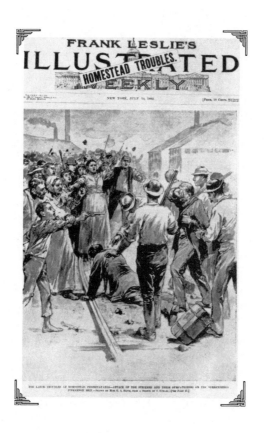

# 10

# STRIKE THREE

A T THE 1889 DEDICATION of the beautifully designed Braddock Public Library—a sprawling sandstone structure more aptly described as a community center, complete with auditorium, swimming pool, and spacious reading rooms—Andrew Carnegie had capped the ceremonies with this observation to the assemblage, many of them the laborers to whom this building was his gift: "Believe me, fellow workmen, the interests of capital and labor are one. . . . I hope you will remember this hereafter and treat me with proper respect as one of the great guild of those who labor and perform a use in the community and who upon that basis alone founds his claim to live in comfort."

It was a typical public utterance for Carnegie, and even if some in the crowd recognized that their adoration was being demanded, many probably nodded along to his words. It was undoubtedly a lovely building, and if the workmen themselves had little time for books and swimming and lounging, perhaps their wives and children could take some pleasure there. Certainly no one in attendance would have anticipated the events of that unfortunate summer day scarcely three years later, when, according to historian

Arthur Burgoyne, "The dictates of law and humanity were alike suspended."

Not even the organizers of the only union to make headway within Carnegie's holdings could have expected the enormity of what would transpire that summer. The Amalgamated Association of Iron and Steel Workers of the United States was, by its own description, decidedly moderate compared to most unions of the day.

Formed in Pittsburgh on August 4, 1876, the year of the Haymarket Riots, the Amalgamated combined three rather marginal local organizations into a sober-minded group that hoped to advance working conditions in the iron and steel industry nationwide, through appeals to owners' logic and common decency, not through the tossing of bombs. The founding organizations included the United Sons of Vulcan, organized in Pittsburgh in 1858; the Associated Brotherhood of Iron and Steel Heaters, Rollers and Roughers of the United States, formed in Chicago in 1865; and the Iron and Steel Roll Hands' Union, also formed in Chicago, in 1870. While operating separately had allowed each to focus on issues pertaining to specific mills in the three principal U.S. steelmaking regions of Chicago, Pittsburgh, and Youngstown, Ohio, it had also meant smaller treasuries, easily depleted resources, and a lack of strength in numbers more readily exploited by owners.

So it was not surprising that, galvanized by the effects of the great depression of the 1870s, officers of the three organizations agreed not only to merge their efforts, but to declare themselves a nonviolent union. As such, they agreed, they were more likely to enjoy the support of the public and elected officials than were such radical groups as the Molly Maguires. As they had hoped, the new organization was far more successful than any of its single predecessors, and while public opinion was still divided—such incidents as Haymarket suggested to many that unions were crawling with wild-eyed anarchists—the Amalgamated had as much difficulty within its own ranks, trying to reconcile the goals of skilled craftsmen with those of laborers, as it did with recalcitrant ownership.

By 1887 the Amalgamated was the most powerful labor organization in the steel industry, and in that year it joined with four other unions to align with Samuel Gompers and form the new American Federation of Labor, which championed higher wages and shorter working days rather than social upheaval. They were heady days for labor: by 1892, the AAISW had boosted its original membership of fewer than four thousand to nearly twenty-one thousand.

In Pittsburgh, Amalgamated officials had been particularly sanguine about their dealings with Andrew Carnegie and Henry Clay Frick, generally regarded as the two most powerful representatives of capital in the steel industry. They well remembered that Frick had been forced to give in to the demands of workers in his coke fields in the mid-1880s, and that Carnegie's manager at the four-thousand-worker Homestead works had recognized the union as the sole bargaining agent during the highly publicized strike of 1889. As the July 1, 1892, expiration date of that latter agreement neared, union officials had hopes that the upcoming negotiations would prove even more fruitful to their rank and file.

They were encouraged when, in January of that year, John Potter, who had taken over at Homestead when Schwab moved to the Edgar Thomson works, sent word to the joint committees of the Amalgamated suggesting that the union draw up a proposed scale for the upcoming negotiations. Potter had gone on to say that it would benefit neither side for the remotest chance of a strike to disrupt operations, and there was nothing in his message that suggested that the union should expect a diminishment of its present position.

The optimism of union leaders would not hold, however, for they had underestimated Henry Frick's long-simmering determination to rectify what he had considered a "softness" on labor within the Carnegie organization. The first of the sticking points had to do with the sliding scale. The 1889 agreement placed no ceiling on the elevation of wages tied to an upswing in steel prices, but there was a floor of twenty-five dollars written in, regardless of how far the market price for steel might plunge, a clause that the company would argue violated the concept of equal partnership. In an article written for the *Pittsburgh Gazette,* Frick stated his position succinctly: "We believe that if earnings based on the selling price of steel can advance without limit, the workmen should be willing to follow the selling price down to a reasonable minimum, and so this figure was finally fixed by the Carnegie Company at the rate of $23 instead of $25. We had originally asked a reduction to $22, but subsequently agreed to compromise the rate at $23." As Frick went on to point out, the Amalgamated refused to budge below twenty-four dollars.

The second major point at issue concerned the anniversary date upon which the scale rate would be determined. The 1889 agreement governing workers at Homestead called for annual recalculation on June 30. Frick insisted that the date be revised to December 31, the same as that at Edgar Thomson, "for the reason that the change would permit us to take our estimate upon the wages we must pay during the year, beginning on January 1, so that we would be able to make contracts for the year accordingly."

It was a purposefully circular justification, allowing Frick to skirt the real reason for the company's desire to change the dates. During the summer months, with construction activity across the country at its peak, steel prices were traditionally high. Demand, and prices, generally reached their nadir in the dead of winter. It was a transparent ploy, of course, and another issue upon which the Amalgamated stood firm.

The final issue, the rate of pay per ton, was particularly galling to Frick. Over the previous decade, production rates at all Carnegie installations, particularly Homestead, had risen dramatically, resulting in a corresponding raise in pay for workers. The company contended that improvements to the physical plant and innovations incorporated by management accounted for the increases. In facilities where such improvements had been made, Frick was demanding a reduction in tonnage rates.

"Where no such improvements had been made, there was no request upon our part for a reduction," he went on to say. "As a rule the men who were making the largest wages in the Homestead mill were the ones who most bitterly denounced the proposed revision of the scale, for out of the 3,800 men employed in every department only 825 were directly affected by this reduction."

The union countered that it was the efforts of the workmen themselves that accounted for the increases, and in any case, bargaining agents were hardly about to give up what they considered a rightful share of this so-called partnership, given the difficulty of the work and the dangers that accompanied it.

As one iron "puddler" described his job: "For twenty-five minutes while the boil goes on I stir it constantly with my long iron rabble. A cook stirring gravy to keep it from scorching in the skillet is done in two minutes and backs off blinking, sweating, and choking, having finished the hardest job of getting dinner. But my hardest job lasts not two minutes but the better part of half an hour. My spoon weighs twenty-five pounds, my porridge is pasty iron, and the heat of my kitchen is so great that if my body was not hardened to it, the ordeal would drop me in my tracks.

"Little spikes of pure iron like frost spars glow white-hot and stick out of the churning slag. These must be stirred under at once. . . . I am like some frantic baker in the inferno kneading a batch of iron bread for the devil's breakfast." Reading such accounts lends credence to the generally accepted notion that in the steel industry, by the time a laborer reached the age of forty, he was essentially "all wore out."

In an account published in the *Homestead Local News* in April 1892, while talks were ongoing, another workman described a fatal accident at the mill that was typical of the day: "When the blast is put on, it forces a terrific blaze containing particles of the molten steel, out against an iron shield. In the course of a few hours there is an accumulation of metal [referred to as "the skull"] on the shield or wall which of course is quite heavy and must be removed at frequent intervals, otherwise it would fall, which it did in this instance. . . . Passing somewhat underneath the shield is a pressure pipe. . . . When the skull fell, it struck the pipe referred to, causing the pressure to escape. Released from control, the vessel containing molten metal tipped over and emptied into the pit below where it came in contact with moisture, resulting in a terrific explosion. The metal was scattered in all directions, some of it striking the opposite wall seventy feet away. It is not surprising that many workmen were burned. Indeed the great wonder is that more were not fatally burned. The list is long enough however."

Balanced against the feelings of workers subjected to such rigors and dangers were the positions taken by Carnegie, Frick, and their superintendents. In response to questions posed by a congressional committee of inquiry, John Potter, superintendent of the Homestead works, did his best to make management's case:

Q: You say the workmen in that mill can turn out twice the product by reason of the improved machinery?

A: Yes sir.

Q: Than any other mill in the world?

A: Yes sir; of the same character.

Q: What do you mean by the same character?

A: The same class of mill.

Q: Well, if there is no mill like it in the world there is no other same class?

A: That is right.

Q: The labor cost of turning out that product at that mill would be one-half what it would be anywhere else where they are paying the same wages?

A: I do not know whether that is true or not.

Q: Does that not follow as a necessary result . . . ? You stated that with your machinery there the men could turn out twice the product, and I ask the simple question whether, if that is true, the labor cost of that product would not be one-half of any other mill having the same rate of wages?

A: I do not think it would.

Q: . . . What kind of machinery is there which increases the facility of labor?

A: Automatic machinery, hydraulic, etc.

Q: Is that the machinery of which there is no mill possessed?

A: We use hydraulic machinery to a greater extent than any other mill.

Q: Then the use of machinery actually reduces the cost of the product, does it not?

A: Well, it should do it; that is what we want it to do.

The interrogator was trying to get past the company's argument that it was the machinery that made all the difference, for the experience of the men on the production line had proven otherwise. As one Amalgamated representative explained, the installation of new equipment had already resulted in a net reduction in wages, by making it possible for ten men to do the work that might previously have required thirty. Not only had twenty men lost their jobs, but the company was insisting that those remaining ought to take a pay cut as well.

If one can sense the frustration of the interrogator trying to get a straight answer out of Potter, however, Frick's responses during the same session probably sent the poor man raving:

Q: Mr. Potter, the general manager of your mills, stated a few moments ago that owing to the improved machinery in your mills . . . you were able to turn out 50 per cent more product with 50 per cent less labor in certain lines. Do you endorse that statement?

A: I think that is substantially correct, in one department.

Q: In other words with the use of that machinery one man does the work that four men did formerly?

A: I think that is correct. . . .

Q: Can you state independently of other costs the labor cost of producing a ton of steel billets?

A: I could get those figures for you, but I think I will have to decline to give them to you.

Q: Upon what ground?

A: Well, I do not think we should be asked to give away those details of our business.

Q: You asked the Government for a duty to compensate between the difference in the American labor cost and the foreign labor cost; then upon what principle, receiving from the Government a protection which is ostensibly and avowedly for that purpose, do you decline to give the information upon which that legislation is based?

A: We did not ask the Government for such protection.

Q: You did not?

A: No, this concern did not.

Q: You are greatly misrepresented then if you did not. The press misrepresents you very much.

THOUGH HIS OUTRIGHT REFUSAL to share what he considered company secrets with Congress was classic hard-nosed Frick, his statements regarding the influence exerted by Carnegie Steel in support of tariffs enacted to protect the steel industry were disingenuous, to say the least. Though it might have been correct to say that he or Carnegie made no direct lobbying efforts, the steel industry as a whole was united in its efforts to uphold the tariffs that were being debated by presidential candidates Cleveland and Harrison. The issue was such a lightning rod in its day that a fair number of ordinary laborers were ready to forsake their natural Democratic leanings and vote for Republican candidate Harrison, a staunch supporter of the tariffs.

And despite such artful public dodging, the truth was that the amendments to the wage scale sought by Frick would have saved the company no more than two cents per ton on a product that sold for between thirty and thirty-five dollars per ton at the time. As Frick had pointed out in his own article, the changes would affect only the skilled craftsmen at the Homestead mill, less than one-quarter of the workforce. While the men paid at tonnage rate might earn somewhere between ten dollars and fifteen dollars per day, the average rate for a laborer was in the neighborhood of $2.00 to $2.25.

Carnegie Steel, moreover, had become the nation's leading producer of steel, its output soaring from 250,000 tons in 1880 to more than 1 million tons in 1890. As profits for that year totaled nearly $5 million, and a two-cents-per-ton write-off would have dented the bottom line by all of $20,000, it seems inexplicable that Frick and Carnegie would not have surrendered the point in a trice.

However, between 1889 and 1892, the period governed by the contract, steel prices had declined nearly 19 percent, despite record profits. In any case, both Carnegie and Frick viewed concessions to labor not as justifiable compromise but as the setting of dangerous precedents sure to be seized upon in other negotiations down the road. Carnegie's view of labor costs was summarized in a letter he had written to Abbott in 1888 before the strike of that year: "I notice that we are paying 14 cents an hour for labor, which is above Edgar Thomson price. The force might perhaps be reduced in number 10 percent so that each man getting more wages would be required to do more work."

In Carnegie's mind, nothing had changed in the intervening years. If costs could be cut, then cut they must be, and never mind if the category read "minerals" or "vegetables" or "men." And if he was tough on matters pertaining to the production line, he was even more demanding when it came to the support staff. Nowhere is this attitude made clearer than in a letter to Frick dated March 31, 1892: "In our experience as manufacturers, we have found that there is more danger of unnecessary increase in clerks than in any other department. I believe that when our consolidation takes place that Mr. Lovejoy's department can be cut down at least one-third. . . . Mr. Lovejoy [Francis Lovejoy, company secretary and business manager] has said that there were now in the building 246 men. It was only two—or it may be three years ago the number was 120. Truly I do not believe there is any department that needs pruning so much as [his]."

While he was at it, Carnegie turned his cold eye upon another area ripe for Frick's shears: "Mr. Abbott also mentioned that Mr. Potter had 18 draughtsmen on his rolls. I cannot see how he employs more than 6. One of the benefits of hard times is, that it requires examination into every branch."

So far as the upcoming negotiations at Homestead were concerned, Carnegie had made up his mind. On April 4, 1892, just before sailing for Europe for the summer, he drafted a notice to all employees at the Homestead works and sent it off to Frick for immediate posting. In light of the upcoming merger of the Edgar Thomson, Duquesne, and Homestead mills, Carnegie wrote that, given that the vast majority of the employees in the newly formed Carnegie Steel were non-union, "the minority must give place to the majority. These Works therefore, will be necessarily Non-Union after the expiration of the present agreement."

Carnegie hastened to add that this would not mean lower wages. Without reference to the unionized skilled workers paid at tonnage rates, he pointed out that most of the workers at non-unionized E.T. and Duquesne were making higher wages than their counterparts at Homestead and that steps would be taken to see that Homestead workers were brought up to par. While admitting that improvements on the production line would mean a reduction in the workforce at Homestead, he "hoped" that such layoffs would prove temporary.

He concluded on a note that was conciliatory but brooked no dissent: "This action is not taken in any spirit of hostility to labor organizations, but every man will see that the firm cannot run Union and Non-Union. It must be either one or the other."

Frick took one look at the notice and determined that posting it would be a terrible tactical blunder—why warn the enemy what was coming when no good could come of it for the company? Instead he reassured representatives of the Amalgamated that negotiations would continue, and at the same time ordered plant superintendent Potter to hike production of steel plates at Homestead to the maximum, thereby ensuring a sizable stockpile of inventory should a strike occur.

Just before he left for Europe, Carnegie summoned Frick to New York for a final strategy session, in which he reminded Frick that if worse came to worst, the ultimate step was simple: they would simply close the plant and wait for the men to come around. He had told Abbott the same thing three years ago, of course, but had seen his manager lose heart in the heat of battle. With Frick in charge, Carnegie had little fear of a recurrence.

Although Frick said nothing to Carnegie during that meeting to suggest that he did not share the majority partner's views, he did write to him soon after in England, warning on April 21 that "it may become necessary to fight it out this summer. No better time can be selected or expected. We will get ready for a fight immediately. If it be unnecessary, all the better. It may be a stubborn one, but if once got into, without regard to cost or time, it will be fought to a finish."

Those were dire words, but Carnegie's reply of May 23 affirmed his faith in Frick: "No doubt you will get Homestead right. You can get anything right with your 'mild persistence.' " And in a follow-up message sent the next day Carnegie seems resigned to the inevitable, fretting that they had probably bought far too much pig iron, "in view of [the] possible shut down at Homestead."

If Carnegie was worried about the economic repercussions of the looming showdown, Frick did his best to reassure him. In late May, Frick wrote again to Carnegie, detailing the pay scales he had directed superintendent Potter to present to the men, adding that he had given a deadline of June 24 for their acceptance. While Frick's offer would have resulted in some modest increases over the previous contract should steel prices stay above twenty-five dollars per ton, he assured Carnegie that his proposal would result in a 15-percent savings overall, with a further wage cut of 4 percent for every dollar the price fell below $26.50.

A skilled heater might see his daily wage rise from $6.37 to $6.67, even with the price of steel at $23, while a melter's helper working on one of the open hearth furnaces would see his pay reduced from $3.60 to $3.26. While the plan would save the company money overall, Frick pointed out that it contained certain features that Homestead plant superintendent John Potter could "spin" to make it seem that he had wrung concessions from the company. "Want to put Potter in the position of having used his influence with us to make a deal with the Association . . . and to have used his influence towards securing for the men as high a rate of wages as possible. In other words, to strengthen him with his men."

Frick went so far as to tell Carnegie, "We do not care whether a man belongs to a union or not, nor do we wish to interfere. He may belong to as many unions or organizations as he chooses." But he was insistent on one thing: no agreement would be put forth giving "the impression upon the minds of people that we were willing to pay Amalgamated men higher wages than others."

Whether Carnegie saw Frick's messages as inspired tactical planning or as documents meant to disguise his true intentions would become a matter of debate between the two. In any case, a cable flew from London to Pittsburgh on June 3 suggesting that far less weighty matters were occupying Carnegie's attention. For some time, Carnegie had been urging Frick to purchase one of the elaborate mechanized musical devices then gaining popularity in Europe and known as the "Orchestrion." The self-playing devices used sheet roll music in the same way as a player piano, but were more complex and sometimes enormous, containing organ pipes, trumpets, trombones, flutes and piccolos, violins, and various percussion instruments, all given life by electrically driven pumps and bellows.

Though they would eventually make their way into saloons and amusement parks everywhere and become known as "nickelodeons" for the coin that activated them, in the early 1890s the devices were still the playthings of kings and sultans, and Carnegie insisted that it was just the thing for a budding tycoon. "Do not think that I have forgotten about the Orchestrion," he wrote Frick, in the midst of all the back-and-forth on Homestead. "On the contrary I have just mailed you pictures of two. The dearer one is by far the best instrument, and the difference will be well spent in buying it." It would cost Frick $6,100 (several hundred thousand contemporary dollars) to have it delivered and ready to play in his Clayton home, Carnegie said, but added, "You will certainly have something that will give great pleasure, and be a marvel in Pittsburgh."

While the matter of the Orchestrion dangled, Carnegie returned to issues at Homestead, making clear his understanding that chances for resolving the matter without a confrontation were virtually nil. On June 10, he wrote Frick, "As I understand matters at Homestead, it is not only the wages paid, but the number of men required by Amalgamated rules which makes our labor rates so much higher than those in the East. Of course you will be asked to confer, and I know you will decline . . . as you have taken your stand and have nothing more to say.

"It is fortunate that only a part of the Works are concerned. Provided you have plenty of plates rolled, I suppose you can keep on with armor. Potter will, no doubt, intimate to the men that refusal of scale means running only as Non-Union. This may cause acceptance, but I do not think so. The chances are, you will have to prepare for a struggle, in which case the notice [i.e., that the works are henceforth to be non-union] should go up promptly on the morning of the 25th. Of course you will win, and win easier than you suppose. . . ."

Carnegie meant his words to be supportive, obviously, but for years afterward he would insist that he had no knowledge of the true manner in which Frick intended to "win." In a June 17 message, Carnegie blithely reaffirmed his support for Frick, then added, "Have ordered the Orchestrion. Please cable whether you wish it finished in light or dark wood. Sorry you had not room for the 'dearer' one."

Frick's attention was elsewhere, however. He wrote back swiftly that all indications pointed to a strike at Homestead. "Regret to say that it does not seem to me that there is any other course open for us. We would better make the fight and be through with it, expensive though it may be."

Two days later, on June 22, he wrote again, even more forcefully: "We will not be trifled with, and are prepared to carry out the policy we have adopted," he told Carnegie. "It may be that we will win without much difficulty, although I am not yet prepared to believe that we will win without a pretty severe struggle, and am not sure, even with the agreement of these men to work, that they will do so, provided we find it necessary to bring in guards."

Despite such statements, Carnegie would, for all the rest of his days, disavow any knowledge of the letter that Frick penned to a third party shortly thereafter. In that very private message of June 25, Frick made it clear exactly how far he was willing to go: "We will want 300 guards for service at our Homestead mills as a measure of prevention against interferrence [*sic*] with our plan to start the operation of the works on July 6, 1892.

"The only trouble we anticipate is that an attempt will be made to prevent such of our men, with whom we will by that time have made satisfactory arrangements, from going to work and possibly some demonstration of violence upon the part of those whose places have been filled, or most likely by an element which usually is attracted to such scenes for the purpose of stirring up trouble.

"We are not desirous that the men you send shall be armed unless the occasion properly calls for such a measure later on for the protection of our employees or property. . . .

"These guards should be assembled at Ashtabula, Ohio, not later than the morning of July 5, when they may be taken by train to McKees Rocks, or some other point upon the Ohio River below Pittsburg [an earlier and accepted variant of the city's spelling] where they can be transferred to boats and landed within the inclosures of our premises at Homestead. We think absolute secrecy essential. . . .

"As soon as your men are upon the premises we will notify the sheriff and ask that they be deputized either at once or immediately upon an ontbreak [*sic*] of such a character as to render such a step desirable."

Frick signed himself "Yours very truly." The person to whom the letter was sent was Robert A. Pinkerton, head of the well-known Pinkerton National Detective Agency, which had provided security forces to management on more than one such previous occasion, including the suppression of the Molly Maguires in the Pennsylvania coalfields during the 1870s.

That Frick had called in the Pinkertons was a sign that the gloves were indeed off, for this was no typical industrial security firm where overaged and overweight types found a place to nod off during after-hours, minimum-wage assignments. Native Scotsman Allan Pinkerton, a former deputy sheriff and the first police detective in Chicago, formed the agency in the early 1850s and made a name for his firm by solving a series of train robberies and forgery cases that had baffled local officials.

In 1861, while investigating a railway case, Pinkerton—an ardent abolitionist who believed that labor unions seldom represented the best interests of the workingman—got wind of a plot to assassinate President Lincoln during a train stop in Baltimore. As a result, Lincoln's train steamed right through Baltimore and on to his inauguration ceremony in Washington. With the plot foiled, Pinkerton became a household name, his firm often called upon to provide presidential security and to direct Secret Service operations for the Union during the Civil War. The company's logo featured a rendering of an unblinking eye with the accompanying legend "We Never Sleep," and gave rise to the term "private eye." One of its most notable employees was hard-boiled crime writer Dashiell Hammett, who learned much of what he knew about the field from a stint as a Pinkerton detective early in the twentieth century. (Hammett would go on to pen *Red Harvest* in 1929, set against the backdrop of labor unrest in a Colorado mining town, with his protagonist a Pinkerton-styled detective.)

In the 1870s Pinkerton used one of his men, James McParlan, to infiltrate the ranks of the Molly Maguires during the coalfield disturbances of the period. It was McParlan's testimony that resulted in the breaking of the Maguires and the execution of twenty of its members, with one commentator noting dryly that "nearly all of them [were] guilty of something."

After the senior Pinkerton's death in 1884, control of the firm passed to his sons, William and Robert, and the Pinkertons became nearly synonymous with strikebreaking activities, often providing large numbers of armed men with military and law enforcement experience to mine and factory owners who wished to supplement local authorities when labor unrest threatened. Pinkerton men had been on the job at the strike at Chicago's McCormick Reaper plant and at Haymarket Square, and now, it seemed, they would come to Homestead as well, en masse.

Despite Carnegie's later protestations, there seems little doubt that Carnegie agreed with Frick's aims, even if he claimed ignorance of the plan's finer details. In fact, Carnegie was hopeful that the defeat of the Amalgamated at Homestead would spell the end of union interference with Carnegie Steel operations once and for all. The same man who had earlier written in *Forum* that "there is no excuse for a strike or a lock out until arbitration of differences has been of-

fered by one party and refused by the other" had only a few days before the call to the Pinkertons sent this to Frick: "Perhaps if Homestead men understand that non-acceptance means Non-Union for
ever, they will accept."

Some commentators, including Carnegie biographer Joseph Frazier Wall, have attempted to explain the apparent contradiction by
arguing that Carnegie would have been comfortable with his men
being organized in what he considered "proper," or local, unions—
that it was only national organizations such as the Amalgamated to
which Carnegie was opposed. But that is tantamount to arguing that
Carnegie saw nothing wrong with men joining any union so long as it
was relatively powerless.

In any case, shortly before leaving England on June 29 for Scot-
land, where he planned to spend the rest of the summer, Carnegie sent
Frick what he considered to be his final word on the troubles at
Homestead.

"One thing we are all sure of: No contest will be entered in that
will fail. It will be harder this time at Homestead than it would have
been last time when we had the matter in our own hands, as you have
always felt. On the other hand, your reputation will shorten it, so
that I really do not believe it will be much of a struggle. We all approve of anything you do, not stopping short of approval of a contest. We are with you to the end."

While Carnegie would in the years to come do his best to disavow all that took place during the "contest" at Homestead, one
finds it hard to imagine marching orders more clearly worded: "We
all approve of anything you do. . . ." Frick would have worn something of a smile as he folded that letter into his breast pocket.

# 11

# THE WAGONS CIRCLE

———◆◆◆———

W
ORKERS AND RESIDENTS of the surrounding community of Homestead were already bracing themselves for
what was to come. In May, Frick had called in workmen
to begin the construction of a tall fence of solid wood, topped by
strands of barbed wire and running for three miles around the
perimeter of the sprawling, 600-acre mill grounds.

By June the fence, strategically placed observation towers, and
other security emplacements had been completed, inspiring workers
to refer to the property as "Fort Frick." As an article in the *Pittsburgh Post* described it, "The great fences that surround the mill are
stronger than any fences one ordinarily sees. They are in reality massive board walls, and strung along the top are two wicked rows of
jagged barbed wire. At each of the gates immense fire plugs have also
been placed with an enormous water pressure in each. In all of the
dark places and exposed portions of the mills are lights of 2,000 can-
dle power each, which have been placed, so that when the strike com-
mences, in the words of the Bible, 'there will be no night there.' "

The *Post* went on to describe the preparations as tantamount to
a declaration of war: "The bridge over the railroad tracks which con-

nects the old city farm grounds . . . and the mill enclosure has not been considered conspicuous enough by the firm, hence they have placed in it an arc light which will reveal the presence of anyone who would try to cross it at night. Port holes with ugly mouths grimly look out upon the peaceful valley from the mill, fort, barricade, stockade, or whatever the Carnegie plant at Homestead could be called to-day, and silently bear witnesses that they are there, not for the peaceful purposes of steel manufacture, but for struggle and fight."

By this time, it seemed, all pretense of a peaceful settlement of the differences at Homestead had vanished. But if Frick was expecting a fight, he evidently thought it would be a short one. On June 2 he wrote Carnegie, "I note that you have taken a place in Scotland. Have no doubt it is a very fine one and I might take a notion to run over for a short time in the latter part of August, say 30 day trip if everything should be going all right."

To customers of Carnegie Steel, he alluded to possible slow-downs in delivery, but in markedly casual terms. To one he wrote, "The mill is going to be all right, but it takes time to break in the men and get things to work smoothly," and to another associate he said, "[The] expiration of the scale, July 1st, and the preparation being made by us to enforce a new scale if necessary, has made the men somewhat careless. So that the product of the mill is not what it should be. We will overcome all this, however, in a short time."

Whether he would be successful was an open question, however, at least in the press. The matter had national implications, for even Frick understood that any major embarrassment to the Republican Party as the champion of steel and other manufacturing tariffs could prove a significant factor in the upcoming presidential elections. It is entirely possible that such thinking led him to purposefully drive matters with the Amalgamated to an impasse so that he could then blame labor for any hostilities that erupted. The alternative was to "give in" to the demands of labor and lend the Democrats support for charges that big business had been shortchanging labor all along.

Whether Frick had such a devious plan in mind or not is impossible to ascertain, especially since he maintained the appearance of serious negotiations with the Amalgamated until the eleventh hour. The union, now sixty thousand strong, had held its annual national meeting—its seventeenth—in Pittsburgh early in June, where it was made clear that whatever happened at Homestead would have a momentous impact on the future of the organization. "[The Amalgamated] is beyond question the most powerful independent labor organization in the world," wrote the *Pittsburgh Post* on June 7, the opening day of the meeting, "and every movement of the manufacturers seems to confirm the belief long held that they aim at its destruction in the coming conflict."

At one point in the proceedings, nearly three thousand men crowded into the Eighth Avenue Opera House in Homestead to hear the town burgess, or mayor, John McLuckie, an AAISW member, express his concerns and his sense of betrayal. As quoted in the *Pittsburgh Post,* McLuckie, a $2.25-a-day employee in the Homestead converter department, had this to say: "The cause of this wage trouble is not generally understood. We were persuaded to vote the Republican ticket four years ago that our wages might be maintained. As soon as the election was over a widespread feeling on the part of manufacturers toward the reduction of wages was exhibited over the land. . . . You men who voted the Republican ticket voted for high tariff and you get high fences, Pinkerton detectives, thugs, and militia."

As one delegate to the convention put it in the *National Labor Tribune,* "[N]ever has there been such a crisis before the organization, as the present. . . . The Carnegie Company have wiped out organization in the Edgar Thomson works at Braddock . . . under the management of Mr. Frick they have wiped out organization in the coke regions, and if they make up their minds to wipe it out at Homestead, who shall say them nay?"

Certainly officials of the Amalgamated, both local and national, were saying "nay." On June 21, three days before the deadline that

Frick had set for a union response to the company's proposal, the Amalgamated called for a meeting. On June 23, Frick convened with national president William Weihe—described by one contemporary chronicler of the strike as "six and a half feet of sound sense, a brawny colossus quite free from pretense"—along with twenty-five local union representatives. At this gathering, Frick offered his compromise: the company would agree to an increase in the floor of steel prices from twenty-two dollars to twenty-three dollars. But the men were adamant at twenty-four dollars and the meeting broke up before there could be any serious discussion of the actual tonnage rates or of the anniversary date for establishing steel prices.

The impasse over a difference of a mere dollar seems to many of us now, as it did then, a tragedy. Surely this minor impediment could have been removed to avert an all-out war. But to workers, the difference of a dollar was a smokescreen that obscured other, equally important issues.

The anniversary date, for example, was more significant than it seemed. In addition to the likelihood that steel prices would be lower when construction was at low ebb, other factors would favor ownership. With less work available, where would unhappy workers go if they did not like what was handed them? And while winter meant no added expense to manufacturers, workmen incurred the extra expenses of heating fuel, warm clothing, and even groceries, which in winter could not be supplemented with homegrown vegetables.

Following the collapse of talks on June 23, some men held out faint hope that there would be another scolding letter from across the Atlantic, in which Carnegie would direct his underling to give in to workers' demands. But despite the fact that Frick had cabled Carnegie on the failure of the meeting—"While harmonious it did not result in anything. . . . We are now preparing for a struggle. . . . Have ordered one of the Lucy furnaces blown out at once . . . we will have no more conferences with them"—no reply was forthcoming from the Scottish Highlands.

The June 24 deadline came and went, and on the morning of the 25th Frick posted notices at Homestead announcing that managers of the company would henceforth deal only with individual workmen. In the company's eyes, the Amalgamated Iron and Steel Workers no longer existed.

Tensions at the plant and in the nearby town were escalating, to say the least. The *Homestead Local News* reported a fight between James Gibson, a steelworker, and John Caddy, a watchman for the Pittsburgh, Virginia, & Charleston Railroad lines that ran through a break in Frick's newly built fence to service the Homestead works. When Gibson attempted to enter the mill grounds by walking along the tracks, Caddy ordered him to stop and a tussle ensued, one "in which Gibson was getting the best of the fight, when Yardmaster James Dovey ran in and caught Gibson, whether to separate the combatants or to hold Gibson while Caddy assaulted him, as some say he did, is not known, but while Gibson was in this disadvantageous position, Watchman Caddy belabored him severely with a club."

The *News* reported that an outraged crowd then pursued watchman Caddy, who fled down the railroad tracks toward the nearby town. Both the watchman and the yardmaster were arrested for assault, with the latter quickly bailed out by Homestead's superintendent, John Potter.

Another incident, reported in the June 28 issue of the *Pittsburgh Post,* suggested that Frick's warning of secrecy to Pinkerton had not been well heeded. The *Post* story said that strangers thought to be Pinkerton men, as well as several believed to be agents of the Coal and Iron police used to break the coke field strikes, had been spotted "lounging about" Homestead. According to the *Post*, "A committee of men was at once appointed to look up the strangers. The two men were found in a saloon. The workmen walked up to them and demanded their business.

" 'Oh, we are only here looking around. We have a little private business to attend to,' said one of the men.

" 'You are only looking around, are you?' queried Carney, one of the committee. 'Well, the best thing you can do is to get out and do your looking around from some other seaport. . . .'

" 'I know you,' broke in another member of the committee, 'I saw you both several years ago. I worked at Joliet then, and you watched the mills there during the strike. Get out.' "

One can imagine the effects of such a confrontation inside a local tavern where every stare had turned as hard as the stuff the patrons made each day. According to the *Post,* the two strangers were given half an hour to get out of town, but "did not consume one-half that time in reaching a train."

The *Post* went on to report that word had been received that "at least 300 Pinkertons and members of the Coal and Iron police will be here Thursday next. It is believed that if trouble ensues here, the company will order down all the men who served as policemen during the coke strike and that a few Pinkertons will be added."

Another *Post* story reported that one M. P. Maverek, a workman suspected of having turned informant for Superintendent Potter in exchange for a raise in pay from $1.75 a day to $2.50, had turned up at a union rally, asking to speak so that he might clear his name. He was snatched up by a burly mechanic who reiterated the men's suspicions of him. Maverek protested that if he had actually done the things he was accused of, he would want to be killed. "You won't want long," someone in the crowd shouted back. "You are just the kind of fellow that will be killed." According to the *Post,* the rising passions of the crowd suggested that Maverek was about to get what he had asked for, when police arrived to break up the disturbance.

Another account in the local press suggested that in addition to Pinkertons and turncoats, local workmen had yet another type of interloper to deal with. It was reported that a stranger had approached a Homestead millworker on the streets on June 28, asking directions to a place where he might find comfortable lodging and decent food. The stranger explained that he was newly arrived in town to begin a new job on July 1. When the millworker asked the man where he was going to be working, the stranger pointed over the shoulder of his interrogator toward the Homestead works.

It was enough to prompt the millworker to invite several of his associates to hear a retelling of these plans, whereupon the crowd grabbed the stunned man and ran with him toward the banks of the Monongahela, where he feared he was about to be drowned. Instead, they tossed the scab into a skiff bound for the Pittsburgh side of the river, with a warning never to return.

By this time, workers in Homestead understood there was no hope of reprieve. With Master Carnegie gone to ground in his Scottish retreat, spies planted in their midst, scabs already summoned from distant points, and three hundred mercenary Pinkertons and Coal Field Police on the way to Homestead, there would be no peaceful settlement. As the headline in the *Post* blared: IT LOOKS LIKE WAR.

# 12

## A FINISH FIGHT

———————◆———————

IF FRICK HAD BEEN COUNTING on the element of surprise, his efforts had failed. The community saw what was coming, and began to prepare its own battle plans. At one point during those last tense days of June, a reporter for the *Pittsburgh Post* overheard a group of tonnage men discussing the use of balloons that could be used to drop bombs directly into the mill. One of the workers described the stakes in simple terms: "My job means my life, and any fellow that takes my job tries to take my life and then his won't be safe."

Frick, meanwhile, was attempting to portray the company's position in terms the American public would find favorable, sending copies of articles lauding the Homestead works to the company's publicity agent as well as to several Pennsylvania newspapers. One such piece, published in the *Pittsburgh Times* in early June of 1892, noted the growing production at the works of armor plating for ships (the company had produced the plates for the ill-fated battleship *Maine,* the explosion of which, in 1898, would trigger the Spanish-American War), and described the work in terms that evoke something of the immensity and odd grandeur of the steelmaking process:

"When the steel is ready, the open hearth furnaces are tapped, and streams of molten steel run into the mold and the ingot is made. The weight varies from 20 to 100 tons. It is then . . . taken from the metal mold while still hot and is transferred on a special car to the press shop. This car has a capacity of 150 tons, five times that of the average freight car. At the press shop, two large cranes that could lift an ordinary house take this mountain of metal and put it in a furnace where it is heated . . . and is carried to the Armor rolling mill . . . a mill so vast that mere figures are powerless to convey a full appreciation of its size."

Mere figures may indeed be "powerless," for what contemporary reader's brain has not gone blank at times when trying to comprehend the number of pixels per inch in a high-definition television screen, or the number of terabytes of data amassed by the leading online search engine? Still, perhaps we can grasp the magnitude of the steelmaking enterprise by contemplating a few old-fashioned numbers:

A cubic foot of steel weighs more than 600 pounds, and, given that there are about 120 cubic feet of steel in an ingot, the typical mass moving down the line weighs more than thirty tons (a military Humvee or a typical pyramid stone tips the scales at about two and a half tons). The rollers flatten that mass into a slab of whatever thickness is called for, and that slab is in turn trundled to the press shop, where its ragged ends are cut off by a hydraulic press with a pressure of 2,500 tons. As the *Press* story noted, that monster would "shear a plate of steel six inches or a foot thick as quickly as a hungry tramp will cut a tenderloin steak."

The piece goes on to describe the endless array of machines and support services necessary to keep such an enterprise functioning. "Nineteen locomotives of all sizes are required to handle the traffic. . . . The blacksmith shop . . . keeps 25 men busy. . . . The open hearth furnaces require 32 skilled melters, one for each furnace for each shift."

Toward the end of this tour, the reporter tosses off one final, telling observation: "It must not be forgotten that this mill never stops except a few hours on Sunday." Unlike lumber milling, coal mining, rock quarrying, rail building, canal excavation, or any other exhausting, mind-numbing, and potentially life-threatening undertaking, halting the process of steelmaking entirely was not a matter of choice. Once lit, the furnaces would burn forever, or until the furnace was no longer fit for duty. It was far too expensive to allow the fires to die and then relight them. In that way, the fires were more precious than the machinery within which they burned.

In many respects, then, the Homestead mill was a self-contained organism, and, if one accepted the view of the *Times* writer, a thriving one at that. "Further removed from the mill are eight handsome residences built for the operative managers, and a handsome club-house for the accommodation of guests and officers. The firm has also erected 40 other houses for their better class workmen.

"All the 3,500 employees appear contented," the piece concludes. "From a little village a few years ago, Homestead has grown to a borough of nearly 12,000 inhabitants, chiefly supported by the great Homestead Steel Works."

If the residents of Homestead had ever supported the view of their employer as "great," things had certainly changed. Effigies of plant superintendent Potter and of Frick were now hanging from the town's telegraph posts, and the Amalgamated had taken possession of a newly laid railroad loading platform to prevent its use for discharging carloads of replacement labor. AAISW officials were reported as promising, however, that "no rioting will be countenanced and that every measure and discipline will be used to insure its utter suppression."

While most speakers at union rallies pleaded with members to stay sober and avoid raucous behavior, one worker interviewed by the *Pittsburgh Post* said, "I have but one life to lose, and that is already far spent, but I am willing to sacrifice it for my little home."

On the evening of June 29, after a delegation of AAISW members gathered outside the main gates of the Homestead mill and appealed to the non-unionized mechanics and laborers to honor the stoppage, the strike formally commenced. "What if we don't want to come out," one of the laborers was reported by the *Pittsburgh Times* as saying. "Come out anyway, or if you don't you'll have to be a rapid runner," was the reply.

Apparently this put an end to any resistance, and the mechanics and laborers returned quietly to the plant to remove their tools. By 9:00 p.m. that evening, the Homestead works had ceased to operate.

Meanwhile, in messages to Carnegie, Frick was resolutely upbeat. "Homestead seems to be the center of attraction, and I do not think anything has been left undone toward securing for us a complete victory at that place. Doubtless by the time this reaches you it will be uninteresting, at least I trust so. . . . We shall, of course, keep within the law, and do nothing that is not entirely legal."

It is hard to imagine, of course, that anyone involved in the matter would find it "uninteresting," let alone Andrew Carnegie. By this time the national press had gotten involved, and on July 1 the *New York World* published an editorial cartoon bearing the legend "The Modern Baron With Ancient Methods." The drawing depicted a likeness of Carnegie atop a set of castlelike battlements on which "Carnegie Steel Works" had been chiseled. In the cartoon, cannons protrude from firing ports in the battlement walls, and a steaming pot of melted pitch sits near Carnegie's feet. In his hands, Carnegie holds a fire hose labeled "hot water," while overhead a banner bearing the words "Protection Castle" flutters in a breeze that courses above a fence that is "electrified."

The coverage was typical; in the national press, it was Carnegie who bore the brunt of responsibility, while the local press focused upon Frick and plant superintendent Potter.

On June 30, the local *Post* carried the headline IT IS A LOCKOUT, and reported that notices had been posted about the plant advising the 3,800 employees to report to the central office on Saturday, July 2, to pick up their final pay. The paper also reported that because the firm had officially declared a shutdown at midnight of June 29, several hours shy of the time that workers had voted to leave their posts, the work stoppage was officially termed a lockout and not a strike.

An editorial-styled sidebar suggested the mood of the surrounding populace: "An undivided sentiment exists, now that the firm has unmistakably shown its hostile attitude and determination to attempt an extermination of the Amalgamated. . . . All expectation of an amicable settlement seems to have vanished, and nothing is now thought of but preparation for the trial that seems bound to come. There is quiet in Homestead, it is true, but it is like the quiet of a town under military surveillance. It is impossible for a stranger to set foot in the town without his presence being noted right away."

One reason strangers were suddenly conspicuous was the determined organization of the workers, who were keeping the river, the roads into the town, and activities within the plant grounds under constant observation. Whether there had been a leak of Frick's communiqués to Pinkerton, or whether it was supposition based on his previous anti-labor tactics, the workers assumed that an attempt would be made to bring hired guards as well as strikebreaking labor into the plant.

Since the burgess, or mayor, of Homestead, John McLuckie, was a skilled worker and thus one of the strikers, there was little distinction between the town's government—or its very population, for that matter—and the organizing body of the strike itself. The millworkers did meet, however, to elect one Hugh O'Donnell, a skilled roller, as the chairman of the strike's advisory committee.

From the moment that the lockout commenced, observers were posted on all the bridges around Pittsburgh and on the banks of the Monongahela to sound the alarm at any suspicious movement toward the area. In an effort to keep matters under control, Mayor McLuckie ordered all the saloons of Homestead closed and saw to it that the effigies of Frick and Potter decorating the town's telegraph poles were cut down.

Frick, meanwhile, had cabled Carnegie to let him know that

outside help was on the way to protect their interests. Of the arrival of the Pinkerton guards, scheduled for July 6, he was once again reassuring to a fault: "We expect to land our guards or watchmen in our property at Homestead without much trouble, and this once accomplished, we are, we think, in good position." The plan was to land the men on the banks of company property abutting the Monongahela and quarter them on mill premises.

The Pinkertons were not the only outside forces that had been summoned. On July 1 the *Pittsburgh Dispatch* reported that a man named James McNeally, a former Pittsburgh police officer, made an appearance at the company offices on mill grounds, then left, making the mistake of walking through downtown Homestead on his way. Whether McNeally's choice of routes was born of an ex-cop's disdain or simple stupidity is hard to tell.

Whatever the case, in accordance with procedures that the union committee had agreed upon, a member of the surveillance team stopped McNeally and demanded to know his business. McNeally suggested that his questioner mind his own, not so delicately described, business.

That was all it took to bring a crowd of union associates who subdued McNeally and searched his pockets. One of the men found a billy club secreted in McNeally's jacket, and asked McNeally if there was anything else they should know about. McNeally repeated the same answer he had offered to earlier questions put to him, and a more vigorous search ensued. This time one of the men in charge found a revolver in one of McNeally's pockets, along with a letter he'd been carrying. McNeally was hauled off to the Homestead jail, where he was charged with carrying concealed weapons, a fact he did not contest.

More important, however, was the wording of the letter he'd been carrying. It had been written on Carnegie, Phipps stationery and was addressed to McNeally, "ex-Police Officer, Pittsburg, Pa." "DEAR SIR," it boldly began. "Please come up to my office tomorrow. Wish to see you. Yours truly, J. A. Potter, Superintendent."

There was no need for workmen to question McNeally as to why he had been summoned. As a Homestead constable escorted Mc-Neally to the Pittsburgh jail following his guilty plea, the pair heard sounds of a disturbance in the distance. The constable rounded a corner, then brought his prisoner to a sudden halt. Outside the downtown station was a crowd of more than a thousand, waiting for McNeally's arrival. Exactly what the mob had in mind would never be known. The constable wisely made an about-face and hurried his frightened prisoner to an outlying station.

Meanwhile, disquieting word of yet another Frick tactic had begun to spread through the streets of Homestead. The Tide Coal Company in Allegheny City had been approached by a known associate of Frick's to arrange for the retrofitting of a pair of barges—the *Monongahela* and the *Iron Mountain*—each 125 feet long by 25 feet wide.

One of the barges was being hastily converted into a floating dormitory, the other into a mess hall with dining tables and a food-preparation area. Though no specific use had been stipulated for the vessels, the Homestead residents had little doubt that they would end up tethered at the wharf on plant grounds and put into service for the scab labor and hired mercenaries said to be on the way.

The Amalgamated had taken the possibility of a "sea assault" into account, of course, and had pressed a number of private watercraft into service as patrol boats up and down the Monongahela River. On the night of July 1, a *New York World* reporter was aboard one such craft, a steam-powered yacht called the *Edna,* along with Hugh O'Donnell, when three sharp blasts sounded from the whistle of the new Homestead power plant.

When O'Donnell and his crew responded to the alarm, they got the news from an exhausted but wild-eyed worker who had just rowed himself across the quarter-mile-wide river from Rankin to the Union Hall in Homestead: the Baltimore & Ohio evening express, due in Rankin in less than twenty minutes, was reported to be loaded with nonunion strikebreakers. In seconds, O'Donnell and his crew were back on board the *Edna,* steaming across the river, followed by crowds of workers in every skiff and rowboat that could be commandeered.

Well before the whistle of the express had sounded its approach, more than a thousand strikers had surrounded the B&O station. The scene resembled an ambush waiting to happen.

"Don't be looking for a battle," O'Donnell told the *World* reporter. "Every man knows the watchword: 'hands down.' No pistols or clubs or stones," he said. "We will simply surround these strangers, whether they be 'black sheep,' workmen or Pinkerton detectives and very gently but very firmly push them away from this locality. If they are content to move in the direction of Pittsburg, well and good. If they choose to resist they may be forced to the river bank. We have flat boats there, which such people may cast themselves adrift in, if they don't listen to reason."

While the reporter gazed about at the quiet but determined faces of the massed men, wondering if in fact reason could prevail under such circumstances, the mighty B&O steam engine hissed to a stop down the tracks. O'Donnell and a knot of his closest advisers stepped forward on the platform beneath the startled gaze of the engineer and his wary crew. When the train's conductor clambered down from the forward car, O'Donnell was quick to assure the nervous man that he meant no trouble. He simply wanted to talk to the men on board before they made any move to disembark in Rankin.

The conductor stared back at O'Donnell, bewildered. Why would a thousand tense steelworkers be surrounding his train, he wondered. And what men did O'Donnell want so badly to talk to? Aside from a few families and businessmen bound for Pittsburgh, there was hardly a soul on board the express.

O'Donnell turned to his men with a questioning look, but a quick search of the cars proved the conductor right. A false alarm, then. The workers melted back into the night.

◆   ◆   ◆

THOUGH THAT PARTICULAR EVENT had proved an empty threat, the question that remained in O'Donnell's mind was not "if" but "when." By the following day, July 2, even the *New York Times* was reporting that the company would attempt to land as many as three hundred "mechanics" on company grounds, in order that "necessary repairs" be made.

No one in Homestead was buying such hogwash concerning "mechanics," however, and O'Donnell had taken extraordinary care to be sure the strikers were not taken by surprise, readying his men like any battlefield commander. As he outlined the measures in a speech, "The Committee has, after mature deliberation, decided to organize their forces on a truly military basis. The force of four thousand men has been divided into three divisions or watches," with each division responsible for an eight-hour surveillance shift.

Each division was headed by a "commander," who in turn supervised eight "captains." "During their hours of duty," O'Donnell explained, "these Captains will have personal charge of the most important posts: the river front, the water gates and pumps, the railway stations, and the main gates of the plant. The girdle of pickets will file reports to the main headquarters every half hour, and . . . the plan is that in ten minutes' time the Committee can communicate with the men at any given point within a radius of five miles."

O'Donnell explained the makeup of a special ancillary group: "In addition to all this, there will be held in reserve a force of eight hundred Slavs and Hungarians. The brigade of foreigners will be under the command of two Hungarians and two interpreters." This was a telling coda, pointing to one of the divisions in the ranks of workers that had traditionally bedeviled labor organization within the mills. Most of the unskilled workers at Homestead, as elsewhere, tended to be recently arrived immigrants from Eastern Europe, many of whom did not even speak English.

To many of the "Huns," the concept of labor organization was unfathomable, and even the lowest wages and scales promised an opportunity to live in circumstances far superior to those left behind in an impoverished European homeland. The interests of such a man, happy to be making $1.50 a day, were hardly the same as those of skilled workers and tonnage men who might earn ten times as much, seasoned workers who had seen how quickly they could be thrown out of work when the price of steel dropped.

Given their druthers, many of the unskilled workers might have chosen to work on at Homestead, but as they quickly learned, that was not an option. In the end, whatever their feelings, almost all of the nearly four thousand workers at Homestead would take an active role in the strike.

Meanwhile, the ramifications of the unrest at Homestead had not gone unnoticed at the highest levels of government. News reports placed Pennsylvania Republican committee chairman Chris Magee in a series of meetings with President Benjamin Harrison on the matter, and it was understood that Harrison had given Magee an unequivocal message to deliver to Carnegie and Frick: patch up the trouble at all hazards. If not, they were to understand, Harrison would undertake a serious review of all federal patronage earmarked for Pennsylvania.

If Frick got Harrison's message, he seemed to pay it no mind. On the morning of July 2, striking workers saw that two of the open-hearth furnaces inside the Homestead works had been lit. When word reached O'Donnell, he quickly fired off a letter to assistant plant superintendent E. F. Wood asking that the furnaces be shut down immediately. "There is a great number of men who, on account of its being pay day, cannot be held in check," O'Donnell advised. "If the gas is not turned off we cannot be responsible for any act that may be committed."

As agitation grew among the pickets outside the plant gates, plant watchmen took it upon themselves to allow a group of workers inside to extinguish the fires. Soon after, another group of workers, realizing that materials already loaded inside the furnaces would be ruined if the heating process was disrupted, reentered the plant and lit the furnaces again. It was a series of events that led several papers covering the strike to suggest that the mill was being better cared for by the strikers than by the company itself.

At the same time, however, the secretary of the newly formed Carnegie Steel Company, Francis Lovejoy, issued a statement carried in the *New York Times* and elsewhere that as of July 2 the Homestead Mill would be operated as a non-union plant and that "no expense is to be spared to gain this point." Lovejoy went on to say that the mills at Homestead "have been closed for repairs, and will remain closed for two or three weeks. About the 15th or 20th of July, it will be published and posted that any of our old employees may return to work and must make application by a certain day as individuals. All who do not apply by the time stipulated will be considered not to desire to work, and their places will be filled by new men."

In the *Times,* Lovejoy predicted that "it will be easy to get new men into the mills, for one of the Vanderbilt [rail] lines passes directly through the property and the men can easily be set down there." Then followed the company's often-repeated refrain: "Only 280 of the 3,800 men employed in the Homestead Mills are affected by the new scales. . . . But so strong is the loyalty of the men to their organization that nearly all of the employees have decided to fight. . . . hereafter we will have nothing to do with trade organizations."

The union's response was equally forceful. O'Donnell claimed that while the new agreement initially applied only to a relatively small group of workers, the intention of the company was to cut wages across the board, anywhere from 20 percent to 60 percent. Just as clearly, he argued, the intention all along had been to abolish the AAISW's right to bargain at Homestead so that wages and working conditions could be set by the company without the need to negotiate. As a result, the union would "fight to the end."

On Sunday, July 3, Homestead mayor John McLuckie told a reporter for the *New York World,* "We do not propose that Andrew Carnegie's representatives shall bulldoze us. We have our homes in this town, we have our churches here, our societies and our cemeteries. . . . They never have imported a man into Homestead, and by [damn] they never will. We shall not permit it."

McLuckie went on to testify that the struggles of Homestead workers had attracted the support of many outside the Monongahela Valley: "Andrew Carnegie may beat us in this struggle, but if he does he beats himself. These mills have large contracts for architectural ironwork to be used in the World's Fair buildings at Chicago. . . . Last Monday the Illinois Central Trades Assembly, which represents sixty thousand workmen, passed resolutions that not a single beam of timber of non-union workmanship should enter these buildings."

McLuckie concluded by holding out hope that a coalition of outside forces, including the governor of the state, might yet carry the day. "We have a united people," he declared, "and I think that we can keep those mills idle till Mr. Carnegie's representatives decide to put us to work again."

On that same Sunday, Reverend J. J. McIlyar of the First Methodist Episcopal Church in Homestead delivered a stinging sermon that made dire predictions should someone not see the light. "A suppressed volcano exists among American workmen," McIlyar said, "and someday there will be an uprising that will become history. The question is often asked, what would Homestead be without the mills? Why not ask, where would Andrew Carnegie be without the millions he has made from his mills? . . . Capitalists should remember that men do not sell their self-respect when they sell their labor."

◆　　◆　　◆

DESPITE ALL THE PLEAS and rhetoric, a coded cable that arrived in Carnegie's London office on the morning of Monday, July 4, suggested how the matter would actually play out: CARNEGIE, MORGAN, LONDON, the message was headed. SMALL POND PONY PLUNGE RE-PAIRING POND PONY CHOKE WATCHMAN ARRIVE PLUNGE MORNING BOARD. EARLY.

The sender of the coded message was Henry Clay Frick. A second message, this one addressed to Robert A. Pinkerton of New York City, offered unmistakable clues as to the news he had actually conveyed to his majority stockholder across the sea.

"My Dear Sir," it began. "I am just in receipt of your favor of the 3rd. In reply would say, that we have all our arrangements perfected to receive your men at Ashtabula [in faraway northern Ohio, on the rail line between New York and Cleveland], and to conduct them to Bellevue Station, a few miles below this City of the Ohio River, where they will be transferred to two boats and two barges [the *Mononga-hela* and the *Iron Mountain*]."

The transfer was to take place at 11:00 p.m. on the evening of July 5, Frick wrote to Pinkerton. "The boats and barges are manned with reliable men, and will at once start for our Homestead works, and should arrive there about 3 o'clock on the morning of the 6th."

He continued in a fashion that made it clear that their planning had been ongoing for some time: "The boats are well provisioned, all the uniforms etc. that you have had shipped to the Union Supply Company, are on board the boat. There will also be on board the boats the Sheriff's Chief Deputy who will accompany and remain with your men."

"We have taken all possible precaution to keep the arrangements quiet," Frick concluded, "but, of course, it is more than likely that we will not be successful in this."

It was typical of Frick, who signed off only as "Chairman," to downplay the possibility of trouble. As understatements go, however, it was one of the greatest magnitude.

# 13

## EARLY WARNING

———◆———

INDEPENDENCE DAY OF 1892 was, by all accounts, a sub-dued affair in Homestead, Pennsylvania. The *Pittsburgh Dispatch* led its story on strike developments with a description of the holiday weather, which seemed emblematic of the prevailing mood:

"The people of Homestead spent a very wet Sunday afternoon. It was none of your new fangled poetic summer showers, but a genuine old-fashioned drizzle, which transformed the dust-carpeted streets into rivers of sticky, yellow mud. It flooded the camps of the men detailed to watch the silent works and made life a moist and heavy burden for the little gang of humanity within the white-washed confines of the steel works."

A story in the *Homestead Local News* struck a note of melodrama. "The thunder of an awful silence pervades in the vicinity of the still works," the piece began. "In the region of Munhall [the neighboring town just to the west of Homestead], that community in which for three years the hum of ponderous machinery has reverberated and almost caused the very earth to tremble, is now ominously silent. . . . Spread out on its broad expanse is the property owned by the Carnegie Steel Company, and for a greater part covered by their

146

mammoth works. It lies there, a monster, sleeping. How different from its waking moment! Where there were ordinarily hundreds now there is not a single puff of smoke or steam."

It was undoubtedly a welcome respite from the usual clouds of foul air and the endless grinding of gears and wheels and the shrieks of escaping gases. At the same time, most residents must have understood what a deceptive calm it was, and how ironic was the holiday being celebrated. Certainly no king or queen held sway over the populace of Munhall and Homestead, but many viewed Carnegie and Frick as rulers whose powers were equally absolute, and the conflict that loomed had taken on revolutionary overtones. "We are asking nothing but our rights," Mayor McLuckie had told a reporter on the previous day, "and we will have them if it requires force to get them."

Faced with a dearth of real news to report, the *Dispatch* gave over space to further description of the military-style preparations made by the advisory committee: "With the aid of a field glass the man in the signal tower [freshly erected atop union headquarters] can gaze over the ramparts and take a leisurely survey of what is going on in the enemy's camp. During the day he can signal by a system of variously colored flags to the pickets stationed on the hills across the river; at night a strong flashlight will be used. The river patrol will send up rockets when necessary and will also make a liberal use of colored fire." Mention was also made of "that hoarse-voiced steam whistle" which had sounded the alarm when the B&O Express was thought to be arriving full of scabs and thugs, and which was to be reserved for "great emergencies."

Meanwhile, assistant plant superintendent E. F. Wood had finally gotten around to issuing a response to the committee's charge that blast furnaces in the plant had been relit with the intention of putting strikebreakers to work. There was no truth whatsoever to those reports, Wood declared. "Saturday morning the regulations which control the pressure of natural gas in the furnace pipes failed to work properly and I ordered the escaping gas to be ignited in order to avoid accident."

Whether anyone bought Wood's story is debatable, but the calm held throughout the afternoon and evening except for one incident, when a pair of workmen burst into union headquarters about 3:00 p.m.

"Black sheep," one of the men shouted, gasping so hard he could hardly squeeze out the words. "Fifty of them, with trunks on their backs, walking right into town."

In moments a force of more than five hundred union men had been mobilized and was on the way down the muddy streets to confront this brazen cadre of strikebreakers. Every street in "Hunkietown," where the scabs were seen taking cover, was blockaded by menacing strikers. Once it was certain that every avenue of escape was blocked, a pair of captains led a group of handpicked men on a house-to-house search. A cry went up in one, and a striker came bursting out a door with a cowering man caught by the nape of his jacket.

As the terrified captive spoke little English, it took some moments to sort the matter out. Once an interpreter had been summoned, however, all became clear. The man was Hungarian, an employee of the Homestead mill, and one of their own. He and nine of his fellow Hungarians, fearful of the violence that seemed sure to erupt, had packed their trunks and were on their way out of town when all the fuss began. Fearful and bewildered, they'd turned back and taken refuge with friends and relatives.

On the way back to headquarters, exasperated union leaders encountered a stoop-shouldered old woman standing before the mouth of a narrow lane between buildings. "The dirty black sheep," she called in a cracking voice. "Did you get them?" Before anyone could respond, the white-haired woman drew a hand from beneath a shawl and produced a cudgel with its thong wrapped around her bony wrist. "I have guarded this point well," she told them proudly.

One of the committee captains turned to a nearby reporter and shook his head in disbelief. "I believe that woman could win the strike for us," he said.

◆　　◆　　◆

RUMORS CONTINUED TO SWIRL through the community. The *Post* reported that upward of one hundred Homestead superintendents had left town, ostensibly on vacation leave during the lull in operations. However, it was suspected that the men had actually been dispatched to various towns and cities in the East and Midwest to recruit non-union workmen. "It is noted that Manager Potter has gone to the company's iron mines near Duluth, where there are brawny men by the hundred," the *Post* story said.

Nor had the concerns outside Pittsburgh lessened. A *Dispatch* story that ran on July 5 reported that U.S. Navy officials had expressed fears that further delays in deliveries of armor plating, already well behind schedule, would bring a halt to work on several new ships under construction. Since Carnegie's contracts with the navy totaled more than $4 million, the matter was of serious concern to the company as well, but as the story noted, the navy brass "cannot believe that the company will be long in reaching an agreement with their men for the reason that any prolonged cessation of work would not only mean an immediate loss, but might jeopardize their chance of getting an additional contract for from five to ten thousand tons of armor soon to be let."

Union leaders took heart from such reports, believing that the pressures would induce the company to cave in. But it was a fine line that they were walking; should Carnegie Steel lose too much business as the result of a prolonged strike, there could be no work to go back to, whatever agreement might be reached.

Soon enough, however, the agonizing would end. Sometime during the evening of July 4, Frick sent a letter to William H. McCleary, the high sheriff of Allegheny County, setting an inevitable chain of events in motion. Citing the veiled threats made by the advisory committee in its letter to assistant superintendent Wood concerning the lighting of the open-hearth furnaces and arguing "that from threats openly made we have reasonable cause to apprehend that an attempt will be made to collect a mob and to destroy and to damage our property aforesaid and to prevent us from its use and enjoyment," Frick went on to say: "We therefore call upon you, as Sheriff of Allegheny County, Pa., to protect our property from violence, damage and destruction, and to protect us in its free use and enjoyment."

In retrospect, this rather showy request to the sheriff seems part of a well-rehearsed scenario. Given his previous experience in handling labor unrest, Frick had little reason to trust the abilities of local law enforcement, and sending out such a call set the stage for the use of the Pinkerton men he had already engaged.

From his point of view, he was the defender of a multimillion-dollar physical plant now surrounded by a well-organized group of four thousand workers, bolstered by the sympathies of just about every workingman in the Monongahela Valley, not to mention the very mayor of the town that lay just outside his gates and through which every means of ingress and egress to his installation passed. He well understood that in a moment's flashpoint, anything might give rise to the sacking and destruction of what most considered the world's flagship steelmaking installation.

From a businessman's standpoint, then, and setting aside the fact that the impasse had been reached as the result of his and Carnegie's intransigence, the decision to import Pinkerton men to bolster an ill-organized, undermanned force of deputies with little stake in standing firm against a howling mob of thousands was not so much an underhanded tactic as a prudent business decision.

Once the decision had been reached not to simply close the plant for whatever length of time it would take for workers to give in, there was no longer any turning back. From then on, he was a general, preparing for an all-out battle. One might imagine a commercial geared to the Fortune 500 crowd of the day: a soot-stained, high-collared actor wearing a suit and sitting on an overturned bucket amid the smoldering ruins of the Homestead works. "Should have brought in the Pinkertons," the Frick stand-in laments. If bringing in the Pinkertons signaled ill will and duplicity to the workers, that was the last concern of Henry Frick.

It seemed likely, then, that the request to Sheriff McCleary was merely a necessary precursor to the deputizing of the Pinkertons, who had already disembarked from their train in Ashtabula and were on their way to Bellevue, an Ohio River hamlet about ten miles downstream from Homestead, not far past the confluence of the Allegheny and the Monongahela.

In any case, McCleary responded dutifully to Chairman Frick's request and, early on the morning of July 5, appeared at union headquarters in Homestead, accompanied by two deputies. According to accounts in the *Pittsburgh Dispatch* and elsewhere, the high sheriff told union leaders about the request he had received from the company. Under the circumstances, he said, "I thought it would be a wise move to come here this morning and personally look over the ground."

O'Donnell and some fifty members of his advisory committee listened to the sheriff, then asked him to wait outside while they convened behind closed doors. When they emerged, O'Donnell had a startling proposition for the sheriff: "The Advisory Committee is not only ready but anxious to assist you in preserving peace and protecting property hereabouts," he began, before dropping his bombshell. The advisory committee would offer as few as one hundred or as many as five hundred men to be deputized on the spot and to serve the high sheriff as sworn officers of the law. The committee would even be willing to post a bond of $10,000 for each man to ensure that their duties were performed properly.

The offer sent McCleary into a hasty conference with his own men, but in short order he had regrouped. He thanked O'Donnell for the union's offer and promised to keep it in mind for the future, "but just now," he said, "I prefer to have my own men and I will send fifty deputies to Homestead this afternoon."

He went on to repeat his request for a look at the mill grounds, and O'Donnell acquiesced, appointing a group of men to escort him there. O'Donnell stayed behind to meet with his trusted advisers and, upon McCleary's return from the tour, called the sheriff in for one final piece of business. McCleary, who professed to find no signs of disorder in or about the plant, was somewhat apologetic as he entered the room where O'Donnell and his men had gathered around a long table. "Still," the sheriff explained, "I must do my duty and I will send the men."

O'Donnell asked the sheriff if that was all he had to say, and McCleary assured him that it was. "Well, then," O'Donnell said, pointing to a great mound of documents that had been piled in the center of the table. "What you see here, Sheriff, is the last meeting of the Advisory Committee of the AAISW. We, as members of that committee, have, after due deliberation, resolved to formally disband this committee, and we have asked you here to witness it.

"The Advisory Committee from now on," he continued, "will not be responsible for any disorder or any lawless act perpetrated either in Homestead Borough or Mifflin Township. Do you understand?" he demanded. "Our responsibility ceases from this very moment. I now declare the Advisory Committee to be dead."

As O'Donnell finished speaking, the members of the committee reached to unfasten their lapel badges and tossed them down on the table. In the words of a *Dispatch* reporter, "The odd bits of narrow ribbon formed a crimson mound in the center of the table." Scarcely had the badges stopped flying than others began to move the pile of documents that had been gathered on the table and place them in the grate of the room's fireplace. O'Donnell struck a match, and in moments the committee's documents were ablaze.

O'Donnell stood and turned to the astonished sheriff. "Have you anything further to say to us?" O'Donnell asked.

McCleary had nothing at all to say. He and his men backed hastily out of the room and hurried through the streets of Homestead to the banks of the Monongahela, where a grim ferryman offered to cross them over to the train station at Rankin for a quarter a head. It wasn't the cheapest price you might find, but McCleary wasn't in the mood for haggling. In short order, he and his men were across the river and at 2:00 p.m. were on a B&O train bound for Pittsburgh.

In the meantime, several members of the now-disbanded advisory committee sent a telegram to the union's legal counsel in Pittsburgh, asking that a court order be sought enjoining the sheriff from sending deputies to the Homestead works. Speaking now as concerned "Citizens of Mifflin," they decried the move as one "calculated to cause unnecessary disturbance."

But by 6:00 p.m., the union's underground telegraph was crackling. Armed men were on board the evening Homestead express. "They are bound for Fort Frick," shouted one man as he jumped down from the train at an intermediary stop. "And they are going to get off at Munhall." By the time the express made its stop in Munhall—about six minutes later, according to newspaper accounts—there were two thousand men gathered about the platform as Sheriff McCleary's chief deputy, Samuel Cluely, stepped down from the train along with nine other officers.

Cluely, a silver-mustached man who cut an able figure, stopped short. No shouts, no catcalls, just a wall of grim-faced men everywhere he looked. In moments the train pulled out, and the crowd began to close in about the platform. Cluely had a pistol holstered at his side, but using it in such circumstances was clearly out of the question.

Finally, a former committeeman stepped forward, speaking in a calm if forceful voice. "Gentlemen, what is your business here?"

Cluely just as calmly handed over a copy of the notice he had been ordered by his boss to post about the town.

Whereas, It has come to my knowledge that certain persons have congregated and assembled at and near the works of the Carnegie Steel Company . . . and that such persons have interfered with workmen employed in said works obtaining access to same, and that certain persons have made threats of injury to employees going to and from said works, and have threatened that if the owners of said works attempt to run the same the property will be injured and destroyed. . . . Now, I, William H. McCleary, High Sheriff of said county, do hereby notify and warn all persons that all acts enumerated are unlawful, and that all persons engaged in the same in any way are liable to arrest and punishment.

The order went on to amplify and extend the terms and conditions, but the import was clear. The gloves were off. The finish fight had begun.

"Our instructions are to proceed to the Homestead Steel Works with all possible speed," Deputy Cluely said, when the committeeman's gaze lifted from the sheriff's order.

The committeeman shook his head. Someone behind him shouted, "You fellows will never get to the gates alive," and a cheer of affirmation rose.

The committeeman turned and raised a hand to the crowd. "Order, boys, order; these gentlemen are now in our care and you must protect them from the unthinking mob." He instructed an aide to clear a path through the crowd and then turned back to Cluely.

"Follow me or I will not be responsible for what may happen," he said.

Cluely turned his own formidable gaze on the nine deputies. No one questioned what they saw there. All fell into line behind the union spokesman, and Cluely and the procession made their way to union headquarters, passing as smoothly and quietly through the assembled multitudes as a hot knife through butter. Cluely and his men were given a choice: they could accept safe passage back to Pittsburgh, or stay on, at their own risk, in Homestead.

It wasn't much of a choice. Before leaving, however, Cluely was quick to point out that there would be many more men returning in his wake.

"And we are not going anywhere," the union representative responded. There would have been no bravado from either side in such an exchange. Only resignation. And, surely, no small amount of sadness.

# 14

## ROCKETS' RED GLARE

———➤◆◄———

T HE EVICTION OF CLUELY and his fellow deputies may
have played directly into company hands. It having proved
impossible to secure the protection of the Homestead works
property from local law enforcement agencies, Frick was now entirely within his legal rights to bring in private guards.

Whether Frick had anticipated as much is impossible to know.
But this much is clear: While Frick slumbered in his upstairs chambers at Clayton, several miles to the north, and while Andrew
Carnegie woke early for a day of fishing on Loch Rannoch, one of the
more remote spots in all of Scotland, events in Homestead, Pennsylvania, spun steadily out of control.

By 11:00 p.m. on the night of July 5, approximately three hundred Pinkerton guards arrived by train at the Bellevue station, just
west of Pittsburgh, on the southerly banks of the Ohio River, and
some ten miles downstream from the Homestead works. Before retir-
ing, Frick had informed High Sheriff McCleary of the imminent arrival of the Pinkerton men; and chief counsel for the firm, Philander
C. Knox (who would later become U.S. attorney general and secretary of state under William Howard Taft), had asked McCleary to

send one of his deputies to meet the train, suggesting that this emissary be given the power to deputize the Pinkertons.

McCleary agreed to send along a deputy, one Colonel Joseph H. Gray. Gray would escort the Pinkerton men from the station at Bellevue to the docks where the *Iron Mountain* and the *Monongahela* were tethered, and accompany them during the short voyage to the company docks in Homestead. McCleary, however, was an elected official, caught between a rock and a hard place in all this. While Carnegie Steel exercised significant political clout in the area, McCleary was well aware of the absolute contempt held by the greater part of his constituency for the Pinkertons.

Ultimately, he balked at deputizing the Pinkertons, warning Gray explicitly that he lacked the power to do so. Although McCleary attempted to justify his actions by reasoning that his office should maintain authority in the matters, his refusal seemed to Frick typical of local politicians.

No matter, Frick must have concluded. Whether deputized or not, the Pinkertons were on the way, and they would handle matters as they should be handled.

It took a bit of time for the transfer to be made in Bellevue, but by 2:00 a.m. on July 6, the loaded barges had been pulled away by tugs and, with Deputy Gray and Superintendent John Potter on board, were on their way to the mill. According to historian Paul Krause, author of *The Battle for Homestead,* the Pinkertons, under the command of Captain Frederick Heinde and his chief deputy, Charles Nordrum, did not plan to arrive defenseless. Along with the distinctive slouch hats and white-bloused Pinkerton uniforms, there were 300 pistols and 250 Winchester rifles on board the barges, as well as crates and crates of ammunition, ancillary armaments, and food enough for a lengthy siege.

Shortly after their departure, one of the tugs was disabled, and both barges had to be hooked up to the remaining craft, the *Little Bill.* Scarcely were they under way again, passing beneath the Smithfield

Street Bridge, than a union sentry posted there peered down through the darkness and spotted the heavily loaded barges making their way upstream.

A runner was dispatched to the nearby telegraph office, and at 2:30 word was relayed to union offices in Homestead: "Watch the river. Steamer with barges left here." Soon the great whistle mounted atop union headquarters was shrieking the alarm, and sleepy citizens of Homestead and Munhall stumbled from their beds, wondering if, this time, the call was real.

The patrol boat *Edna,* launched from the Homestead docks and churning quickly downstream toward the mouth of the Mononga-hela, soon spotted the *Little Bill* with the barges in tow. Marksmen on the *Edna*'s decks fired warning shots across the bow of the tug and barges, and the pilot of the *Edna* sounded the prearranged signal on his craft's sharp whistle. There was no doubt. The long-feared inva-sion was under way.

It was 4:00 a.m. now, and thousands of workers and citizens of Homestead and Munhall had rushed to the southern banks of the river. As the tug began to turn toward shore, angry shouts rose up from the crowd, followed soon after by shots. One volley blew out the windows of the tug's pilot house, sending the crew sprawling to the decks.

On shore, Hugh O'Donnell and his division commanders and captains raced about, imploring the crowds for calm, but the situa-tion had careened beyond anyone's control. "There was no method, no leadership apparent in the response to the [whistle] blast from the light works," said a report in the *New York Herald.* "It was the up-rising of a population. . . . Not men alone, but women, too; women armed with clubs as they joined the throng which streamed up the Pennsylvania and Pittsburg and McKeesport tracks picking its way with a fleet footedness born of long practice over the ties."

William B. Rodgers, the frightened captain of the *Little Bill,* had managed to steer his craft past the massed crowds in Homestead proper. The mob had managed to keep pace as they passed along the town, but finally Rodgers had gained the deserted grounds of the Homestead works, where the infernal mob was stymied by the high fence that Frick had built. It was hardly the sort of thing a tugboat captain was trained for—he had been told by Frick that he would be transporting a number of "watchmen" from Bellevue to the plant grounds—but he was a dedicated man, and no coward, either. His intent was to reach the company docks looming in the darkness just ahead, land the barges that he towed, and make haste away, back to the blessed calm of the normal tugboating life.

The frenzied crowd was only momentarily frustrated by the battlements of Fort Frick, however. When they saw the *Little Bill* make its turn toward the company docks, another mighty cry rose up, and men began to batter down the undefended walls. In short order, the fence was flattened and hordes of workers stampeded through the breach, crying wildly as they went. "We'll send them home on stretchers," came the cry, according to the *Herald* report. "Hell will be full of new pictures in the morning."

Others streamed into the plant along the unguarded railway tracks that scant days before had carried mundane carloads of ore and coke in, armor plate and rails and steel beams out. According to press accounts, one of the leaders of the mob, no less compelling for having appointed himself to the fore, was a middle-aged Britisher named Billy Foy, whose former "command" had been as chief of the corps of the Homestead Salvation Army. As the *Herald* put it, "All the fervor of his wild religious training, spent hitherto in emptiness in denouncing the intangible devil and the invisible powers of evil, seemed to find a long looked for object upon which to wreak its will. The man had been longing for a chance for years to grapple with the powers of darkness in bodily form. Now it was coming—coming up the river to rob him and his mates of their very homes and beds."

While Foy led the charge through the shattered fences at the waterline of company property, another, even more colorful character stood out in the melee. This was Mrs. Finch, the apparent leader of the women who had joined the pack, that same white-haired grand-mother who had guarded the alleyways of Homestead from the first days of the gathering storm.

"The dirty black sheep," she cried, brandishing her famous cudgel above her head. "Let me get at them."

Mrs. Finch's fervor had drawn a contingent of followers, some carrying babies, others clutching clubs, as she led the way toward the mill. "High and shrill and strong for her years as the voice of the lustiest fisherwoman who marched on Versailles," as the *Herald* re-porter put it, "a foolish mob going to war against hopeless odds of arms and discipline, the cries seemed then terrible as the charging cry of the black fanatics of the Sudanese desert."

By the time the mob caught up, the captain of the *Little Bill* had managed to complete his bounden duty. The *Monongahela* and the *Iron Mountain* had been docked, and though no men had yet ven-tured onto shore, gangplanks had been readied for that purpose.

As the crowds surged toward the tethered barges, an odd quiet descended over what had been bedlam. So much hatred had been brewed over the past weeks, so much invective hurled. Now the masses stood in a state of astonished anticipation, as though awaiting the emergence of creatures from a newly landed spaceship. Hatred palpitated there, no doubt. But also there was awe, and fear.

One man wearing the slouch hat of a Pinkerton appeared on the deck of the *Monongahela,* and a murmur swept through the crowd. A woman bent to pick up a stone, then hurled it at the barge. "Don't you land," another called, "you must not land."

A man's voice followed. "Go back, go back, or we'll not answer for your lives." Another voice cried, "Don't come on land or we'll brain you."

The situation threatened to boil over once again when Hugh O'Donnell finally arrived, shouting mightily over the crowd for si-lence. Amazingly enough, he was obeyed.

O'Donnell, portrayed in a widely published *New York World* sketch as a tall, angular man with a full, dark mustache and striking good looks, turned from the crowd and called out across the ominously quiet waters to the barges: "On behalf of five thousand men, I beg of you to leave here at once. I don't know who you are nor from whence you came, but I do know that you have no business here."

There was no immediate response, of course, and O'Donnell pressed on: "We, the workers in these mills, are peaceably inclined. We have not damaged any property, and we do not intend to. If you will send a committee with us, we will take them through the works . . . and promise them a safe return to their boats. But in the name of God and humanity, don't attempt to land! Don't attempt to enter these works by force."

Perhaps the last sounded like a challenge, or perhaps he had simply been biding his time, but at that, Captain Heinde, leader of the Pinkerton force, stepped finally onto the decks of the *Iron Mountain* to deliver his response, unequivocally and imperturbably: "We were sent here to take possession of this property and to guard it for this company. . . . We don't wish to shed blood, but . . . if you men don't withdraw, we will mow every one of you down and enter in spite of you. You had better disperse, for land we will."

O'Donnell surveyed the scene around him. In addition to the armed thousands who had occupied the steep banks of the river where the barges were tied off, hundreds more looked down upon the scene from the vantage of the Pmickey (Pennsylvania, McKeesport, and Youghiogheny) Railroad Bridge just upstream. On the opposite side of the Monongahela, more sympathizers had gathered. O'Donnell had spent weeks and months in the attempt to engineer a peaceful resolution to a dispute that, in his mind, cried out for a meeting of reasonable minds. How had it come to this?

What could he say now that had not already been said? What could he do but accept the inevitable?

Finally he took a breath and shouted back to Heinde. "I have no more to say," he called. "What you do here is at the risk of many lives. Before you enter those mills, you will trample over the dead bodies of three thousand honest workingmen."

With that, O'Donnell turned away.

# 15

## OVER THE EDGE

———▶◆◀———

HAD THIS BEEN A MODERN-DAY standoff, with Frick in close touch with his emissaries by cell phone and Carnegie observing the scene via CNN satellite feed, there might have been some last-minute intercession, some barked command to send history down a different path. But for the slumbering Frick, the matter was out of his hands. His terms had been dictated, and events would proceed however they would.

As for Carnegie, he had given Frick free rein. If he glimpsed any dire omens in the mists above a secluded lake in Scotland's wilderness that early July morning, there was little he could do about it.

As it was, the exchange between Heinde and O'Donnell was followed by a period of motionless silence on the banks of the Monongahela, broken finally when Heinde ordered a group of his men to lower the *Iron Mountain*'s gangplank to the shore. The moment the plank hit ground, William Foy, the former Salvation Army commander, strode to its foot, followed by a group of striking workers.

Heinde, with a riot stick in hand, stepped onto the gangplank. "Now, men," he warned, "we are coming ashore to guard these works and we want to come without bloodshed. There are three hundred men behind me and you cannot stop us. . . ."

"Come on, and you'll come over my dead carcass," Foy shouted back.

It was enough for Heinde, who stepped forward suddenly, slashing his stick at Foy's temple. Foy managed to duck in time, but Heinde's momentum sent him stumbling down the gangplank, his men surging after.

Heinde's foot clipped the flat end of an oar left untended on the dock, sending its knotted handle flying upward. The knurled end of the oar cracked against the cheek of one of Foy's companions, who went down with a cry of pain. Another of Foy's men jumped forward and drove a club of his own into Heinde, sending him onto his back.

Accounts differ as to what exactly happened next—historians, trial transcripts, newspaper articles, and eyewitness accounts debate who fired first according to their predispositions. The only certainty is that two shots were fired in quick succession.

One hit Foy, the other Heinde. And the battle was on.

Pinkerton captain J. W. Cooper shouted his orders, and from a row of Winchester rifle barrels poised from the *Monongahela*'s stem to its stern, flashes of fire shot out. Incredibly, only two men on the tightly packed shore, scant yards from the tethered barges, were dropped by that first wave of Winchester fire.

Hugh O'Donnell had just raised his hands in a futile attempt to quell the crowd. "For God's sake put down your guns and look to the protection of your families," he cried, when he felt a burning sensation on one of his hands. He snatched it down to see that the flesh of his thumb had been notched by a rifle bullet, taking along with it the last hope of reason. As O'Donnell clutched his bloody hand, the men on shore opened up with return fire of their own, riddling the *Iron Mountain*, the *Monongahela*, and the *Little Bill* with an array of fire from pistols, shotguns, rifles, even antique muskets.

One of the first steelworkers to go down was a man named Martin Murray. He lay bleeding and semiconscious while the bullets continued to fly above him and his friends ran screaming for cover. There was a momentary lull in the firing, then, and Murray realized that someone was standing over him now. He felt hands go under his shoulders, felt himself being lifted up.

He heard a familiar voice, encouraging him to hang on, that they would find help soon. It was his friend and fellow striker Joseph Sotak who had come to rescue him, Murray realized. He had no idea how badly he had been wounded, or if Sotak's words were the kind of commonplace assurances you gave a dying man, but still Murray was comforted—until he heard another shot and he felt Sotak's hands go limp.

"Joseph?" Murray cried, but there was only a moment's gurgling in response. Sotak had taken a round squarely in the mouth. He was dead by the time the two of them hit the ground.

For ten minutes the firing continued. In addition to Foy and Heinde and Sotak and Murray, at least twenty-three others—eleven union men and another dozen of the Pinkertons—fell.

The men on shore had scrambled behind hastily thrown together barricades of scrap iron and lumber scavenged from the mill grounds, and with their targets hidden, the Pinkertons were holding fire. While the wounded were being dragged away and tended to, Superintendent Potter held a heated strategy session with the Pinkerton captains.

The Pinkertons wanted to mount a fresh assault and gain a foothold on dry land; they were sitting ducks on the barges, they argued. But Potter, a factory manager in the everyday world that seemed so far away now, was adamant. "I will not take the responsibility for any further bloodshed," he said, staring in disbelief at the carnage that surrounded him. He insisted that no further initiatives be taken until High Sheriff McCleary arrived from Pittsburgh.

Reluctantly the Pinkertons went along. It was agreed that the *Little Bill* would quit the scene immediately, taking the badly bleeding

Captain Heinde and the other wounded Pinkerton men across the Monongahela, where they could be put on board a train and taken to a hospital in Pittsburgh. The barges would stay where they were, and the rest of the men would remain on board.

Captains Cooper and Nordrum issued the orders, and their men retreated from the decks. Soon the union men on shore could see the Pinkertons hard at work chiseling firing ports in the hulls of the barges, whether to prepare for an assault of sniper fire or to repel anyone who might attempt to board, it was impossible to tell.

For their part, the men on shore went about fortifying their positions, supplanting their hastily formed barricades with a long battlement built, ironically, of steel beams taken from company stockpiles. Others were sent to scour the surrounding neighborhoods for more stores of guns and ammunition. Word of the battle had meanwhile reached Pittsburgh, and several hundred armed sympathizers were on the way to reinforce the strikers' ranks.

Though much of the armed resistance went on as if by reflex, Hugh O'Donnell bound up his hand and did what he could to bring reason to bear. His first task was to persuade the five hundred or more women who had gathered at the scene to go home. When that was finally accomplished, and the wounded men had been removed for medical care, O'Donnell prevailed upon McLuckie to issue word that all saloons in Homestead would remain closed until further notice.

By 6:00 a.m., a relative calm had descended upon the scene. The early-morning fog had burned off, allowing onlookers gathered atop the hills overlooking the plant and the river to view the spectacle from a safe vantage point. A few skiffs now surrounded the Pinkerton barges, firing occasional rounds at their quarry and taking desultory fire in return.

By 8:00 a.m., the frustrated Pinkertons had had enough of being pinned down. One of the captains shouted their intention to come ashore, but he received no reply from an emplacement of union men close by. When a door on one of the barges began to creak open, a shot from somewhere on shore rattled off the planks.

In moments the firing was once again at full bore. John Morris, a twenty-eight-year-old Welsh immigrant and a skilled worker in the plant's blooming mill, the place where steel is given its first preliminary shape, had taken a position atop the pump house overlooking the wharf. When Morris squeezed off a round that he thought had struck one of the Pinkertons, he raised his head just to seek confirmation.

His timing could not have been worse. As he rose, a rifle bullet split his forehead, the force of the shot catapulting him off the tower. He fell sixty feet, dead before he hit the ground.

Another young man, Henry Striegel, just nineteen and a sympathizing Teamster who had heard about what was happening at Homestead, ran toward the front lines of the conflict with a pistol in hand. Before he could get off a shot, he tripped on a spar of iron and tumbled to the ground. As he fell, his pistol went off and the bullet bored into his leg. Striegel was writhing on the ground, clutching at his leg in agony, as a seasoned striker started up from his cover to drag the lad to cover. There was a shot from one of the barges, then, and a bullet tore through Striegel's throat, killing him instantly.

Only moments before the shooting had begun, Peter Fares, a twenty-eight-year-old Slovak who worked as a helper on one of the open-hearth furnaces, had come to the mill yard, curious to see for himself what was going on. Fares carried no weapon. In fact, he had a loaf of bread in one hand, and was about to tear off a chunk for a bit of breakfast, when a bullet from a Pinkerton sniper's rifle hit him just above the lip. As the slug flattened and proceeded on, it took Fares's brain matter, and the back of his skull, along with it.

The fourth member of the union garrison to die met the most ironic fate of all. One group of men had "borrowed" a twenty-pound cannon from the Homestead chapter of the Grand Army of the Republic, the Union Army Civil War veterans' association. The antique brass weapon had been ferried across to the opposite bank of the Monongahela, set up at what was deemed a better vantage point for firing on the barges.

When the second round of fighting began, the neophyte cannoneers joined in. Amazingly enough, the first of the three-pound balls they launched struck one of the barges with a thundering crash of wood and debris. They hurriedly reloaded and fired again, but as true as the first shot had flown, the second went equally awry. The ball flew far above the barges and into the plant grounds, far from the combat lines, where a twenty-three-year-old laborer named Silas Wain, a recent immigrant from England, was standing beside the boiler house, engaged in earnest conversation with his brother William.

To William it was an impossible sight. One instant he was talking to Silas about their uncertain prospects in this "land of opportunity." In the next instant there was a heated rush of air that seemed to atomize his brother before his eyes. It took William, who was unscathed, some moments to realize. But soon enough his astonished eyes traveled to where Silas had been driven by the errant cannonball. His brother's corpse lay before him, as one newsman put it, "a mangled mass of bloody flesh . . . stretched in the dust of the mill yard."

The deaths of these four men, representing a veritable cross-section of the union membership, seemed only to galvanize an already enraged group of strikers. But their marksmanship had done little to elevate the mood on board the Pinkerton barges. The commanders of the force, frustrated by the confines of their position, were aching for the chance to establish a beachhead from which they felt they could mount a successful offensive on their less experienced opponents.

Among the general rank and file on the barges, however, there was far less unity of purpose. As it turned out, only about 40 of the total force were Pinkerton regulars who knew what to expect. The other 260 were recent conscripts, the usual assortment of would-be toughs, aimless drifters, and otherwise unemployed men who had signed up for a job promising good pay and the prospect of "three squares" a day. Perhaps there were a few among them who relished the prospect of a knock-down, drag-out fight, but it was beginning to look as if there were not nearly enough.

Many of the men had actually refused the orders of their superiors to open fire, and had run into the holds of the barges to cower under beds and behind tables when the fighting began. And many of those same men had earlier pleaded to be allowed to join the ranks of the wounded taken away by the *Little Bill*.

Now they complained bitterly that they had been marooned there on the barges to die. "They were the worst sort of cowards I ever saw," second-in-command Nordrum would later testify. When the cannonball blew through the side of one barge, it was all he could do to keep many of those cowering belowdecks from jumping overboard on the spot.

At approximately 11:00 a.m., however, a ray of hope appeared to the less eager among the mercenaries. Like some angel of mercy in mechanical form, the *Little Bill* was spotted, steaming across the waters toward their embattled position, eliciting a great cheer from the men.

Captain Rodgers was at the helm of the *Little Bill,* the Stars and Stripes fluttering from the flagstaff. It had been his idea to raise the flag—"I did not think the workers would fire upon a vessel flying Old Glory"—but his hopes, and those of the anxious Pinkertons, were soon put to rest.

The moment the *Little Bill* got within range, a furious barrage issued from the riverbank. One shot blew through the side of the pilothouse, narrowly missing Rodgers and plowing into the groin of a crewman who stood beside him. From a prone position on the deck, Rodgers swung the *Little Bill* hard about, guiding his craft downstream as quickly as a tug might go.

If the disappearance of the *Little Bill* was not dismaying enough, what the Pinkerton men saw next was something out of a nightmare. Just upstream from the company docks, strikers had loaded a raft high with timbers and creosote-soaked railway ties. Then someone tossed a torch amid the pile and soon the entire raft was engulfed in flames.

The Pinkertons could only gape in fear as the floating inferno was cut loose and sent drifting toward them. Several of those on board the *Iron Mountain* and the *Monongahela* donned life jackets and rushed toward the rails to jump, but grim Pinkerton regulars raised their Winchesters and threatened to shoot anyone who tried to desert. One can only imagine the predicament: take a rifle bullet in the breast from your fellow combatant, or wait to be incinerated alive?

Fortunately for the frightened men staring into those rifle bores, the strikers had miscalculated. The fire aboard the floating pyre grew so fierce, so quickly, that the pile consumed itself down to the water-line and sank, just as it was about to careen into the barges.

Hardly had that threat been extinguished, however, than another hellish spectacle presented itself. Workers high atop the hill near the mill itself loaded a railroad flatcar with casks of oil and set the whole thing ablaze. The car's brakes were released and yet another portable conflagration was loosed, hurtling along the track that led down to the docks from the mill.

There seemed no possibility of escape this time. The car was meant to fly off the end of the tracks and launch itself atop the wooden barges that lay squarely in its path. Even the Pinkerton regulars were ready to jump ship at this prospect, when, somehow, fate intervened once more. The ponderous car would not hurtle anywhere; its bulk was its own undoing. At the bottom of the tracks it abruptly stopped dead, leaving the Pinkertons to stare as it burned it-self harmlessly to cinders on shore.

It was not the end of the attacks on the *Iron Mountain* and the *Monongahela,* however. As John Holway, a student who had had the misfortune to sign up for the siege, would later testify, "There seemed to be sharpshooters picking us off. At first they fired straight at us, but after a while they fired through the aisles on the side, and they would shoot men who thought they were safe. The bullets would come, zip, and you would hear some man yell, and you would know they were not cautious. . . .

"About 12 o'clock barrels of burning oil were floating around the bank to burn us up, to compel us to go on the wharf and there shoot us down, but they didn't succeed because the oil was taken up by the water. . . . At about 3 o'clock we heard something; we thought it was a cannon, but it was dynamite. . . . It partially wrecked the other boat. A stick of it fell near me. It broke open the door of the aisles, and it smashed open the door, and the sharpshooters were firing directly at any man in sight. . . .

"Most of the men were for surrender at this time, but the old detectives held out and said, 'If you surrender you will be shot down like dogs; the best thing is to stay here.' We could not cut our barges loose because there was a fall below, where we would be sunk. We were deserted by our captains and by our tug, and left there to [die]."

One of Holway's fellow conscripts was a man named Tom Connors. He was hunched under a table nearby, a life jacket tied about his chest, his hands thrown over his head in terror. A slug whistled through a gap in the barge's siding, and Connors cried out. Men who ran to Connors's aid found blood spurting from a severed artery in his arm. His agonized screams began the moment he was hit, and continued unabated for the long minutes it took for him to lapse into unconsciousness.

It was enough for even the most seasoned of the Pinkertons. If they did not surrender, they all would lose their lives.

A white flag was thrust up from a gap in one barge's side. In seconds, a marksman's bullet shot it down. Disbelieving Pinkertons raised a second flag, and another volley from the riverbank blew it to smithereens as well. According to historian Krause, there was a reason for such disregard: workers had learned that a call had gone out from company headquarters to Pennsylvania governor Robert E. Pattison requesting that state militia be sent in. The workers wanted to finish off the hated Pinkertons before outside aid could arrive.

As early as nine o'clock that morning, once he had learned of the casualties at Homestead, William Weihe, national president of the Amalgamated, hurried to the Pittsburgh offices of High Sheriff Mc-Cleary, imploring him to arrange a negotiating session with Frick. Despite a briefing on the terrible events of the previous night, Frick dismissed Weihe's appeals out of hand.

"I told the gentleman who called that we would not confer with the Amalgamated association officials," he told a Philadelphia reporter. "It was their followers who were rioting and destroying our property, and we would not accept his proposition. At the same time this representative of our former workmen said they were willing to accept the terms offered, and concede everything we asked except the date of the termination of the scale, which they insisted should be June 30 in place of December 31."

When the reporter pressed Frick about whether that would resolve the conflict, Frick brushed the possibility aside: "It is in the hands of the authorities of Allegheny County. If they are unable to cope with it, it certainly is the duty of the Governor of the State to see that we are permitted to operate our establishment unmolested. The men engaged by us through the Pinkerton agencies were sent up to Homestead with the full knowledge of the sheriff and by him placed in charge of his chief deputy, Colonel Gray, and as we know, with instructions to deputize them in case it became necessary."

In other words, it seemed, even the Pinkertons had become dispensable pawns in a ploy to bring the irresistible force of the militia into play. Frick was washing his hands of responsibility altogether, shunting everything off onto elected officials. The company's official statement was published in the press later that day, concluding, "We are not taking any active part in the matter at present, as we cannot interfere with the Sheriff in the discharge of his duty and are now awaiting his further action."

While Frick awaited favorable word of direct intervention from Harrisburg, strikers continued their siege on the hapless Pinkertons. At 4:00 p.m., Amalgamated president Weihe made his way to the mill yard in Homestead and managed to attract the attention of a significant number of the forces arrayed there. He begged the men to lay down their arms and allow the Pinkertons to leave the barges without fear of harm.

All the while that Weihe spoke, gunfire and dynamite explosions continued from the hillside behind them. He warned the men that if they persisted, the militia would be sent in, but this inflamed as many as it frightened.

Hugh O'Donnell had arrived by then, and took his place beside Weihe. A rescue boat bearing a white flag was on its way to the barges, O'Donnell announced. They should let the tug hitch up to the barges and pull the Pinkertons away.

"No," one of the self-appointed leaders of the more militant strikers replied. "Let the Pinkertons lay down their arms and march out."

This brought a cheer from the assemblage, and O'Donnell asked if in fact that would solve the impasse. A quick straw vote seemed to indicate that it would. The only question that remained was how to convey this offer to the men on the barges. "Go down yourself," someone called to O'Donnell.

Meanwhile, a great shouting had sprung up from the battlements on the riverbank and the crowd rushed to see what had caused the alarm. O'Donnell and Weihe ran with the others to the edge of the hilltop to find that two Pinkerton men had emerged on the decks of one of the barges, white handkerchiefs held in their upraised hands. Hundreds of rifles were trained upon the pair, and an ominous silence held.

"Don't shoot," O'Donnell cried, and others echoed the command as he made his way quickly down the steep hillside and climbed up the gangplank to confer with the two Pinkerton men. Workers on the hillside stood with their trigger fingers poised, ready to strike at the first sign of treachery.

After a moment, O'Donnell turned back to shore and withdrew a handkerchief from his own pocket. He raised his hand and waved the white square above his head for everyone to see. Surrender had finally been brokered. The bloody "Battle of Homestead" was at an end, or so it seemed.

# 16

## THE BETTER PART OF VALOR

—▶◆◀—

THE DECISION TO SURRENDER had not been easily made aboard the barges. According to a report in the *St. Louis Post-Dispatch,* one of the Pinkerton men remained adamantly opposed to going ashore, even with their ammunition virtually gone and most of his colleagues joined against him. Death was preferable to crawling ashore like a whipped dog, he said. He would stay on board and fight it out to the end.

Another Pinkerton, a hard-bitten veteran, hefted the Winchester that he carried under one arm. "You'll come in or I will blow your brains out," he told the holdout, adding a few choice epithets that contemporary sources declined to specify.

The holdout stared back contemptuously, then turned and began to walk away, toward the stern of the boat. As the other men looked on, he suddenly stopped and whipped his Colt pistol from his holster. Before anyone could react, he raised the Colt's barrel to his head and fired. He toppled over as the stunned men looked on, "his brains oozing out on the already blood-soaked boards."

If there had been any fight left in them, this display squelched it.

To a man, the rest of them turned and raised their hands and watched the strikers pour on board.

◆     ◆     ◆

AS THE NEW YORK WORLD REPORTED, "The mob started for the boat . . . and took complete possession. They ran like wild men about the edges and in a twinkling of an eye filled the cabins of both boats from both ends. The Pinkerton guards shook like the traditional aspen leaf. They huddled in groups in the corners and waited for death. Of mercy they expected none, but they were pleasantly disappointed.

"They were jostled about, kicked and cuffed and sworn at but their lives were spared, although rougher treatment was in store for them at the hands of the main army of the mob still left on the river bank."

For a disbelieving American public, the "gauntlet" that the Pinkertons were forced to run on shore may have constituted the most indelible and shocking images associated with the Homestead battle. According to press accounts, things went reasonably well for the Pinkertons as they were led down the barges' gangplanks and up the opposite shore, suffering little more than jeers and catcalls as they hurried along with their gazes cast down.

It was when they reached the top of the bank and were forced to pass between two large piles of discarded scrap that things changed. There they were forced, as the World put it, "to enter a lane formed by two long lines of infuriated men who did not act like human beings." Exhausted and sleepless, their nerves frayed by the tensions of some twelve hours of armed combat and their passions inflamed by witnessing the shooting of scores of their fellows, this group of strikers snapped.

The Pinkerton men "screamed for mercy," said the World. "They were beaten over the head with clubs and the butt ends of rifles. You could almost hear the skulls crack. They were kicked, knocked down and jumped upon. Their clothes were torn from their backs, and when they finally escaped it was with faces of ashen paleness and with the blood in streams rushing down the backs of their heads staining their clothes. It ran in rivulets down their faces, which in the melee they had covered with their hands."

John Holway, the unfortunate student turned Pinkerton guard, lent his own voice to the description of the scene. "What we wanted was that our steam tug pull us away, but instead of that the strikers held that we should depart by way of the depot. . . . I started up the embankment with the men who went out . . . but I looked up the hill and there were our men being struck as they went up, and it looked rather disheartening. I . . . went about halfway down to the mill yards without being hurt, when three fellows sprang at me and knocked me down twice. One said, 'You have killed two men this morning; I saw you.' I dropped my satchel, and [ran]. . . . I got on further toward the depot and there were tremendous crowds on both sides and the men were just hauling and striking our men, and you would see them stumble as they passed."

With his satchel gone, Holway hit upon a means of escape. He simply pulled his hat low and walked out of the line of Pinkerton men, hoping to blend in with the mob. He had passed through the first lines of the mob and thought he had made it when he heard a shout rise up behind him. "A Pinkerton," someone cried. "He's getting away!"

Holway didn't hesitate. He burst between a pair of astonished workers in front of him, making for the gap that the mob had torn in the company fence. As he jumped over the debris, he risked a backward glance to find a crowd of at least a hundred men running after him.

"I ran down a side street and through a yard," Holway said. "I ran about half a mile I suppose, but I was weak and had had nothing to eat or drink and my legs gave out. I could not run any further. Some man got hold of me by the back of my coat, and about twenty or thirty men came up and kicked me and pounded me with stones. I lost control of myself then. I thought I was about [to die] and commenced to scream. There were two or three strikers with rifles rushed up then and kept off the crowd and rushed me forward to a theater. I . . . found about 150 of the Pinkerton men there, and that was the last violence offered me."

It was the end of the physical threats to Holway, but it certainly wasn't the end of his worries. "That evening," Holway continued, "I was told we were going to be arrested for murder and put in jail."

Such rumors quickly swept through the fearful group of captives, making for a harrowing night, especially for Holway and others like him, who had had little intention of signing on for such a nightmare. Finally, at about 1:00 a.m., the doors to the opera house where the Pinkertons had been detained flew open and Hugh O'Donnell entered, along with AAISW president William Weihe and Sheriff McCleary.

O'Donnell raised his hands to quell the excited questions directed his way. The Pinkertons would be given safe passage from the opera house to a special train that waited at the Homestead station, he announced. From there they would be taken back to Pittsburgh, escorted by Sheriff McCleary.

At first the captives resisted. They wanted no part of another parade through the streets of this bloodthirsty town, but O'Donnell and Sheriff McCleary reassured them. It was late, and the streets were clear. That's why this time had been chosen. Were the captives to linger in the opera house, who could say what a new dawn would bring?

The debate did not last long. In moments the Pinkertons were filing out of the opera house, two by two, surrounded by moderate workers who were faithful to O'Donnell and Weihe. In short order, the train, accompanied by a great shout of triumph from the workers who had escorted them, was off to Pittsburgh.

Though some of the men feared that they would be held for trial, there proved to be no need for concern. After a brief layover, the trainload of Pinkertons was moving again, this time hell-bent for

New Jersey. Nor would there be any stops in Pennsylvania along the way, for word of what had happened at Homestead was out, and workingmen everywhere were joined in outrage and were gathering along the line, itching for a chance to get their hands on a Pinkerton.

On that train, one of the wounded conscripts found himself sharing a seat with a reporter for the *New York World*. He held out a pair of thickly callused hands and told the correspondent that he was a workingman himself, a maker of organ bellows in a factory in Chicago.

He didn't even know the name of the river that ran alongside the grounds of the Homestead works where he had nearly died, he told the reporter. "We were engaged as private watchmen, but we did not know we were to be used to shoot down honest workingmen," the man insisted. "We are workingmen ourselves and sympathize with the strikers now that we know the truth."

According to his version of the facts, the rank-and-file Pinkertons had no idea of what awaited them at Homestead until the barges had reached the outskirts of the town and the firing began. By the time the barges had been tied off and the first men shot, it was too late to do anything.

"All our men were not armed," this maker of bellows continued. "Those who had rifles used them. . . . They were desperate. It was a case of being shot to death on one side or drowning on the other."

Another of the more experienced "watchmen," a Philadelphian named Ed Spear, allowed that he and his fellow Easterners suspected that they were bound for the troubled Carnegie works, but that no one expected what they had encountered. "I have had plenty of experience," Spear said, "but this is the worst. I was in the New York Central strike and other big ones, but this one beats them all. It was an awful day. By God, but those men did shoot. I never saw and heard so many missiles in all my life. . . . I never saw anything like it and don't want to see the like again."

# 17

# WHILE ROME BURNED

―――――▶◆◀―――――

THE STRIKERS AND THE RESIDENTS of Homestead viewed the rout of the Pinkertons from completely different perspectives, of course. To the former, a hated enemy had invaded, armed to the teeth, attempting to take their jobs and their homes and, by extension, to obliterate their very community, and these invaders had not stopped short of anything, not even murder.

Moreover, the intentions of the Pinkertons had been foiled, their leaders sent packing, their ranks reduced to sniveling bands of cowards who, though they had shot down sons and brothers of the mill-workers, then begged for mercy as they were driven from their dens and chased back from whence they came. It must have seemed a glorious victory, especially to those who had seen fellow strikers and loved ones maimed or killed by Pinkerton fire.

But for Weihe and O'Donnell, and the more perceptive of the union leadership, the calm that descended over the Homestead works was clearly temporary. For throughout the afternoon of July 6, telegrams had flown back and forth from Pittsburgh to Harrisburg, and they suggested no cause for the workers to celebrate.

As the standoff continued into the day, High Sheriff McCleary sent a formal request to the governor, stating that he lacked the resources to maintain order in Homestead and requesting that the militia be sent in. While the exact number of casualties was still in question, it appeared that six workers had been killed and seventeen wounded; only two of the Pinkerton men were reported to have died, though more than two hundred of them were said to have been wounded.

Despite the alarming tally and McCleary's desperate tone, the governor responded that he could not—and would not—entertain such a request until he could be satisfied that all available resources of the local authorities had been exhausted. An exasperated McCleary posted a call to the local citizenry, offering to deputize anyone who would immediately join ranks to help quell the disturbance in Homestead. All of sixty men responded.

Frick, meantime, was steadfast in his contention that the matter was in the hands of the sheriff and the governor. He claimed to be "satisfied without a doubt that the watchmen employed by us were fired upon by our former workmen and friends for twenty-five minutes before they reached our property, and . . . they did not return the fire until after the boats had touched the shore and after three of the watchmen had been wounded, one fatally."

Frick went on to tell reporters that no man who had been known to raise a rifle or pistol in the battle would ever again be employed in his operations. Nor would any man asserting any claims to union membership. Carnegie Steel would not be dictated to. Nonunion replacements would take the places of every man who had joined the fray.

WHILE BLOOD FLOWED, FRICK SMOKED, ran one headline in the July 7 edition of the *New York World,* and the lede described Frick as one of the coolest men in Pittsburgh during the strife: "While the men whom he had locked out and the men he had employed to force an entrance into the mill were killing each other at Homestead the steel king sat in his magnificently furnished office and smoked cigars, gave orders to subordinates or chatted with visitors." When he was told that the Pinkerton men had surrendered and that the mill grounds had been left in control of the mob, the report continued, Frick expressed little emotion.

"I was very sorry to hear of the disturbance at Homestead," he was quoted as saying. "We are entirely out of the deal now so far as protecting our interests up there are concerned. The matter now rests entirely with the Sheriff, and to him we look for protection of our property."

Pressed to explain just what he meant, Frick asserted that as the mob had broken down fences and trespassed onto company property of their own accord, the firm could in no way be deemed responsible for any subsequent damage. He intended, in fact, to present a bill for repairs to Allegheny County, once a proper assessment was complete.

How much of this was bravado is difficult to know, but Frick had never been one to equivocate. A cable he sent to Carnegie, meant to bring his majority stockholder up to speed, sheds further light on his state of mind. Dated July 7 and dictated to the company's agent in New York for relay by transatlantic cable, the message was addressed to Carnegie care of the London offices of J. P. Morgan: SMALL PLUNGE, OUR ACTIONS AND POSITION THERE UNASSAILABLE AND WILL WORK OUT SATISFACTORILY.

Perhaps the message was intended simply to placate Carnegie, but given Frick's history, it is just as likely that matters had developed at Homestead more or less as anticipated. After all, his marching orders from Carnegie had been unequivocal: "We are with you, no matter what, and not stopping short of a contest."

It might be debated what, if anything, would have constituted a real crisis in Frick's view. Suffice it to say that Frick's pose was generally one of equanimity, and the message was apparently well received by Carnegie. He wrote back immediately, to "Frick, Pittsburgh. Cable just received. All anxiety gone since know you stand firm.

Never employ one of these rioters. Let grass grow over works. Must not fail now. You will win easily next trial. Only stand firm. Law and order. Wish I could support you in any form."

Not everyone saw it Frick and Carnegie's way, certainly, and some influential outsiders took it upon themselves to weigh in. During an impromptu discussion on the Senate floor on July 7, Senator John Palmer of Illinois declared that the millworkers were well within their rights in driving off the Pinkertons. Manufacturing establishments were public institutions just as railroads were, Palmer reasoned, and while owners had a right to defend their property, workers had an equal right to defend their employment and means of livelihood.

Nor was criticism directed solely at Frick. On July 8, the *St. Louis Post-Dispatch* carried an editorial letter addressed to "My Lord of Cluny Castle," and signed by "Uncle Tom." The writer skewered Carnegie as "My lord," and went on to say that he had seen fit "to throw his gauntlet at those who produced for him the colossal fortune which he legally enjoys, and when they manfully resist . . . the author conclusively proves that 'Triumphant Democracy' is a huge swindle."

On July 9, a correspondent sent by the *Post-Dispatch* actually made his way to the grounds of the country shooting estate in rural Scotland where Carnegie was spending the remainder of his summer, far from any madding crowds. The correspondent was ushered by a liveried servant inside the reception hall of a two-story fieldstone building overlooking a sprawling loch and its surrounding forests and grouse moor.

While the reporter idled about the trophy-filled room of a house said to be costing the steel magnate $10,000 for its eight-week rental, he discovered on a table a copy of the *Times* of London with a story detailing the riot at Homestead circled in pencil. Twelve strikers and nine Pinkertons were reported as dead by the *Times,* and the reporter was still holding the paper when Carnegie entered the room.

Did Mr. Carnegie have anything to say regarding these troubles at his mills, the correspondent inquired.

Carnegie gave the reporter a scathing look. "I have nothing whatever to say," he responded. "I have given up all active control of the business, and I do not care to interfere in any way with the present management's conduct of this affair."

So far, so good, one could imagine Frick murmuring, had he enjoyed the perspective of a fly on a nearby wall.

"But do you not still exercise a supervision of the affairs of the company?" the reporter persisted.

"I have nothing whatever to say on that point. The business management is in the hands of those who are fully competent to deal with any question that may arise."

"Have you heard from Homestead since the riot occurred?"

"I have received several cables and among them several asking my interference with the parties in control."

"But you must have some opinion. . . ." the reporter tried.

Carnegie shook his head decisively. "No sir. I am not willing to express any opinion. The men have chosen their course and I am powerless to change it. The handling of the case on the part of the company has my full approbation and sanction."

It was Carnegie's final word, and with it he turned and left the room, his heels echoing on the hard floors. The correspondent watched him go, then turned to make his own exit. He was met on the stairs of the shooting house by the servant who had shown him in earlier.

He had found Mr. Carnegie in his garden, the servant smoothly intoned, and his master wished him to convey that he had nothing to say on the matter.

The reporter thanked the servant. "So I've heard," he said. And made his way out.

◆　　　◆　　　◆

IN HOMESTEAD, MEANWHILE, scores of broadsides and ballads had already been published damning the Pinkertons and the company, and celebrating the triumph. "Tyrant Frick," one was titled. "A man named Carnegie, who owns us, controls us, his cattle, at will," went another. "Fort Frick's Defenders" began with this: "Hurrah for the light of Truth and Right!"

But exultation had turned to grief, and to some trepidation as well. IN THE HOUSES OF MOURNING, read one headline. Another story was titled OVER THE BIER. A *New York World* piece titled BURIAL OF THE DEAD detailed the funerals given Henry Striegel, Thomas Weldon, and Joseph Sotak, the man who had been shot in the throat as he ran to help his fallen comrade.

At Weldon's service, Father John J. Bullion, a Catholic priest, echoed the remarks of Illinois senator John Palmer, saying that "the workman has a certain right on account of the length of time he has been employed . . . and when he protects that property he is doing only what is right. . . . [I]t is wrong for a mob to come here and deprive the workman of the right that is his."

The service for John Morris, the twenty-eight-year-old skilled laborer who had been shot off the top of the mill's pump house, was conducted by the pastor of the Fourth Avenue Methodist Episcopal Church, Reverend James J. McIlyar, who excoriated the company generally, and Frick specifically, in his remarks: "This town is bathed in tears to-day, and it is all brought about by one man, who is the least respected by the laboring people of any man in the country. There is no more sense of excitement in that man than there is in a toad."

While the remarks were rousing to those in attendance, they would not find favor among McIlyar's superiors. In less than a year they would force McIlyar's retirement.

Local churchmen were not the only ones to condemn company tactics; a New York City minister denounced the Pinkertons and said that "if every man of them were taken out and hanged the only loss to the nation would be the wear and tear of rope." And a pastor in Newark, New Jersey, chimed in: "The manager of the Carnegie company is morally, if not legally, guilty of the bloodshed which has taken place."

The *Pittsburgh Commercial Gazette* published what claimed to be a comprehensive list of the dead, including two Pinkerton men and twelve workers. The list of the seriously injured included thirty-four names, most of them workers, though the paper also reported that all 305 Pinkerton men had sustained injuries of one degree or another.

At the mill grounds and on the streets, order seemed to have regained a foothold. The *Commercial Gazette* reported that all damage at the Homestead mill had been repaired. The breached fence had been boarded up, the makeshift fortifications and other debris had been cleared, even "the hose used in throwing oil on the water restored to its place."

Reports claimed that control of company property had been restored to that of the company's watchmen, and that no damage to buildings or machinery was apparent. The streets of Homestead were quiet, according to the *Gazette,* with order assured by a special contingent of workers under the direction of moderate strike leaders.

Still, the mood was one of great uncertainty, as residents shared bits of news gleaned from the streets along with their fears of another pending invasion. "But the slightest attempt to break through the guard line of the strikers around the mill property will precipitate a battle in comparison with which the conflict of Wednesday will be a mere skirmish," the *Gazette* reported. Telegrams pledging support from other union groups and sympathizers arrived at union headquarters by the hundreds, along with one detailed missive from an anarchist detailing methods for the construction of more effective dynamite bombs than had been employed in the assault on the barges.

On July 8, a contingent of Homestead citizens, headed by Hugh O'Donnell, traveled to the Pennsylvania capital in Harrisburg to meet with Governor Robert Pattison. The delegation pleaded with Pattison to hold off sending troops in, arguing that such a move would only encourage a fresh round of fighting.

The company's fence had been repaired, O'Donnell argued, and while pickets once again surrounded company property, they were only exercising their established rights to strike. The union's advisory committee had been reestablished and even the town's saloons remained closed, a sure sign that the locals were serious in their intention to maintain order.

Pattison agreed to take the matter under advisement, though he warned O'Donnell that he would not delay in sending in the militia if the slightest act of violence was reported. Since Pattison had clearly been hesitant to respond to Sheriff McCleary's entreaties from the outset, O'Donnell and his men could be forgiven for hoping the governor was sympathetic to their position. Pattison was actually in something of a quandary. He was, like McCleary, an elected official, and though he was a staunch Democrat, he owed a great political debt to Allegheny County Republican chairman Christopher Magee, who had been in league with the interests of Frick and Carnegie for some time. According to political historian Paul Krause, Magee, owing to a dispute within his own party, had actually delivered his county's swing vote to Pattison during the 1890 gubernatorial election and now was ready for payback.

But Pattison owed an equal debt to rank-and-file working Democrats across the state. Like High Sheriff McCleary, he was not eager to alienate his traditional base of support, and thus was dragging his feet as long as possible, hoping that somehow the situation would right itself.

Late on the afternoon of July 6, Pattison had issued a public statement calculated to appease the workers: "It is not the purpose of the military to act as police officers," he declared. "The civil authorities must in the end settle the differences. I look for a speedy adjustment." But at the same time, as the *New York Herald* reported in a

July 7 story, Pattison was busy making contingency plans for mobilizing state troops for transport to Pittsburgh.

Meanwhile, the finger-pointing within company ranks had already begun. Despite his avowed support of "company officials," Carnegie was furious. Had it been his decision, he reminded partners Phipps and Lauder, he would simply have closed the plant and waited the workers out.

Furthermore, given the fact that the Pinkertons had been called in, how could things have been bungled so badly? As Carnegie put it in a message to his cousin and partner George Lauder, "Matters at home bad—such a fiasco trying to send guards by Boat and then leaving space between River & fences for the men to get opposite landing and fire. Still we must keep quiet & do all we can to support Frick & those at Seat of War. I have been besieged by interviewing Cables from N York but have not said a word. Silence is best. We shall win, of course, but may have to shut down for months."

Carnegie even threatened to return to Pittsburgh at once and take over the situation himself, a possibility that dismayed both Phipps and Lauder. Carnegie's return would signal an unequivocal loss of confidence in Frick. Any such action might easily prompt another resignation on the part of the volatile Frick, and thereby send a signal to the union that they had won yet another victory.

No, they quickly responded to Carnegie. What had been done was done. The best thing to do now was sit pat, continue to support Frick, and keep up the pressure on the governor to send in troops so that the mill could be reopened without any concessions to the union.

Meanwhile, Frick had already begun his own campaign of damage control. In a long cable to Carnegie, he reiterated that he had made no secret of his intentions from the outset. "My letter of July 4th informed you of the arrangement made to introduce watchmen into our works," Frick reminded his superior, then went on to some blame-shifting of his own:

"There is no question but what the firing was begun by the strikers. All that I have to regret is that our guard did not land, and between ourselves, think that Potter [the plant superintendent who had accompanied the Pinkertons] was to blame. He did not show the nerve I expected he would. He . . . failed at the critical time."

Frick, well aware of Carnegie's affinity for the "close the plant" strategy, went on to defend his decision to bring the situation to a head. "Would like to say just here that I had not overlooked the fact that an effort to introduce guards at Homestead so soon might cause trouble, but was just as well satisfied that it would cause trouble if done at any later date, and we were only letting our property lie idle awaiting the pleasure of one of the worst bodies of men that ever worked in a mill, so concluded it was better to have trouble, if we were to have it, at once."

Frick went on to reassure Carnegie that despite the unflattering press coverage, not everyone was distressed with the company's handling of matters. "We have been in receipt of numerous letters and telegrams commending our position, particularly so since the people have become acquainted with it. At first there was [a] wrong impression, and a strong pressure brought to bear to get us to have a conference [with the union], but it is now almost all the other way."

He closed with one last defense of his decision to bring in the Pinkertons: "Feel sure that when you become thoroughly acquainted with all the details, you will be satisfied with every action taken in this lamentable matter," he told Carnegie. "The best evidence of the character of the men employed at Homestead is shown by the manner in which they treated the watchmen after they had surrendered, and also it would not have mattered who the men were that were in those boats, their treatment would have been just the same. They did not know that they were obtained through Pinkerton at the time they fired upon them."

Disingenuous as Frick's letter may sound, it was entirely consistent with Frick's utterances concerning the labor issues at the Homestead works from first to last.

In Frick's view, the responsibility for the continued success of Carnegie Steel was his and his alone. Concessions to the union had nothing to do with fairness. Once granted, whatever the issues and no matter how limited the scope, a deadly precedent would have been set, one that would spread like a cancer through every level of the ranks of the flagship operation and from there throughout the whole of the Carnegie empire.

From this perspective, Carnegie Steel would ultimately find itself paying higher wages than competitors who had not been compelled to submit to union demands, and that would spell doom, for the company and for the workers as well. Whether anyone thought him sincere as to the latter was of no concern to Frick. He had been given a job to do and he intended to do it.

As for Carnegie's favored tactic of simply closing the works down until starving workers cried to be brought back to work, where was the sense of that? Weeks or months of production lost, and the effect on the lives of workers and their families just as debilitating in the end. No, there would be no glad-handing from Henry Clay Frick, no smile and wink and handshake while the knife was slipped into the ribs from behind.

Frick's choice had been to dismiss the union summarily—a troublesome, potentially disastrous choke in the labor input valve—and to bring in the Pinkertons to ensure that his factory would continue to operate. That the workers had responded with violence had been their own unfortunate choice. Of one thing he was certain: the law was on his side.

Meanwhile, Governor Pattison was looking for the best way out of a situation he surely found "lamentable" as well. Following his visit from the AAISW delegation, Pattison ordered George Snowden, the commander of the Pennsylvania National Guard, to send an emissary of his own on a secret mission to Homestead to try to determine whether there was any hope that the dispute could be settled by peaceful means.

Accordingly, Major General Snowden dispatched one of his

trusted adjutants, who traveled to the area and returned quickly with his report. Indeed, things in Homestead and on the lines surrounding the mill were quiet, the adjutant found. But in his opinion the mood of the strikers was clear. Any attempt to reopen the plant by bringing non-union men through the gates would result in a disaster that would make the battle with the Pinkertons seem tame.

When the adjutant met with Frick in his downtown offices, he received the same pronouncement that Frick had already delivered to the press. There would be no more meetings with union representatives. There was nothing to discuss. So far as Carnegie Steel was concerned, the Amalgamated Association of Iron and Steel Workers had ceased to exist.

After contemplating this gloomy report, Pattison—another elected official who drew support from the capital and owners alike—determined that attempts to sway Frick would be fruitless. He could pay the piper now, or pay him later. And to delay further might only allow the strikers' resolve to harden, and their ranks to swell with sympathizers from far and wide. It was a calamitous situation that must have had him wondering why he had ever entered politics, but nonetheless he returned to his desk and prepared the fateful proclamation, addressed to George R. Snowden, Major General Commanding, National Guard of Pennsylvania:

"Put the division under arms and move at once, with ammunition, to the support of the Sheriff of Allegheny county at Homestead. Maintain the peace. Protect all persons in their rights under the constitution and laws of the State. Communicate with me."

The order was issued just after midnight on July 10, and was accompanied by another addressed to William H. McCleary, Sheriff of Allegheny County, Pittsburgh:

"Have ordered Major General George R. Snowden, with the division of the National Guard of Pennsylvania, to your support. At once put yourself in communication with him. Communicate with me further particulars."

◆　　◆　　◆

THERE HAD BEEN SPECULATION IN the local press that the guard's two Pittsburgh regiments, 2,500 strong and comprising primarily area workingmen, might refuse the call. In fact, during the railroad strikes of 1877, local guardsmen called in to control the protestors at the Pennsylvania Railroad yards had simply lowered their weapons and dispersed into the crowd. This time, however, Snowden and the governor were taking no chances.

The call to the guard was for the mobilization of the entire force, some 8,500 men, a display of force meant to overwhelm the slightest thought of resistance. Nor would there be any delay in carrying out Pattison's orders. The troops began to arrive at the Munhall station, close to the Homestead works, at 9:00 a.m. on July 12, while others streamed off cars at nearly every Pittsburgh area station.

One contingent was immediately dispatched to surround the mill grounds, installing themselves between the pickets and the looming fences of "Fort Frick," while the main body of the force, some five thousand troops, took up a position on the hilltop about three hundred yards south of the mill, the same vantage point from which spectators had gathered to watch the clash between workers and Pinkertons just a few days before.

The response of the strikers and the union to the deployment, reported to be costing the state of Pennsylvania about $22,000 per day, was restrained. The *New York Times* reported that Hugh O'Donnell appeared before a public meeting held at the Homestead Opera House to declare that the troops were to be viewed as "friends and allies." O'Donnell and McLuckie counseled the men to treat the troops with respect and threatened punishment to anyone—man, woman, or child—who so much as issued catcalls.

Once this approach had been put to a vote and overwhelmingly approved, O'Donnell put together an advisory group for the purpose of effecting communication between the strikers and General Snowden. At midday on July 12, shortly after the national guard troops had been installed atop the hill overlooking the mill grounds, O'Donnell led his contingent, which included a former militia captain, one Ollie Coon, into the camp to confer with the commander, a meeting observed by a reporter for the *Times*.

"General Snowden, I believe," O'Donnell began.

Snowden's response was a stony stare.

O'Donnell spotted High Sheriff McCleary standing in a group of militiamen nearby and called out, asking for an introduction to the general. The sheriff acknowledged O'Donnell with a nod, but maintained silence as well.

At that point, Ollie Coon spoke up. "We have come to speak for the citizens and for the locked-out men of the Amalgamated Association of Iron and Steel Workers—" he began, but Snowden cut him off abruptly.

"I neither know nor care anything about them," said Snowden, an unmistakable edge in his voice. "I am not here to look after the strike or the Amalgamated Association or to pay any attention to either. I do not accept and do not need at your hands the freedom of Homestead. I have that now in my possession, and I propose to keep the peace."

He turned to O'Donnell to make sure he was making himself clear. "I want no strikers to come near the troops as strikers, and I want it distinctly understood that I am in absolute control of the situation."

O'Donnell, stunned by this reception, did his best to make amends. "General," he said, stepping in front of Coon, "I think that the Captain's reference to the Association and the strikers was accidental. We came as representing the citizens of Homestead as well as the Amalgamated strikers. I will amend Captain Coon's speech, and withdraw his reference to the Amalgamated Association. We are citizens of Homestead and of Allegheny County."

General Snowden allowed himself a civil bow. "I am always

glad," he told O'Donnell, "to meet the citizens—the good citizens—of any community."

"We have been peaceful and law-abiding citizens—" O'Donnell started to say.

"No, you have not," a brusque General Snowden cut in.

He turned to gesture behind him at McCleary. "Sir, you have defied and insulted this Sheriff, and I want to say to you and to the strikers that the Governor has instructed me to announce to you that we are here to aid the Sheriff. You have refused to deal with him, but it is he with whom you will have to deal now. If you insist on it, I can go further into the conduct of you and your men. You had better not insist."

He gave McCleary a glance, and then turned back to a speechless O'Donnell. "I want to assure you, however, once more that we care nothing about your association or your strike. The peace will be preserved at any cost."

If O'Donnell had harbored any illusions about what the arrival of the troops meant, they had certainly vanished by now. Snowden cared nothing about the goodwill of the workers. He was no politician, but a military man, and he had defined his mission in no uncertain terms.

O'Donnell, heartsick at what he'd experienced, was grasping at straws now. "We've got four brass bands, down below," he told the general, pointing down the hill toward the streets of Homestead. "We would like to have them and a parade of our friends pass in review before the camp."

The general didn't bother to follow O'Donnell's gesture. "I don't want any brass-band business while I'm here," Snowden snapped. "I want you to distinctly understand that I am master of this situation."

In the face of such a dressing-down, O'Donnell could do little more than stare. He turned to give his men a nod, and their group filed quickly away.

"We'll show him before we get through," Ollie Coon muttered

bravely at O'Donnell's shoulder. "He doesn't run this town." Perhaps O'Donnell heard Coon, perhaps he did not. In any case, the crest-fallen union leader had nothing more to say.

Less than one week before, it seemed that labor had secured a monumental victory in Homestead. On this afternoon, however, the tide had very clearly turned.

The Frick Building in Pittsburgh ca. 1901, designed by the noted architect Daniel Burnham, towering over the adjacent Carnegie Building and epitomizing Frick's undying drive to outdo his former partner. The Frick Building still stands. (*Carnegie Library of Pittsburgh*)

# PART THREE

# UNRAVELING

# 18

## THE OCCUPATION
## OF HOMESTEAD

———◆———

I F HUGH O'DONNELL HAD BEEN humiliated by his treatment at the hands of General Snowden, he had little time to dwell upon it. Among the things on his mind, as he made the long and dreary march back down the hill from his encounter with the general, was the rumor now sweeping through the town that Carnegie Steel would soon press charges against the strikers for conspiracy and murder.

Word was circulating on the streets and in the local and national press that the company had retained any number of top criminal attorneys in Pittsburgh, and that one of the newly developed flash cameras had been used during the riots to take pictures of those destined to be charged. In fact, the *New York Times* reported that Sheriff McCleary had sworn in a special group of deputies for the sole purpose of issuing arrest warrants to strikers.

The financial concerns of thousands of displaced workers also loomed large. While the AAISW reported that sufficient funds were in its coffers to cover the living expenses of its members, that membership accounted for fewer than 10 percent of those out of work.

Most of the unskilled labor force lived—then as now—from payday to payday, dependent on their earnings for food, housing, clothing, and medicine.

Nor was outrage at the installation of the troops universal. As a July 13 *New York Times* article began, "Mob rule in Homestead has come to an inglorious end. The town has been wrested without bloodshed or struggle from the rioting locked-out Amalgamated workmen, who have ruled with absolute and despotic sway for two weeks, and has been taken under the protecting care of the National Guard."

Certainly, Carnegie seemed relieved that Governor Pattison had finally sent in the troops: "Governor's action settles matter," he cabled Frick the day the militia arrived. "All right now. No compromise."

Perhaps the long-awaited intervention of the governor validated Frick's actions in Carnegie's mind. At any rate, he wrote this soon after, in an apparent effort to smooth the feathers of his treasured manager: "*Paris Herald* published bogus cable from me to [Allegheny County Republican chairman] Magee," a reference to a story in which his support for Frick had been called into question. "Have not spoken, written or cabled one word to anybody," he declared. "Shall continue silent. Am with you to end whether works run this year next or ever. No longer question of wages or dollars."

Frick seemed grateful for this show of support. He shot back a cable to Carnegie at his Rannoch Lodge: "Much pleased with your cable," he told Carnegie. "Never had a doubt but what you would thoroughly approve of every action taken in this matter when you would once be made acquainted with all of the facts."

If Carnegie gave grudging approval to Frick, not everyone else did. Even the editors of the staid and generally supportive *New York Times* were moved to opine, "It will be a mistake for Mr. Frick and the company to hold obstinately to the position that they will not treat with these men, and that they will replace them with others who are not connected with the Amalgamated Association. There are matters to be considered in this case besides the cold-blooded principles of supply and demand."

The same piece brought up the issue of tariff protections enjoyed by the company, wondering why the government should offer such guarantees to owners if the benefits were not to be shared with workers. In fact, many of the union men believed that Frick and Carnegie were originally motivated to lower the wage floor as a result of a recent lowering of the tariff on iron billets, a charge the company vigorously denied.

Criticism of the company's handling of the matter was widespread in the British press as well, where it was reported that a July 14 meeting of the London Trades Council had unanimously passed a resolution condemning the employment of "a gang of irresponsible armed bullies to coerce men struggling against a reduction of wages." One member of the National Liberal Club was quoted as saying that if Carnegie were still a member of that organization, "he ought to be kicked out."

The United States Congress had also become involved. As early as May, the House Judiciary Committee had launched an investigation into the practices of the Pinkerton Detective Agency, fueled by complaints that the agency had been employed unlawfully by various railroad companies in strikebreaking practices. The investigation, carried out under the pretext that rail lines were involved in interstate commerce and delivery of the U.S. mail, was extended to Homestead when news of the riots reached Washington, and a subcommittee under the aegis of Representative William C. Oates, a seven-term Democrat from Alabama, began hearings in Pittsburgh on July 11, a day before the arrival of the militia.

The first witness called was Frick, whose message to the subcommittee was resolute: "I can say with the greatest emphasis that under no circumstances will we have any further dealings with the Amalgamated Association as an organization. That is final."

The subcommittee heard as well from sheriff's deputy Joseph

Gray, who had accompanied the Pinkertons on the barges and who insisted that the workers on shore had precipitated the firing on the night in question. Gray's contentions were supported by later testimony from William and Robert Pinkerton, as well as by Pinkerton commanders and employees on the barges themselves, including the unsuspecting student, John Holway.

Arrayed against the company's witnesses were Homestead town burgess John McLuckie, strikers' advisory committee chairman Hugh O'Donnell, and union president William Weihe, as well as a number of strikers and citizens of Homestead, all of whom were certain that it was the men on the barges who had commenced the firing.

The subcommittee completed its investigation in Pittsburgh and returned to Washington on July 15, where Chairman Oates, a former colonel in the Confederate Army, was quoted in press accounts as saying, "I think we got all the information possible. We got down to the bottom of the trouble. It will not take long to prepare the report."

He characterized Frick as "remarkably cunning" and union leaders as intelligent and capable, calling the workmen as a group "the most intelligent lot of manual workers I have ever seen." The subcommittee had learned that the workmen earned anywhere between $1.00 and $1.50 a day for unskilled labor, to as much as $65 to $275 a month for the most demanding positions. Oates admitted, however, that he had been unable to pry from Frick or anyone else the actual cost to the company of making a ton of steel billets.

Pressed to say how the matter would be resolved, Oates was equally vague. He did say that he feared that an attempt to introduce non-union workingmen to restart operations at Homestead would inevitably result in a fresh wave of bloodshed, "and a great deal of it." But Oates, who would become the only congressman subsequently elected governor of his state, also suggested that the committee would likely conclude that the Homestead case was outside the scope of federal jurisdiction.

Frick, meanwhile, had written Carnegie with his own summation of the investigation and its import: "Congressional inquiry ended. Business men and the impartial public without exception concede that we substantiated by good reasons our position." He ended with a coded suggestion that the strikebound works would soon be back in operation, "Proper slowly tomorrow at Plunge," he told Carnegie. He would start slowly, but start the Homestead works he would.

Meantime, one of those dire rumors circulating in Homestead had proven true. On July 18, three Pittsburgh constables bearing arrest warrants for Hugh O'Donnell, John McLuckie, and five other union leaders on charges of murder were escorted through the streets of the town by two companies of militiamen. While General Snowden used binoculars to keep careful watch from his perch atop the nearby hill, the procession wound its way through the warren of streets below to the homes of the seven men. In every case they were stymied: the doors were locked and the windows shuttered.

Tipped off by informants, all seven had left town, with O'Donnell said to be on his way to New York on union business. Evading the warrants was at best a temporary measure, however, designed to buy time and prepare something of a defense strategy.

Late on the evening of July 18, McLuckie, swaggering drunk and full of brave declarations that it was nothing but a put-up job, surrendered himself to authorities and was hustled to the Allegheny County Jail. On the following day, constables returned to Homestead and issued subpoenas to forty persons expected to testify to McLuckie's part in the riots.

On July 20, McLuckie was released on $10,000 bail when the presiding judge stated that second-degree murder was likely the most serious charge that could be leveled against him. However, the judge made no secret of his essential reading of the matter to the assembled crowd of spectators. "The law makes every man guilty of rioting who stands idly by without any effort to suppress the disorder," the court stated. "If the mob designs and commits murder, each man in it is guilty of murder."

Late that same evening, Hugh O'Donnell returned to Homestead from New York, accompanied by a representative of the national labor organization called the Knights of Labor. O'Donnell told reporters that he would travel to Pittsburgh on the following morning to turn himself in, along with three others of the accused.

Two of the workers who would not be turning themselves in were Anthony Flaherty and James Flanagan. Both had fled the state, fearing that charges of first-degree murder would be leveled against them.

The appearance of the Knights of Labor representative fueled speculation that O'Donnell's trip to New York had been made to consult with political strategists for the Democratic Party and prepare for a national strike of sympathy by every major union in the country.

Meanwhile, Carnegie, fearful of any renewed violence, counseled Frick to abandon the idea of bringing Homestead back on line immediately. "Your last cable received, in which you think that Plunge will be running again soon," he wrote. "I wish I could share this view. You should announce that the works will not run this year. . . . Starting a few months sooner or later is nothing compared with starting with the right class of men. The only danger is that you may be tempted to start too soon. Nothing will cure the disease so thoroughly and give you peace in the future as a long stoppage now. I should be tempted, if in your place, to announce that the works will be closed . . . for the remainder of the year if the military departs and leaves an excited populace."

Frick seemed not to listen. Certainly he had no fears of any "excited populace," whether or not the military stood guard. His reply of July 18 suggested that, in his mind, all difficulties at Homestead were not only behind them, but had almost never existed: "Looking back over the transactions of this month so far, or previous to that, I cannot see where we have made any serious blunders, or done anything that was not proper and right. . . . It will be of course our earnest effort to convict all of the men engaged in the riot and in law breaking . . . but it will all blow over before long, and when we do get started at our several works they will be all non-union, and if we treat the men as we always have done . . . it certainly will be a long while before we will have any more labor trouble."

In short order the company mailed notices to nearly all of the 3,800 employees at the Homestead works, informing them that they had until 6:00 p.m. on Thursday, July 21, to reapply for employment at the mill. "It is our desire to retain in our service all of our old employes [*sic*] whose past record is satisfactory and who did not take part in the [riots]," the notice read. "Such of our old employes as do not apply by the time above named will be considered as having no desire to re-enter our employment." The document was signed by H. C. Frick, chairman of the Carnegie Steel Company.

A reporter for the Associated Press toured the Homestead mill on July 19 and reported that about 150 men were at work. Four of the furnaces in the area given over to the manufacture of armor plating had been fired up and fires were still being tended in the open-hearth furnaces that had been relit earlier.

Company secretary Lovejoy was quoted in a *New York Times* story on that same day as predicting a break in the ranks of the union within a week. "There is no doubt of the existence of a large conservative element among the locked-out men," Lovejoy said. "When one moves, others will follow like sheep."

Frick was himself hard at work, preparing for any contingency that might prevent the immediate return of the Homestead works to operation. In a letter to one of his associates, he pondered the wisdom of building fifty to one hundred houses as well as one or two large boardinghouses on mill property so that outside workers could more readily be enticed to come to work at the plant. Local press accounts claimed that cots and provisions sufficient to house four hundred men had been carried to the mill grounds. Large contingents of workmen were reported to be on the way to use those cots and foodstuffs: two hundred from Cincinnati, and hundreds more from Cleveland, Youngstown, even Chicago.

Frick also had to contend with sympathy strikes on the part of workers at his Beaver Falls, Union Iron, and Duquesne works, where men walked out for a week. To Sheriff McCleary he sent yet another request for deputies, noting, "We are just in receipt of information that a crowd, aggregating probably 150, are congregated about the entrance of our works at Duquesne, intercepting workmen and preventing them from going to work."

Frick's concerns did not end with the strikes and the strikers themselves. When he learned that in the battle's aftermath the Munhall postmaster had boasted to a reporter, "We cleared the Pinkertons out," Frick dashed off a telegram to the U.S. postmaster general demanding an investigation into the Munhall postal chief's fitness for office.

If the postmaster demurred, it did not keep Frick from pursuing other means of "handling" the situation. Dismayed at the arrival of more than one hundred press correspondents in the strike's aftermath, Frick did what he could to court the coverage of papers more likely to favor the company's position. He was certainly partial to the *New York Times,* which used the terms "strikers" and "rioters" interchangeably, and which disparaged the local press in one lengthy article that claimed the advisory committee bullied local writers into conforming to the union view of the situation. Frick, annoyed at the unfettered access that all reporters seemed to enjoy at the Homestead works, took the time to write to a colleague at the offices of the Pittsburgh & Lake Erie Railroad, asking that all nonemployees be prohibited from using the railroad's supply tracks that led into the mill grounds.

Meanwhile, dissension was growing within the ranks of the strikers. Hugh O'Donnell, perhaps overwhelmed by his encounter with General Snowden at what was now known as "Camp Sam Black," and by the prospect of facing murder charges, had begun to talk of an "almost unconditional surrender" in the face of daunting odds. Though O'Donnell's stated aims were to put the men of Homestead back to work, his apparent willingness to accept a settlement on company terms was anathema to men who had been willing to risk their lives in defense of the union's position.

According to a story carried in the *Pittsburgh Post*, O'Donnell went so far as to meet with two reporters, F. D. Madeira of the *New York Recorder* and J. Hampton Moore of the *Philadelphia Public Ledger*, and authorize them to approach plant superintendent Potter to find out under what terms the striking workers might return to their jobs. According to the *Post* account, Potter received the two in a cordial fashion and said that, apart from "certain objectionable strife makers," the company was prepared to take back any man. Even some of those "strife makers" might be welcomed back, Potter suggested, if the charges against them proved to be unfounded.

Furthermore, Potter said, while the company would under no circumstances recognize or deal with representatives of any union or association, a man was free to join any organization he wished. Meanwhile, any man who wished to return to work would simply have to sign an agreement that fixed the initial floor of iron billets at twenty-three dollars, with the terms to be renegotiated on December 31 of the following year.

The relative bonhomie with which the proposal was outlined could not obscure the fact that Potter was simply repeating what Frick had already laid out so bluntly: a twenty-three-dollar floor for wages, a wintertime anniversary date for the agreement, and, most significant, the end of the AAISW as a bargaining entity within Carnegie Steel forevermore.

While a downcast O'Donnell tried to sell his men on this dreary prospect, Henry Frick went on with his preparations to reopen Homestead one way or another, and Andrew Carnegie continued to stew in his Highlands retreat, no longer so sure that he'd placed his trust in a "management genius" after all.

How long the stalemate might have continued at Homestead is a matter of conjecture. But then the Russian assassin arrived upon the scene.

# 19

# ANARCHY IN PITTSBURGH

I T IS NEARLY 2:00 P.M. ON SATURDAY, July 23, 1892, a typically smoky and ash-strewn afternoon in downtown Pittsburgh, for Saturday constitutes no break in the everlasting work week, and the stacks of the various industries that line the banks of the Allegheny and the Monongahela and the Ohio pump their effluent into the confines of the high-walled valley with the indifference of a thousand domesticated dragons.

In the Fifth Avenue building where the operations of Carnegie Steel and the Frick Coke Company are housed sits Henry Frick, engaged at this moment in a conversation with Carnegie Company vice-president John G. Leishman. Hearing a sound at the door behind him, Frick turns from the conference table with some annoyance at the interruption, to find a man he had dismissed from his offices only a day or two before.

Though the man has earlier represented himself as Simon Bachman, employment agent, he is neither employment agent, reporter, striker, officer of law, nor business confidant. He is in fact one Alexander Berkman, age twenty-five, and he has come all the way from Worcester, Massachusetts—where he has lived with the radical

Andrew Carnegie in 1862, age twenty-six and still in the employ of Thomas Scott at the Pennsylvania Railroad. (*Carnegie Library of Pittsburgh*)

Henry Clay Frick in 1875, age twenty-six and about to embark on the mining career that would earn him the title "King of Coke." (*Courtesy of the Frick Collection*)

Carnegie (still unmarried at forty-five) and his mother make their triumphal return to Dunfermline, Scotland, to mark the 1881 groundbreaking for the first Carnegie Library. (*Carnegie Library of Pittsburgh*)

Workmen pulling coke from ovens in the vast coal fields of western Pennsylvania. It was coal and coke that enabled Pittsburgh to become the "Iron City." (*Rivers of Steel Archives*)

A detail from the Charles Graham engraving "Making Steel at Pittsburgh," evoking the otherworldly aspect of a massive Bessemer converter in full blow, ca. 1886. (*Rivers of Steel Archives*)

A BESSEMER STEEL CONVERTER.

Aftermath of the catastrophic flood that engulfed Johnstown, Pennsylvania, on May 31, 1889. More than two thousand were killed. (*Carnegie Library of Pittsburgh*)

The walls of "Fort Frick" encircled the Homestead works and were erected by Carnegie's no-nonsense manager in anticipation of the labor strife to come. (*Carnegie Library of Pittsburgh*)

The Homestead works, site of the deadly labor clash of 1892. Onlookers watched from the railroad bridge spanning the Monongahela River *(left midground)* as gunfire broke out between strikers and Pinkerton detectives at the company docks *(center midground.)* The ferry *Little Bill,* called to rescue the strike breakers when their landing craft were burned, is visible in the right midground. *(Carnegie Library of Pittsburgh)*

Workers line up for their pay at the Homestead works following the restoration of order. Stereoscopic images like this one became popular in the mid–nineteenth century. (*Library of Congress*)

Alexander Berkman, the twenty-one-year-old anarchist who shot and stabbed Henry Clay Frick in a failed assassination attempt. (*Library of Congress*)

A rare shot of Carnegie and Frick together, taken during a visit in Scotland in the brief halcyon period following the Homestead debacle. Seated beside Frick are his daughter Helen, and his wife, Adelaide. At Carnegie's knee are Frick's sister-in-law, Martha, and his son Childs. *(Courtesy of the Frick Collection)*

The Carnegie Library in Homestead, an imposing sandstone structure, was completed in 1897. In all, Carnegie donated nearly three thousand public libraries worldwide. *(Homestead and Mifflin Township Historical Society)*

Skibo Castle, part of a 22,000-acre estate in the Scottish Highlands that Andrew Carnegie purchased as a summer home for $425,000 in 1898. Guests might be awakened each day by a skirling bagpipe player traversing the misted grounds or by a rousing pipe organ concert issuing from the great hall below. Today Skibo is the site of an exclusive hotel and private club. *(Carnegie Library of Pittsburgh)*

Carnegie's sixty-four-room mansion at East 91st Street and Fifth Avenue in New York City, into which he and his wife moved in 1902. The six-story structure was the first private home to feature an elevator. (*Museum of the City of New York, Wurts Collection*)

Frick's block-long, sixty-room mansion at East 70th Street and Fifth Avenue, completed in 1914, now the home of the fabled Frick Collection. "I'm going to make Carnegie's place look like a miner's shack," Frick reportedly told confidants. *(Courtesy of the Frick Collection)*

Andrew Carnegie at seventy-nine with faithful companion, in the Scottish Highlands in 1914. In later life, Carnegie's principal occupations were golfing and the nearly impossible task of giving away the world's largest private fortune. *(Carnegie Library of Pittsburgh)*

Henry Clay Frick at Eagle Rock, his summer home in Pride's Crossing, Massachusetts, in 1914, with his first grandchild, Adelaide, upon whom he doted. *(Courtesy of the Frick Collection)*

social reformer Emma Goldman—on an urgent errand, the true nature of which can scarcely be announced. . . . But wait, let us now turn to the words of this unexpected man himself:

> The door of Frick's private office, to the left of the reception-room, swings open as the colored attendant emerges, and I catch a flitting glimpse of a black-bearded, well knit figure at a table in the back of the room.
>
> "Mistah Frick is engaged. He can't see you now, sah," the Negro says, handing back my card.
>
> I take the pasteboard, return it to my case, and walk slowly out of the reception-room. But quickly retracing my steps, I pass through the gate separating the clerks from the visitors, and brushing the astounded attendant aside, I step into the office on the left, and find myself facing Frick.
>
> For an instant the sunlight, streaming through the windows, dazzles me. I discern two men at the further end of the long table.
>
> "Fr—," I begin. The look of terror on his face strikes me speechless. It is the dread of the conscious presence of death. "He understands," it flashes through my mind. With a quick motion I draw the revolver. As I raise the weapon, I see Frick clutch with both hands the arm of the chair, and attempt to rise. I aim at his head. "Perhaps he wears armor," I reflect. With a look of horror he quickly averts his face, as I pull the trigger. There is a flash, and the high-ceilinged room reverberates as with the booming of cannon. I hear a sharp, piercing cry, and see Frick on his knees, his head against the arm of the chair. I feel calm and possessed, intent upon every movement of the man. He is lying head and shoulders under the large armchair, without sound or motion. "Dead?" I wonder. I must make sure.

FRICK WAS NOT YET DEAD, as it turned out. As Berkman describes it, he advanced upon the prone Frick, who roused himself and began to crawl weakly toward the door. "Murder!" Frick cried. "Help."

Berkman raised his pistol and aimed it between Frick's shoulder blades. Again he pulled the trigger, but as he did, the hand of Leishman struck Berkman's arm and the second shot went astray.

Berkman and Leishman struggled, but Berkman gained the upper hand. By now Frick was cowering behind his chair, with Berkman just inches away. He pointed the pistol at a spot between Frick's eyes and pulled the trigger again. There was a dull click, but no explosion came.

Berkman stared at his pistol in disbelief. Frick's eyes rose to something over Berkman's shoulder. Berkman would have shot again, but felt a rush of air, then a thunderous crack as a hammer, wielded by a company carpenter, drove into the back of his head. The man who would have killed Henry Clay Frick slumped unconscious to the floor.

◆    ◆    ◆

OTHERS WHO WITNESSED THE INCIDENT described it somewhat differently. James Bridge reported in his 1903 *Inside History of the Carnegie Steel Company* that Berkman's first shot had grazed Frick's ear and lodged in his neck. The second shot, said Bridge—by the time of his writing a confidant of Frick—did not miss, in fact, but had entered Frick's neck as well.

When this failed to dispatch his quarry, Bridge said, Berkman pulled out a dagger fashioned from a steel file and began to stab Frick, first in the hip, then in the side, and a third time just below the knee. According to Bridge's account, Frick shrugged off his injuries and threw himself upon the would-be assassin, holding his knife hand down until frightened clerks and assistants finally came to their superior's aid. As Frick steadied himself on the edge of his desk, the others dragged Berkman into a chair, where he seemed to be mumbling incoherently.

A deputy sheriff rushed into the room at that point, his revolver drawn as if he were ready to shoot Berkman on the spot. According to Bridge, Frick lunged forward. "No, don't kill him," Frick cried.

He stumbled forward. "Raise his head and let me see his face."

The surprised group obeyed, and Berkman's jaws were forced open. All stopped to stare in surprise. On the assassin's tongue lay a capsule of fulminate of mercury, a suicide device that—had Berkman managed to crush it between his teeth, Bridge tells us—would have blown them all to kingdom come.

Bridge's account and George Harvey's 1928 biography, commissioned by Frick and titled *Henry Clay Frick: The Man,* paint a picture of near-superhuman behavior by Frick on that day. When a surgeon was rushed to the office to tend to his wounds, it was said that Frick refused any anesthetic, and calmly assisted the doctor as he probed the wounds for the bullets.

"There, that feels like it, Doctor," Frick said, on two different occasions. And each time, the doctor extracted a slug with his tongs.

With the removal of the bullets, the doctor advised that his patient be removed immediately to the nearest hospital, but, according to Harvey, Frick would have none of it. He insisted that his wounds be sewed up then and there, and next had himself propped up in his chair, where he completed the letter he had been working on when Berkman attacked, stipulating the final terms for a loan he sought. After that task had been completed and he had signed the rest of the day's essential correspondence, he took the time to dictate two cables, one assuring his ailing mother that he was all right, then another to Carnegie.

"Was shot twice but not dangerously," the message to Scotland read. "There is no necessity for you to come home. I am still in shape to fight the battle out."

Only after he was finished with his day's work did Frick permit himself to be carried from the office to an ambulance that would take him to his East End home, and even then he had his litter bearers stop so that he might issue a statement to reporters:

"This incident will not change the attitude of the Carnegie Steel Company toward the Amalgamated Association. I do not think I shall die, but whether I do or not, the Company will pursue the same policy and it will win."

No wonder that Hugh O'Donnell was ready to submit. He and his men were only human. Their adversary was clearly as invincible as Vulcan himself.

# 20

# NOT AN INCH

◂—◂◆▸—▸

NOT SURPRISINGLY, SPECULATION arose immediately that Berkman had been acting in league with the strikers. And shortly after the would-be assassin was taken into custody, Pittsburgh police arrested two local men long suspected of unsavory activity. The arrests of Carl Nold and Henry Bauer, identified by police as the leaders of a group known as the "Northside Anarchists," were presented to the *Pittsburgh Post* and other media as evidence of a "carefully laid conspiracy against the life of Chairman Frick."

A cache of anarchist literature was confiscated from the homes of the men, including plans for the making of dynamite bombs, a discovery much ballyhooed in the local press. It was the observation of the *Post* that such an instrument could be carried about "in perfect safety by any person who took care to avoid a collision."

As his September trial would bear out, however, Berkman had acted on his own, drawn to Homestead by press accounts that he and Emma Goldman had pored over as they worked the counter of the luncheonette they operated in Worcester. Berkman and Goldman were Russian immigrants who had arrived in the United States in the

1880s, both profoundly affected by the radical anarchist tradition that had grown exponentially in Europe during the last half of the century, resulting in the assassination of Czar Alexander II in 1881.

Goldman, who would one day be labeled by the press as "the high priestess of anarchism" and by J. Edgar Hoover as "one of the most dangerous women in America," followed the accounts of the 1886 Haymarket incident closely, and was appalled by the opening declaration of the judge presiding at the trial of those accused of killing Chicago police officers: "Not because you [threw] the Haymarket bomb, but because you are anarchists, you are on trial."

When four of the Haymarket defendants were hanged, the seventeen-year-old Goldman made a decision. She would dedicate her life to avenging what she saw as a heinous miscarriage of justice, and would do everything in her power to seek the overthrow of a government that ruled principally by coercion. When she and Berkman read of the Pinkertons who had been summoned to Homestead and the occupation of the town by the state militia, they found a target for their outrage. Frick must die, they determined, and Goldman even went so far as to offer her services as a prostitute to secure the funds to buy the necessary pistol.

While the use of Pinkertons to quash a strike had become something of a negative to most Americans, the appearance of bomb-throwing, pistol-blazing radicals as representatives of labor was even more damning. Though certain of Goldman's tenets—opposition to the draft, free love, equality between the sexes, and birth control— have earned her adherents to this day, a cold-blooded murder plot went too far, and even steadfast friends of labor drew the line.

Berkman's attempt on Frick's life, then, exerted an incalculable influence on the public's perception of the Homestead strikers' cause. Though his trial would bear out Berkman's lack of connections with Nold or Bauer, or with any other labor activist in Pittsburgh, the damage was done.

No one on the side of ownership benefited more than Henry

Frick. "Say what you will of Frick," the *St. Louis Post-Dispatch* wrote, "he is a brave man."

By July 28, *The Nation* was reporting that there seemed to be no connection between Berkman and the Homestead strikers, but went on to state that the attempt on Frick's life was the natural extension of the attitude taken by them: "If it was right to murder the Pinkertons—and nobody among the strikers, from O'Donnell down, has ever admitted that it was wrong—it was right and logical to try to kill the employer of the Pinkertons."

Berkman's actions moved the local *Pittsburgh Catholic* to suggest, however, that perhaps the freedoms so prized by Americans went too far: "The attempt on Mr. Frick's life is an eye opener. We are no better, no safer, no securer, than the people residing in France, or Germany, or Russia. Our lax laws have given these Anarchists a foothold here."

Even the *National Labor Tribune* would write of Berkman's prospects, "Whatever the term of imprisonment may be it will be inadequate to fit this crime—a crime that is against both capital and workman."

Had either Nold or Bauer known Berkman, their suspicions as to his true errand in the city would have likely been aroused: The *New York Times* reported that for a period of time following his immigration, Berkman had worked in the city on radical anarchist John Most's publication, *Die Freiheit*. It was said that Berkman often told co-workers that any capitalist who refused to give up his property should be murdered, a sentiment that alarmed even the hard-bitten Most, who fired Berkman.

In her 1931 memoir, *Living My Life,* Emma Goldman wrote that Sasha, as she referred to Berkman, had originally intended to carry out a far more dramatic plan. The two had decided Berkman should build and carry a bomb to Pittsburgh for the purposes of annihilating Frick. Berkman's mechanical abilities were unequal to his passions, however. When a test of the bomb design carried out in a remote section of Staten Island failed, the plan to use a pistol evolved in its place.

In the end, Nold and Bauer received five-year sentences for having sheltered Berkman before the assassination attempt, and Berkman, who conducted his own defense, received a twenty-two-year sentence, which exceeded the usual attempted manslaughter sentence by a factor of three.

Berkman, who had announced to the judge at the outset that he expected no justice and that he dedicated his actions to those workers "murdered" by the state in the aftermath of the Haymarket trials, would stay in prison until 1907. Upon his release, he returned to New York and became editor of Goldman's *Mother Earth,* a radical journal that was produced until 1919, when the two—staunch opponents of the World War I draft—were deported by the U.S. government, along with several hundred other "subversives." Berkman died in the south of France in 1936, of a gunshot from his own hand, following a long and debilitating illness.

Meanwhile, the political fallout in Homestead and its environs was intense. When news of the assassination attempt reached the ranks of the newly installed state militia, one man, Private W. L. Iams, jumped up from a group of twenty or so comrades with whom he had been conversing to shout, "Three cheers for the man who shot Frick."

As the incident was reported by the *Pittsburgh Commercial Gazette,* none of his surprised colleagues was moved to respond to Iams's call. Undaunted, Iams went on to deliver the three cheers himself. At that juncture, the regimental commander, one Lieutenant Colonel James Streator, came out from his tent and angrily called the men to attention.

"Who spoke those words about Frick?" the commander shouted.

Iams stepped forward without hesitation, proudly claiming responsibility.

The commander stared at him in disbelief. Such words flew in the face of the guardsman's oath to protect and defend the laws of the state. In effect, Iams had just publicly confessed to treason. The commander asked for an apology, to himself and to the regiment of which Iams was a part.

Iams, however, was resolute. "I refuse," he said, and Commander Streator ordered his immediate arrest.

As Iams was being dragged away, Streator, a veteran of the coke region labor confrontations of the 1880s, ordered the immediate formation of a court-martial, which sat at once, and took almost no time in reaching a verdict of guilty. As punishment, Iams was sentenced to be hung by his thumbs. Following that, he was to be dishonorably discharged from the militia.

Though Iams was to have been suspended for thirty minutes by slender cords fastened to his digits, he passed out from pain after twenty. He was cut down and thrown into the guardhouse for the remainder of the evening, then hauled out the next morning so that the signs of treason might be inflicted upon him before his dismissal was made final.

A barber shaved half of Iams's head bald and half his mustache as well. His rifle and pistol were taken from him, as was his uniform, the latter replaced by a threadbare suit and hat. Following the reading of the charges against him and the subsequent judgment, Iams was marched to the edge of the camp and out of sight while the regimental band played "The Rogue's March."

"He was always a troublesome fellow," Colonel Streator was reported to say, as Iams disappeared.

WHILE ALL THIS WAS GOING ON, Frick was making a near-miraculous recovery at Clayton, his fashionable home in the suburbs, and carrying on business as usual from his bedroom. From Rannoch Lodge, Carnegie had cabled his reassurances that Frick was still his man: "Too glad at your escape to think of anything. Never fear my brave and dear friend my appearing on the scene as long as you are able to direct matters from house and unless partners call. We know too well what is due to you. Am subject to your orders. . . . Be careful of yourself is all we ask."

One of the first matters Frick attended to on the morning following the attempt on his life was to dictate a notice to the five hundred or so men who had joined the company after the strike was announced on July first.

"In no case and under no circumstances will a single one of you be discharged to make room for another man," Frick's announcement read. "You will keep your respective positions so long as you attend to your duties. Positive orders to this effect have been given to the general superintendent." What conflicts this directive might occasion with Superintendent Potter's earlier assurances to those other-than "strife-makers" that they could have their old jobs back were not addressed.

For nearly two weeks Frick stayed at home, a telephone at one side of his bed, a secretary on the other, attending to his duties as chairman of Carnegie Steel as though nothing had happened to him. On Thursday, August 4, however, he was required to leave his bed for an event that troubled him far more than any strike or assassin's bullet.

Less than one month before, on July 6, 1892, the very day of the Battle of Homestead, Frick's wife, Ada, had given birth to Henry Clay Frick Jr., their fourth child and second son. Ada had gone into labor slightly prematurely, owing, some said, to the stresses surrounding the events at Homestead. From the moment of the child's delivery, both mother and son were in ill health, and while doctors were unable to make a diagnosis, the child took little nourishment and there were fears for Ada's life as well as the newborn's.

Early on the morning of August 3, Henry Clay Frick Jr. went into convulsions and died of internal hemorrhaging. It was a devastating blow to Frick, even though he was no stranger to such loss. One year previously, his seven-year-old daughter, Martha, had died as the result of an abdominal infection that had festered inside her since the age of two, when she swallowed a pin during a family vacation to Paris.

Over the years, Martha's health had had its ups and downs, and Frick had agonized over the possibility of an operation that might alleviate her condition. Today no parent would hesitate to authorize such a procedure, serious though it might be. In the late 1880s, however, an operation of that nature could as easily have killed young Martha as saved her. Frick, a resolute believer in the practice of homeopathy, resisted the surgery until the last. By the time he relented and called physicians in, it was too late. The doctors who examined young Martha explained that while an operation was called for, she was now too weak to survive. Shortly after the surgeons had delivered this prognosis, young Martha Frick died.

Whether or not Frick felt that his delay made him complicit in Martha's death, the loss affected him profoundly. He commissioned a bust of Martha that was displayed prominently at Clayton, and had printed a series of checks bearing her likeness, which he often used for charitable causes. And his granddaughter Martha Frick Symington Sanger would later speculate that much of the art collected by Frick was acquired in conscious or unconscious tribute to the memory of his beloved young Martha. In fact, Frick would later confide to a reporter that when Berkman had aimed the pistol at his head, a radiant vision of Martha had appeared suddenly at his side, an apparition so vivid that Frick had been convinced she was real.

Reeling now from the loss of two children, Frick forced himself from his bed to attend the funeral service of his infant son on August 4, held in the downstairs parlor at Clayton. On the following morning, as if driven away by death or resolved to defy it, he rose to leave the house for the first time since the attack. He rode a streetcar to his downtown offices and began his day promptly at 8:00 a.m., thirteen days after being gunned down. "At office feeling first class," he cabled Carnegie. "Everything assuming good shape."

Carnegie cabled back, "Hearty congratulations from all here upon your return to the post of duty. Every thing is right when you and Mrs. Frick are right. Every other consideration insignificant."

When Frick returned home that evening, he found that local policemen had been stationed outside his home, "for the family's peace of mind." Frick thanked the officers, then immediately sent them home. "If an honest American cannot live in his own home without being surrounded by a bodyguard," he told a reporter for the *New York Times*, "it is time to quit."

Difficult as his week had been, the bad news was not over for Frick. On August 3, the day of his son's death, Hugh Ross, one of the strikers who had been charged with murder, appeared in the offices of Pittsburgh alderman Festus M. King and swore out warrants for the arrest of William and Robert Pinkerton, Frederick Heinde, Superintendent Potter, Secretary Lovejoy, and several other Pinkertons and company officials on charges of murder. Most prominent among the others named was Henry Clay Frick.

Murder warrants were issued, and Frick and the others were forced to appear before a Judge Ewing in Criminal Court. Ewing released Frick on $10,000 bail and gave some sense of his feelings on the matter during the hearing. "This information is made by a man who himself is charged with murder, and is now on bail," Ewing said. "It would have been better had it been made by some other person. I think, if the story in the newspapers is true, none of the men charged . . . can be held for murder and certainly not in the first degree. The men on shore were there illegally and unless you can show me there was a malicious and deliberate killing there is no use wasting any more time. The men on the barges were there legally and the others were there illegally."

In this regard, Ewing was following the line of defense that Frick and his counsel had held as their trump card from the beginning. Once the mob broke down the fences on that night and entered onto company property, they were trespassers, and in that light, all the actions they undertook from that point on were illegal.

While the cases against both company and Pinkerton officials and the strikers wended their way through the courts, Frick stayed focused on his plan to bring the Homestead mills back on line. By early August there were said to be as many as one thousand men at work at Homestead. General Snowden announced that there was little likelihood of further violence and sent several regiments of his militia home.

Though Hugh O'Donnell had long seen the writing on the wall and continued his efforts to contact Frick as well as members of his own advisory board, attempting some settlement between the union and the company, neither side was willing to listen. The union remained formally on strike, and Frick continued to bring in outside workers as well as a number of former Homestead employees who had never aligned with the AAISW, including more than one hundred of the plant's mechanics and maintenance men.

During his visit to New York, O'Donnell had managed to prevail upon Whitelaw Reid, the Republican vice-presidential candidate in the upcoming election, to approach Carnegie and let him know that the union was willing to accede to all the terms of the contract originally offered. Reid cabled Carnegie, who quickly wrote to Frick urging that this proposal be accepted. Then, when Carnegie realized that this would have the unfortunate effect of leaving the union as the legal bargaining agent at Homestead, he quickly wrote Frick back, urging him to disregard O'Donnell's offer. "Use your own discretion," Carnegie finished by saying.

Even if Carnegie hadn't contradicted himself, it is doubtful Frick would have done anything *but* use his own discretion. When a representative of Reid's visited Frick at Clayton during his convalescence, Frick told him that while he was certainly a Republican and a devoted one at that, he would not meet with the union ever again, even if President Harrison himself should request it. "I will never recognize the Union," Frick thundered, "never, never!"

By this point O'Donnell had essentially given up, observing to a friend that Berkman's shots may not have killed Frick, but they had certainly killed the last hopes of the union. In essence, O'Donnell was now a man without a country, facing charges of murder, despised by capital, and disdained by his own men for trying too hard to appease their oppressors.

O'Donnell was not the only one being pilloried by the public, of course. In England, virtually every newspaper had carried daily accounts of the strike and associated developments, and most issued scathing editorials aimed principally at Carnegie. Even the staid London *Times* condemned the use of a private police force as a deliberate provocation to labor. "Here we have this Scotch-Yankee plutocrat meandering through Scotland in a four-in-hand opening public libraries, while the wretched workmen who supply him with ways and means for his self-glorification are starving in Pittsburgh."

The *Edinburgh Dispatch* joined this chorus: "We on this side of the Atlantic . . . may well feel thankful that neither our capitalists nor our labourers have any inclination to imitate the methods which prevail in the land of 'Triumphant Democracy.' "

And the *St. Louis Post-Dispatch* editorial that had begun with that grudging line, "Say what you will of Frick, he is a brave man," concluded with this: "Say what you will of Carnegie, he is a coward. And gods and men hate cowards."

Despite all his proclamations of support for Frick, the criticism he received stung Carnegie badly. As he would write to his friend, the British prime minister William Gladstone, in the aftermath, "The Works are not worth one drop of human blood. I wish they had sunk."

Later, in his posthumously published autobiography, Carnegie would add, "Nothing I have ever had to meet in all my life, before or since, wounded me so deeply. No pangs remain of any wound received in my business career save that of Homestead."

No doubt Carnegie was greatly troubled by what had taken place, and no doubt he would have handled matters somewhat differently had he remained in Pittsburgh that summer. But the fact is that he had chosen to absent himself from Homestead when he was well aware of what was coming. For better or for worse, he had placed his trust in Frick, and he would not return to the scene of this momentous conflict for many months more.

◆　　◆　　◆

ON AUGUST 31, FRICK MADE HIS first return to Homestead in more than two months, accompanied by one detective. He received no abuse entering or leaving the mill grounds, nor did he receive any from the men on the job. In an interview with reporters, he contended that his tour of the facilities showed everything to be in order and that the strike was a thing of the past. He had written to Carnegie shortly beforehand, declaring, "We have been having a rather exciting time for the last forty days, but I feel confident that we will be amply repaid for all of our trouble in this world, and in the near future. We shall be able to get closer to our men, and when they once become acquainted with us, they will find that we are probably the best friends they have."

Even if no one had fallen upon Frick with fists or weapons, it was a bold overstatement, of course. Although production was once again under way, shipments from Homestead for the month of September would total less than half of what they had in previous years, and Frick was forced to make arrangements with rival manufacturers to supply him with steel for fabrication. Such negotiations had to be handled secretly for the most part, owing to fears that sympathetic laborers would strike against their own bosses if they learned they were producing steel for Carnegie and Frick.

In a series of letters he sent to Carnegie, Frick reiterated his hopes that the workers would one day thank them for their efforts to place the company's operations on solid, if paternalistic, footing. In a mid-September message, he assured Carnegie that the strike would soon end and that eventually the public and their workers alike would see things their way. "We cannot expect that the public should understand just how kindly we do feel toward those who are in our service; that we are just as anxious for their welfare as we are for our own," Frick wrote. "We must expect to be misrepresented, but time will cure this all."

To Carnegie's cousin and company partner George "Dod" Lauder, Frick expressed similar optimism. "Am hoping to hear every day that a break has occurred among old men but it may take four months—not more—probably less. Don't expect too much. *It will come.*"

Carnegie, eager to resolve matters, may not have been convinced by such sanguine notions, but still he refrained from any direct remonstrations with Frick. His counsel was consistent: move slowly, wait the men out. "Nothing but time will give you victory; but this will do it, and we know that we have all the time we want." In that same message, Carnegie offered his condolences to Frick on having inherited a difficult situation at the Homestead plant. "Captain Jones always told me there was the worst set of men at Homestead that he ever knew," Carnegie wrote. "The worst in the world.

"Nothing will ever be right at Homestead until a great manager of men takes charge there," Carnegie continued. "Skilled workmen are the race horses, laborers the cart horses; the former have to be driven with a rein although firm, yet gentle."

And in a follow-up letter dated September 28, he went so far as to shift blame for the continuing rift onto Superintendent Potter: "I am expecting daily to hear that a break has occurred. . . . [H]e is a poor manager who has not sufficient influence over part of his men to draw them to him."

Nor did the mental stress of dealing with the continuing difficulty at Homestead escape Carnegie's attention. He closed one memo on the strike by wondering if that Orchestrion had yet made its way to Clayton: "I hope you will find some respite from care in its music," Carnegie told Frick, then went on to suggest there were other ways to find relief: "I recommend you make up a whist club to meet at your house at least once a week." And as for himself, "I caught a trout yesterday that weighed five pounds one and one-half ounces, had only my light rod, and had to play with him an hour and a quarter up and down the Loch." Added as a postscript in his own hand were the underlined words, "That's my record."

◆    ◆    ◆

PERHAPS WHAT FRICK DID NEXT was in response to the hint of impatience in Carnegie's notes concerning the situation at Homestead; but more likely it was the result of his own desire to rid that installation of the influence of the AAISW once and for all.

In any case, on September 30, the last of the bombshells to explode at Homestead was dropped. The entire advisory board of the AAISW—Hugh O'Donnell, John McLuckie, and twenty-seven others, including those already facing murder charges—were accused in a warrant of treason issued by the Pennsylvania Supreme Court. To the men and to the residents of Homestead, such a charge was dumbfounding.

Murder, riot, conspiracy, trespass, these were charges they could understand. But *treason?*

In an October 10 appearance before an Allegheny County grand jury, Chief Justice Edward Paxson explained that the military precision and organization of the strikers into divisions with "captains," "commanders," and the like made the union guilty of setting up an alien invasion force designed to foment a "state of war" and "to deprive their fellow-citizens of their rights under the Constitutions and laws."

The grand jury was apparently swayed by such arguments, and on October 11 it returned indictments against all accused. Yet some sense of fairness seemed to come into play. While the grand jury returned those indictments as well as those against the workmen and union officials accused of murder during the riots, so they also returned murder indictments against Frick and the other company officials.

The populace was apparently exhausted by the long struggle. In an article that detailed the grand-jury indictments, the *New York Times* reported that the announcement "did not cause much excitement among the people, and the defendants themselves took it quite coolly." The story closed by noting that officials at Carnegie Steel would make no comment regarding their own indictments.

On October 13, the last of the Pennsylvania guardsmen were withdrawn from the city, another action that was met by calm. It was as if everyone knew that the game was up, and while the association remained officially on strike, there was a sense that it meant little. Still, the workers were tenacious, even if their cause was lost, and Frick himself was moved to write Carnegie on October 31, noting that "the firmness with which these strikers hold on is surprising to everyone."

Hang on they did, but for not much longer. At the regular Saturday meeting held on November 12, striking workers heard an address from William T. Roberts, one of the most devoted committee members. When Roberts pointed out that the recent defection of the skilled finishers from the ranks constituted a major breach in their unity, most men in attendance seemed to sag.

On November 17, some two thousand mechanics and laborers met and voted to petition the Amalgamated to end the strike. The union members, under the direction of now their national president, William Weihe, rejected the proposal, voting 224–129 to continue. But in a separate action, the union gave notice to the laborers and mechanics that they were free to deal with the company as they liked.

It was an action that amounted to capitulation. On the following morning the laborers and mechanics descended upon the mill en masse, clamoring to be returned to their jobs. Though some mechanics had to be turned away owing to the replacements now holding their jobs, nearly every one of the unskilled laborers was immediately restored to work. On hand as the processing took place was Chairman Henry Clay Frick, who had at last seen his mission accomplished.

On the following Sunday, November 20, local members of the AAISW gathered at union headquarters to hear Weihe advise them that without question the strike had been lost. By a vote of 101–91, the men agreed. On the following day, the local lodge called the strike at an end. The headline of the *Pittsburgh Post*'s lead story put it simply: THEY SURRENDER.

"Through with the war at last, what a relief," Carnegie wrote to Frick from Florence. ". . . think I'm about ten years older than when with you last. Europe has rung with Homestead, Homestead. We are all sick of the name. But it is all over now . . . now for long years of peace and prosperity."

Indeed, the Battle of Homestead was finally at an end. A different kind of battle, however, had just begun.

# 21

## BURY THE PAST

———◆———

THERE WAS SOME TIDYING UP to follow the return of the last of the strikers so inclined during those dreary, late-November days of 1892. Although three of the strikers accused of murder—Sylvester Critchlow, Jack Clifford, and Hugh O'Donnell—were eventually tried, all three were swiftly acquitted, at which point the company declined to pursue further prosecutions.

The indictments for treason were also dropped, and, as had been expected, no company official was forced to stand trial for murder. But the strike had taken its toll. While 1892 production for Carnegie Steel as a whole was up about 80,000 tons overall, production at the Homestead mill was significantly diminished, even though the facility was up and fully running soon after the formal surrender of the union.

According to company reports, total crude steel production at Homestead dipped from 253,000 tons in 1891 to about 190,000 for 1892; steel plate tonnage was down from 44,000 tons to about 33,000; and beams were down from approximately 34,000 tons to about 22,000. Carnegie wrote to Frick that, by his reckoning, "We have lost a million in ore and another [million] trying to run Homestead with new men."

Overall profits for Carnegie Steel were down by about $300,000, a bit less than 10 percent, and the AAISW estimated that the workforce had lost about $1.25 million in wages. The cost to taxpayers for sending in the state militia was estimated at about $500,000. In the final analysis, and including not only direct casualties but ensuing accident, disease, and suicide, it was determined that the battle had taken thirty-five lives in total.

The intangible costs, of course, were beyond reckoning.

In January 1893, a weary-looking Carnegie made a return visit to Homestead, where he delivered what was intended as a conciliatory address to the workforce. In the speech, Carnegie reiterated his confidence in Frick, saying, "Of his ability, fairness and pluck, no one has now the slightest question. . . . I would not exchange him for any other manager I know."

Carnegie also told the men, however, that he had come to "bury the past"—a past with which, he suggested, he had had little to do. Following his fulsome praise for Frick, Carnegie went on to say, "I hope after this statement that the public will understand that the officials of the Carnegie Steel Company, Limited, with Mr. Frick at their head, are not dependent upon me . . . and that I have neither power nor disposition to interfere with them in the management of the business."

Shortly after delivering this disclaimer, Carnegie sat down to write his old friend John Morley, publisher of Britain's *Fortnightly Review,* "I went to Homestead and shook hands with the old men, tears in their eyes and mine. Oh, that Homestead blunder—but it's fading as all events do and we are at work selling steel one pound for a half penny."

Even if one were to accept Carnegie's words at face value, the general circumstances for workers in Homestead had deteriorated significantly. Within a year of the strike's failure, wages for many skilled workers had fallen by more than half, and the much-debated "minimum" floor upon which wages were to be based was abolished altogether. The eight-hour day was a thing of the past; shifts were once again twelve hours long, and the plant operated seven days a week.

In the aftermath of the strike, the noted author Hamlin Garland journeyed to Homestead on an assignment from *McClure's Magazine,* a liberal-leaning publication of the day. Garland, who had gained notoriety in 1891 with the publication of *Main-Travelled Roads,* a collection of stories depicting the harsh conditions of Midwestern farm life, found conditions equally grim in Homestead. Though the place had grown and the homes and businesses were the property of the citizenry, Homestead was as bleak as any "company town."

"The streets of the town were horrible," Garland wrote in "Homestead and Its Perilous Trades." "The buildings were poor; the sidewalks were sunken, swaying, and full of holes, and the crossings were sharp-edged stones set like rocks in a river bed. Everywhere the yellow mud of the street lay kneaded into a sticky mass, through which groups of pale, lean men slouched in faded garments, grimy with the soot and grease of the mills."

While Garland's descriptions of the surroundings were gloomy enough, his observations of the work itself seemed drawn from a tour of Hell: "We moved toward the mouths of the pits, where a group of men stood with long shovels and bars in their hands. They were touched with orange light, which rose out of the pits. The pits looked like wells or cisterns of white-hot metal. The men signaled a boy, and the huge covers, which hung on wheels, were moved to allow them to peer in at the metal. They threw up their elbows before their eyes, to shield their faces from the heat, while they studied the ingots within."

Garland's tone from first to last is one of awe: "I watched the men as they stirred the deeps. I could not help admiring the swift and splendid action of their bodies. They had the silence and certainty one admires in the tiger's action. I dared not move for fear of flying metal, the swift swing of a crane, or the sudden lurch of a great carrier. The men could not look out for me. They worked with a sort of desperate attention and alertness."

When he admits to his guide that the work seems hard, the man can only stare at Garland's naïveté. He lost forty pounds in the first three weeks he worked at the mill, the man tells him, his sweat often puddling in his shoes, and that for the rate of $2.25 per day, not nearly what a tonnage man might make at $10 under the revised rates, but not so bad when compared to shovelers and other bottom-rung laborers who made less than $1.50 for their dozen hours in hell.

Garland seems overwhelmed by the very observation of the process: "Everywhere dim figures with grappling hooks worked silently and desperately guiding, measuring, controlling, moving masses of white-hot metal. High up the superintending foremen, by whistle or shout, arrested the movement of the machinery and the gnome-like figures beneath."

It was a spectacle that called forth any number of ironies from the writer's pen, but none more pointed than this: "Upon such toil rests the splendor of American civilization."

Garland spent the following morning at breakfast with a few of the workers. He found himself hardly surprised that, conditioned by a life that was a dozen hours a day of exhausting and dangerous labor, along with another ten for sleeping and eating to fuel the un-ending cycle, there was precious little to distinguish them from the machines with which they worked.

In the end, it seems, Garland could not leave Homestead and its perils quickly enough. "The ferryboat left a wake of blue that shone like the neck of a dove," he wrote as he made his way back toward his waiting train, "and over the hills swept a fresh moist wind. In the midst of God's bright morning, beside the beautiful river, the town and its industries lay like a cancer on the breast of a human body."

Hellish though the conditions were, Garland found little sympa-thy for the strike among the laborers with whom he spoke. "It was the tonnage men brought it on," one of the men told him. "They can afford to strike, but we couldn't."

When Garland probed, the man shrugged. "We can't hurt

Carnegie by six months' starving. It's *our* ribs that'll show through our shirts. A man working for fourteen cents an hour hasn't got any surplus for a strike." This line of inquiry also led more than one worker to point out that neither Carnegie nor the steel industry itself offered the worst employment opportunities around. "There are lots of other jobs as bad," one worker said.

"A man'll do most anything to live," remarked another, lamenting only the length of the work shift and not what was done within it. "A man could stand this for six hours," he said, and others readily agreed. If six hours a day in Hell would afford them a living, then *that* was a bargain that all agreed would be fair.

Unfortunately, their employers did not see it their way, and nothing in the legacy of the strike seemed to change matters in any significant way. It is true that Carnegie and Frick had been personally vilified by the press, and any number of congressmen and their committees published denunciations and reports that excoriated capital and sympathized with labor. And in the aftermath of Homestead, more than half the states enacted laws that prohibited the employment of private police for use during labor disputes.

But the most profound effect of the unwinding at Homestead was to put an ignominious end to unionization within the industry. When contracts with management expired at the great Jones & Laughlin and Illinois Steel works later in the 1890s, the Amalgamated gave in without protest; and when the mighty U.S. Steel was formed in 1901, efforts to rally workers under the banner of the AAISW were summarily crushed. According to historian John A. Fitch, the last union lodge within a U.S. steel plant surrendered its charter in 1903. None would exist again until 1937, thirty-four years later.

As for men such as Hugh O'Donnell and John McLuckie, they may have escaped prison sentences, but their lives within steel, and as they had known them, were ended forever. They and other leaders were not only denied reemployment with Carnegie Steel, but were blacklisted throughout the entire industry. McLuckie lost his home, said to be worth $30,000, and soon after, his wife died of illness exacerbated by her sorrow.

In 1900, a friend of Carnegie's, a Rutgers professor visiting a shooting ranch in the Sonoran Mountains of northern Mexico, reportedly ran across McLuckie, who had made his way there in desperation, seeking work in the nearby mines. Down to his last pennies, McLuckie related his travails to Professor John C. Van Dyke, who listened with sympathy and fascination.

Upon his return to the States, Van Dyke got in touch with Carnegie, who asked that the professor offer McLuckie whatever funds he needed to get back on his feet, with one condition: under no circumstances was he to divulge Carnegie's name. Van Dyke wrote to offer McLuckie help, but though the proud former burgess thanked him for the offer, he declined. No handouts would be needed. He would make his own way, somehow.

Van Dyke then got in touch with another friend, the superintendent of the Sonoran Railway, who offered McLuckie a job. This time, McLuckie accepted and, according to Van Dyke, went on to prosper in Mexico, advancing within the new company and remarrying. As the story goes, when Van Dyke visited McLuckie sometime later, he felt he could at last let the former Homestead burgess know who his original benefactor had been.

Told the news, McLuckie stared at Van Dyke in astonishment. "Well," he told Van Dyke finally. "That was damned white of Andy, wasn't it?"

While some historians doubt the veracity of the Van Dyke report, it was a story that Carnegie was fond of repeating. He even went so far as to suggest that McLuckie's words be carved upon his tombstone as proof that he had been kind to at least one of his workmen.

It was a comment by Carnegie to British prime minister William Gladstone, however, that seemed chiseled permanently upon his unconscious when it came to Homestead: "The pain I suffer increases daily."

# 22

## DEATH DO US PART

———◆———

IF THE HOMESTEAD DEBACLE SET BACK efforts to organize American industrial labor for some forty years, as most agree, it also opened up a rift between Andrew Carnegie and Henry Clay Frick. In some ways, what happened between them is as fascinating and consequential as the events of those fateful days in 1892.

On the day of the union's formal capitulation, Frick wrote to Carnegie, crowing, "Our victory is now complete and most gratifying. Do not think we will ever have any serious labor trouble again." When Carnegie suggested that the victory had not exactly come cheap, Frick followed up on November 28 with grudging agreement that the cost might have been a bit high, but that "we had to teach our employees a lesson and we have taught them one they will never forget."

To Frick, still smarting from Whitelaw Reid's attempts to invoke President Harrison's influence, the implication that he had acted at all improperly was outrageous. In the days following his return to his office in August, Frick had written to Carnegie more than once to complain that a more forceful posture with Reid would have aided the company's position with the union and the public. There had been no good to come of Carnegie's apparent kowtowing to Reid. The fact that the Republicans had gone on to lose the election was simply proof that Reid and his cronies were out of touch with the mood of the country.

While Carnegie was not yet ready to rebuke Frick openly, he was nonetheless writing friends outside his business circles to insist that what had happened at Homestead was nothing he had sanctioned or would ever have condoned. He insisted to Gladstone that he would have simply closed the mill and waited for the men to return, and went so far as to say he had sent such orders to Frick, only to have the letter go astray.

It seemed that word of Carnegie's damage-control campaign was getting back to Frick, who fought to rally his chief stockholder. On October 12 he wrote to Carnegie to insist that victory was nearly upon them. "If we had adopted the policy of sitting down and waiting," Frick added, "we would have still been sitting, waiting, and the fight would yet have to be made, and then we would have been accused of trying to starve our men into submission."

As Charles Schwab would characterize his old mentor some years later, Frick was a fighter, and when war loomed, he prepared himself for it. In Frick's mind, the fact that shooting had started at Homestead was the fault of the union; if the men had listened to reason and behaved in a law-abiding fashion, there would have been no violence. And the end result would have been the same. Frick saw his own approach as direct and at least honest, if brutal. He viewed Carnegie's tactics as underhanded by comparison.

From all appearances, Frick was sincere in his beliefs—though, as Carnegie's old secretary James Bridge would later contend, he was not immune to the stresses associated with Homestead. In a matter of months, Bridge noted, Frick's full brown beard had gone nearly as white as Carnegie's.

Upon his receipt of Frick's October 12 letter, Carnegie wrote back a letter that was characteristically paternal in tone—calculated, apparently, to further the perception that it was Frick who was solely responsible for the company's situation.

While Carnegie was not without sympathy for his manager, one could be forgiven for wondering about his true motives for offering his condolences: "This fight is too much against our Chairman," Carnegie wrote Frick, "[and] partakes of personal issue. It is very bad indeed for you—very, and also bad for the interests of the firm. . . . There is another point which troubles me on your account, the danger that the public, and hence all our men, get the impression that it is all Frick. . . . You don't deserve a bad name, but then one is sometimes wrongfully got. Your partners should be as much identified with this struggle as you. Think over this counsel. It is from a very wise man, as you know, and a true friend."

Frick's response, in which he was quick to apologize lest any action of his seem to reflect badly on the firm, apparently missed the essential thrust of Carnegie's self-serving "advice" altogether. Instead of pointing out that Carnegie was the chief "partner" who had condoned everything and anything from the beginning, Frick seemed to think Carnegie was questioning his ability to buck up his subordinates. "I am not naturally inclined to push myself into prominence under any circumstances," Frick wrote back. "It seems to me wherever it was possible to put any of our people forward I have not let the opportunity go by."

Whatever Carnegie thought of that reply, it did not deter him from continuing his practice of sending generally supportive messages to his chairman while hedging his bets with others outside the company. After his late January visit to Homestead, Carnegie wrote to Whitelaw Reid, "I have been in misery since July, but I am reconciled somewhat since I have visited Homestead. . . . No one knows the virtues, the noble traits of the working-man who has not lived with them, as I have, and there's one consolation in all my sorrow; not one of them but said, 'Ah, Mr. Carnegie, if you had only been here it never would have happened.' "

For his part, Frick had already embarked upon what he felt was a necessary development for the good of Carnegie Steel occasioned by the lessons of Homestead—namely, the removal of John Potter as plant superintendent. While Frick had made noises to other Carnegie partners about Potter early in the strike, he wisely bided his time, believing that any such change during the actual conflict would be perceived as a sign of weakness by the men.

Once the union was clearly broken, however, Frick went swiftly to work. In mid-October he met with Charles Schwab, who had proven his abilities as both an able manager and a devoted company man at the Edgar Thomson works, and told him what he had in mind. While Schwab was a bit uncomfortable with the prospect of displacing Potter, he was not too uncomfortable to be persuaded by Frick's assurances that Potter would be well taken care of. So, on October 18, it was announced that Potter was being "promoted" to a newly created position as superintendent of general engineering for all Carnegie Steel operations. Taking Potter's place as plant superintendent at Homestead was that thirty-year-old legend-to-be, Charles Schwab.

When he got the news, Carnegie cabled Frick back immediately: "Delighted at content. Await results. You are wonderful at surgical operations without pain."

An eager young man who had pulled himself up by his bootstraps, Schwab was in many ways the mirror image of Frick, especially in energy, devotion to duty, and attention to detail; nor were his abundant good humor and distinct eagerness to please a handicap. If there was anyone who might rally the troops at downtrodden Homestead, it was Schwab, who had long been a favorite of Carnegie's.

When the new superintendent arrived at the plant and took up residence in one of the executive homes built on the grounds, the first thing he did was write Frick a letter begging for advice and suggesting that Frick come out to the plant and show him the ropes. Frick declined, however, pointing out that such a visit might undermine Schwab's authority.

Schwab dutifully returned to his rounds, but soon wrote to Frick again, lamenting that the workforce was utterly demoralized. During one morning in which Schwab went out with a pair of foremen to try to ratchet up production on a line, he watched in dismay as the entire department's labor gang simply quit, leaving two of the old-timers to stare back at him with expressions that said, "What did you expect?"

Furthermore, the problem was not limited to the ranks of laborers. As Schwab wrote to Frick, "All our Foremen and Superintendents here lack energy, vitality, and it seems impossible to get them started up, in fact, the men seem completely worked out." Again he appealed to Frick for a visit.

If he had been expecting miracles from Schwab, the patient reply that Frick sent did not suggest so. "You must not allow anything to discourage you in the least," he wrote Schwab, "even if things do not go well for some time to come, or even if they should get much worse. . . . [J]ust keep at it, doing the best you can, and as I said to you before, do not allow the fact that you are not getting along as well as you would like, to lead you to put yourself in a compromising position with any of the old employees."

Bolstered by such words, Schwab set aside his dismay at the abysmal level of morale, and turned his attention to the physical plant at Homestead. Within days he had analyzed any number of problems with the construction and layout of the mill, and was writing Frick detailed proposals for the upgrading of facilities and the resultant savings and increased outputs to be gained as a result. Before long, Schwab was on his way to Scotland to secure Carnegie's blessings for the improvements as well. In this regard, Schwab was talking with kindred spirits, for when it came to increased efficiency, there were no more ready ears than those of Frick and Carnegie.

Within five years, Schwab raised production at the plant more than 25 percent above its highest previous levels, and by the turn of the twentieth century, the Homestead works were far and away the largest steel manufacturing facility in the world. The fact that he was able to do this without any significant progress on the labor relations front is a testimony to his organizational and cost-accounting skills.

Although Frick had been patient and supportive with Schwab from the outset, there was one subject he refused to discuss, and that was the matter of labor organization within the plant. "I like the way you are going about this matter," Frick said, "treating the men kindly, and considerately, but at the same time keeping in view that, as the Democrats have been overwhelmingly successful on a platform plainly against a tariff for protection, we must expect a great reduction in the tariff on the article we make, and of course in order to live, we must manufacture at very much less cost than heretofore."

In other words, they would have to keep labor costs under strict control, and any negotiations or agitation among the ranks would only interfere with the goal of getting the last ounce of value for the cost expended, in men as well as matériel. To this end, Frick encouraged Schwab to dismiss inefficient men—new employees as well as old—and to keep his ear to the ground for any news of resurgent organizing activity among those strikers who had been permitted to return to work.

Apparently Schwab took heed, and despite his reputation as a good-humored sort, did not hesitate to "nip trouble in the bud," as Frick put it. In a letter he wrote to Frick in May 1893, he told of hearing that one of the original skilled employees, a shearer who had returned to his duties in the Plate Mill, had called one of the new hires a "scab." Schwab called the two men together and asked if the charge was true. The shearer glanced at the hire, then back at Schwab. It was true, he admitted. He had called the man a scab. "Then you're discharged," Schwab replied.

As the shearer strode away, Schwab turned to the men who'd been watching and announced the reasons for the firing in no uncertain terms. Anyone who behaved similarly would meet the same summary fate.

Schwab's zeal apparently went beyond the limits of plant grounds. Told by a new hire that certain of the old employees had been known to parade past his house, shouting threats and imprecations, Schwab ordered that a Homestead constable hide himself behind the new hire's fence. The next time the troublemakers showed up to make a ruckus, the policeman darted from his hiding place to arrest them. "They were fined and discharged from our employ," a proud Schwab reported to his chairman. "The labor situation could not be in better shape . . . and men are working in greater harmony than ever before."

Whether or not Frick believed such sanguine proclamations, he was happy with Schwab's comportment and with the increased level of production. It seemed that Schwab had repaid his confidence every bit as richly as he had imagined.

As the anniversary of the strike neared, Frick determined that 46 percent of the men employed at Homestead were new hires, and 54 percent had been employed before the strike. Only 18 percent of the latter were still in their former positions, however, suggesting that the company exercised near-complete control over the disposition of the labor force.

Frick was ever alert to threat, however, and as the summer of 1893 approached, he urged that Schwab gather whatever information he could concerning the rumored organizing of a "picnic" to commemorate the strike. When it was discovered that the man spearheading the proposed event was still under indictment for riot, Frick had the information passed along to local reporters. Whether Frick also suggested headlines for the stories he envisioned—FORMER RIOTER PLANS PICNIC—is not clear. In any case, word got around and the anniversary date came and went, without picnic and without incident.

A year later, when the Hamlin Garland piece appeared in *McClure's,* Frick was outraged. He wrote an angry letter to Schwab, demanding to know how such a man—along with an *illustrator,* no less—had managed to gain access to the plant.

Despite such occasional distractions, however, matters at Homestead seemed "all well and getting better." Between 1892 and 1897, Schwab managed to reduce the labor force at Homestead by 25 percent, even as production rose to record levels. In 1897 alone, the plant made 28 percent more steel than in 1896, and yet Schwab had cut his payroll by nearly $500,000 in the process.

Even with such gains, and despite the fact that net profits for Carnegie Steel in 1896 totaled more than $6 million, the demand to cut costs was constant. While some of the gains were attributable to better plant design and more efficient machinery, Schwab lamented to Frick in an 1897 memo that some of the tonnage men continued to be paid at rates he considered outlandish. If he could just reduce the daily wages of plate rollers from $15 to $9 and those of beam mill workers from $12 to $6, as he believed was just and possible, he could save the company $20,000 to $25,000 a month, he reported. The reply he got from Frick was a hearty "Godspeed!"

Schwab stayed in contact with Carnegie as well as Frick, of course, and with the former he was apt to discuss his attempts to keep their men reasonably contented. "Homestead shall never again have strikes, if I can avoid it," he told Carnegie in an 1896 letter, "and I think I can."

It was music to Carnegie, who was watching his empire grow to become the largest employer in the state, with the exception of the great railroad where he had gotten his start. Carnegie took pride in the fact that he was paying *his* laborers an average of $1.40 a day at a time when the average for the area was $1.35. He also took great satisfaction in a report published by *Iron Age* that in 1898 he had paid out a total of $13.5 million in wages; the fact that profits for Carnegie Steel were said to be $11.5 million for the same period probably did not please him any less.

"Splendid," Carnegie wrote back to his rapidly rising star in Homestead. "No strikes in future. There would not have been any had you been in charge."

It was doubtless not a message intended to be shared with Frick.

# 23

## GREAT DIVIDE

WHILE FRICK'S CHOICE OF SCHWAB proved to be inspired, and the fortunes of Carnegie Steel soared during the remaining years of the 1890s, Frick's own position within the company was not a happy one. One of the first difficulties in the aftermath of Homestead involved the new armor-plating mill that Carnegie had agreed to install at the behest of President Benjamin Harrison.

Carnegie had never been particularly enthusiastic about producing anything under the hectoring terms of a government contract. Successful bidding and compliance, then as now, involved endless paperwork, and the actual production and delivery of armored plating that would meet government standards was a maddening process. When the U.S. Navy refused to bend on certain specifications for a plating contract in the late 1880s, Carnegie simply withdrew his bid and let the contract go to his competitor, Bethlehem Steel. If Bethlehem could find a way to make money doing business the way the government demanded, then more power to them.

But when Bethlehem found that it could not comply, either, President Harrison appealed directly to Carnegie, who gave in and agreed to complete the plate mill. The installation was completed at Homestead, just months before the strike, under the direction of a longtime Carnegie manager named William Corey. With the experienced Corey and a bevy of government inspectors overseeing the smooth operation of the highly specialized unit, new plant superintendent Schwab was happy to leave well enough alone.

All that changed when, in September 1893, a Pittsburgh attorney contacted Secretary of the Navy Hilary Herbert, representing four unnamed employees who wished to sell information concerning acts of fraud at the Homestead armor installation. Plating that did not conform to contract standards was being manufactured, they claimed. And test results were being cooked to cover the matter up.

As it turned out, the group had also approached Frick with the same offer, but the chairman, believing the matter to be yet another bogus plot by disgruntled ex-workers, had run the attorney out of his office. Nonetheless, Frick had warned Schwab to be on the lookout for funny business at the plating mill and to make certain that production was being carried out with strict adherence to government specifications. Frick also directed the navy's own inspectors to inform him of the slightest suspected impropriety.

Frick's precautions seemed for naught, however, as Secretary Herbert offered the informants 25 percent of any penalties assessed against Carnegie Steel, then convened a secret navy panel to investigate the claimants' charges. Without ever contacting the company, the panel declared the charges accurate. Herbert summoned Frick to Washington, where he announced his summary judgment: a fine of 15 percent of the value of the armor delivered by the company to date.

Frick and Carnegie were furious, of course, certain that they were suffering a backlash at the hands of disgruntled employees and inexperienced bureaucrats eager to retaliate for the loss of the election of 1892. Carnegie wrote to President Cleveland to express his outrage and ask for a new panel, but Cleveland only offered to reduce the penalty to 10 percent.

The offer was an insult to the aggrieved Carnegie, who was aghast that anyone would question his patriotism. It was unthinkable to him that he or his company would defraud the government by producing shoddy armor plating, Carnegie declared. In an angry note to Frick, Carnegie blamed the events of 1892.

"The ghost of Homestead is not yet laid," Carnegie said. "If statement ever necessary, I think you should state that you had to employ best men you could find [in the aftermath of the strike], among them some miserable wretches of course—these spies. They could not and did not do the work to our standard and shirked some parts as was discovered."

A statement would indeed be required. A House Committee on Naval Affairs conducted an investigation, churning out a final report of more than one thousand pages in which the judgment was mixed. While it was difficult to ascertain an intention to defraud, it seemed irrefutable that certain tests of the plating had been "helped along." In the end, the House committee ruled that the navy had been correct in levying a fine upon Carnegie Steel, although the amount was reduced to 10 percent, as the president had proposed.

The resulting scandal, gleefully reported by the newspapers that had vilified the company during the strike, depressed Carnegie, infuriated Frick, and led Schwab to offer his resignation—though all would eventually recover. The fine was paid as part of a five-year renewal of the navy contract, several key plating mill employees were dismissed, and Carnegie Steel went back to making enormous profits. However, the once-rosy relationship between Frick and Schwab had been irreparably damaged.

Frick blamed Schwab's carelessness for the situation, and was further outraged when an emboldened Schwab refused his order to dismiss summarily a number of plating mill subordinates. "This armor mess handicaps us in many ways," Frick wrote to Carnegie, "as the Navy Department are anything but friendly to Schwab and have no confidence in him."

Despite that and other mildly derogatory reports on Schwab that Frick sent Carnegie's way, Schwab's position within the company was assured. In Schwab, Carnegie had found a manager who was as able and detail-oriented as Frick, and who had the added advantage of being unfailingly congenial. What likely annoyed Frick most was the realization that his former protégé was gaining influence within the company nearly equal to his own.

◆　　◆　　◆

ABOUT A YEAR LATER CAME THE INCIDENT that would alter Frick's relationship with Carnegie as profoundly as had been his relationship with Schwab. For some time, Carnegie had been interested in acquiring the coke holdings of W. J. Rainey, a former competitor of Frick's, for much the same reason he had coveted Frick's ovens years before. Frick, however, considered Rainey "a thief" and saw the acquisition as a threat to his own role as the company's primary supplier of coke.

When he learned that Carnegie had actually met with Rainey without informing him, Frick tendered his resignation from the chairmanship. Company affairs were in "splendid shape," Frick wrote on December 18, 1894, so this action should have no adverse effect on operations. He advised Carnegie to purchase his shares in the company and begin an immediate search for his successor.

Frick closed by invoking reasons for his decision that, coming from a noted workaholic, were surprising. The past six years, he told Carnegie, had been extremely taxing, "and my mind from necessity has been so absorbed in looking after the interests of this great concern I have not had time for anything else and feel now that I need such a rest as is only obtained by almost complete freedom from business affairs."

Perhaps Carnegie saw in this last a chance to salvage the situation. He had already written Henry Phipps, "Frick is not well," underlining that first sentence. "He is breaking down and is not of his former power, believe me, to us at present," concluding that Frick might profit from some time away. "What rest will do we know not, but I hope he will return to us again."

Carnegie wrote back to Frick, dismissing his chairman's abrupt threat of resignation as unrealistic, given his responsibility to their great enterprise, and suggested that Frick take an extended vacation, preferably to Egypt. "You will soon return and smile at matters which now in your tired state seem gigantic and amazing," Carnegie wrote, "and your partners will be unable to contain their joy."

But Frick would have none of it. In the little time that passed between his letter of resignation and Carnegie's reply, Frick had learned that a broker was attempting to sell a block of 32,000 Frick Coke Company bonds—bonds that Carnegie had received as part of their original partnership agreement.

To Frick it was treachery beyond bounds, selling H. C. Frick Coke and marrying a thief from the same industry! Despite Carnegie's insistence that he knew nothing of such a divestiture, Frick was beside himself. Worse yet, Phipps had passed along the memo in which Carnegie had shared his concerns about their chairman's mental state.

On December 30, Frick penned a five-page memorandum that can only be described as a jaw-dropper: "Mr. Carnegie, it is high time you should stop this nonsensical talk about me being unwell, overstrained, etc., and treat this matter between us in a rational business-like way. . . . Why do you write such stuff? . . . I warn you to carry this no farther with me but come forward like a man and purchase my interest, and let us part before it becomes impossible to continue to be friends. . . . I desire to quietly withdraw, doing as little harm as possible to the interests of others, because I have become tired of your business methods, your absurd newspaper interviews and personal remarks and unwarranted interference in matters you know nothing about."

If his intent was to get Carnegie's attention, Frick succeeded. Shortly after New Year's Day, Carnegie wrote back that it was "not the first time you have resigned," and that, furthermore, there seemed little point in continuing to correspond about the matter. Though Carnegie cautioned Frick that this time it would not be as easy to reinstate him should he change his mind, he seemed philosophical: "All right. I am forced to agree that the work of the Carnegie Steel Company and the Frick Coke Company is too much for any man."

A meeting of the board was convened on January 11, 1895, at which John Leishman, a former steel broker and a Carnegie partner since 1886, was named to the newly created post of president. While Frick would remain as chairman, his participation in the day-to-day management of company affairs would be significantly lessened and his 11-percent ownership in Carnegie Steel reduced to 6 percent, with the balance transferred to Leishman.

Historians differ on the meaning of this reorganization. Some argue that Carnegie strove to emasculate Frick, and point to a memorandum he wrote to board secretary Francis Lovejoy. As the company now had a president, Carnegie asserted, they could not have a chairman as well. In essence, then, Frick was merely the chairman of the board of directors.

Carnegie biographer Burton J. Hendrick quotes from a Carnegie memo that suggests he had tossed the sop of the "Chairmanship" to a contrite and haggard Frick, who had arrived, Carnegie said, in his chambers begging for reinstatement and desperate to retain some measure of influence in the company's affairs. Still others have said that Frick was sanguine about these developments, especially the ability to convert that 5 percent of Carnegie Steel assets into cash, a move that would significantly reduce his personal debts and allow him to enjoy the "freedom" he alluded to in his letter to Carnegie.

In the end, this restructuring seemed to make everyone happy. Frick retained his influence and yet was no longer consumed by the minutiae that for years had occupied his every waking moment. He began to travel, as Carnegie had long counseled, and renewed his interest in acquiring fine art—an avocation that would provide benefits beyond measure to future generations.

And despite Carnegie's skewed recollections, he too seemed relieved that a way had been found to keep Frick's expertise. The two were even able to meet shortly after the reorganization to discuss the previously taboo topic of the Rainey coke holdings.

By early 1896, Frick was able to write to Carnegie, in the midst of difficult negotiations for favorable freight rates from the Pennsylvania RR, "[I] may view the whole question differently from you, but that is no reason why we should quarrel about it. What we are both after is the ultimate best interest of the Companies."

Perhaps "rest" had done well for Frick, then. He closed by adding what Carnegie must have viewed as an understatement: "In all my dealings want of frankness with you on all subjects has not been a failing. [Though] it might from some points of view be considered a fault."

Meanwhile, business remained steadily on the rise for Carnegie Steel. In 1896 the company produced more than one-quarter of all the steel manufactured in the United States. Profits rose from $5 million in 1895 to $6 million in 1896, then to $7 million in 1897.

Yet, despite such staggering success, there were signs that Carnegie missed his former "management genius" at the helm. From the very beginning he wrote scolding notes to Leishman, urging the new chairman to keep a closer eye on costs, warning, "If you do not look out, you will bring even our firm into serious trouble."

During his annual retreat to Scotland, Carnegie wrote again to Leishman, complaining that "Mr. Frick used to send me monthly costs and also monthly reports of Blast Furnace products and these were very interesting. . . . Please remember how much you can oblige us by keeping us in touch with important events."

Accordingly, Leishman had the necessary figures compiled and the report sent off to Cluny Castle, but it is doubtful that the reply he got from Carnegie filled him with confidence. Though Carnegie thanked Leishman for his trouble, he concluded, "You can scarcely realize how anxious in these times your absent partners necessarily are, and how much they have missed Mr. Frick's admirable correspondence and statements."

Leishman, who had begun as a salesman within the Carnegie ranks, no doubt aspired to reach the same unassailable position enjoyed by many of the long-term partners. If he had, for all intents, taken Henry Frick's place, then why shouldn't he accrue an equal measure of wealth and respect, and a similar place at the roundtable of the titans?

Leishman's motives might have been understandable or even laudable by Carnegie's own standards, but his methods were anything but. When word reached Carnegie that Leishman had run up considerable debt speculating in the stock market and in dubious ventures in iron ore, the game was up.

"We all appreciate your ability in some directions," Carnegie wrote Leishman, "but you have much to do before you regain the confidence of your partners as a safe man to be the Executive head."

In December 1896, following the company's acquisition of two failed coke furnaces, Carnegie wrote again to Leishman, complaining that he could not stand by and see their great concern reduced to the level of "speculators and Jim Cracks, men who pass as manufacturers, but who look to the market and not to manufacturing, and who buy up bankrupt concerns only to show their incapacity."

It all took its toll upon Leishman, who sought out none other than Henry Clay Frick for advice. At this meeting Frick suggested a way out that Leishman found palatable.

Less than two weeks later Carnegie wrote the press release for a Frick-engineered scenario. The very able Mr. Leishman, it was tactfully explained, had resigned the presidency of Carnegie Steel and was about to embark on a cruise to Europe, where, following a suitable period of rest and recuperation, he would undertake to represent the company in its expanded and important operations on the Continent.

In other words, Leishman had been "sent abroad," a favorite euphemism among Carnegie insiders. Out was a man of questionable pedigree, in was a mover and shaker, and Frick remained the man to be entrusted with such maneuvers. As Carnegie would write shortly after, while the board was pondering the acquisition of a floundering competitor, "I am sure the Bessemer which is now waddling can easily be made to fly. Her case is respectfully submitted to the attention of Dr. Henry Clay Frick, Surgeon and Physician—amputations may be necessary."

# 24

# GATHERING STORM

———◆——

A GLANCE AT THE BALANCE SHEETS issued during the tenure of Charles Schwab as president of Carnegie Steel shows that his accomplishments were remarkable indeed. Net profits rose from $7 million in 1897 to an astounding $11.5 million in 1898. In 1899 the figure was $21 million. By 1900, Carnegie Steel would produce nearly 30 percent of the nation's steel and show net earnings of $40 million.

Another statistic is nearly as telling. In 1892 the company's profit of about $4 million represented a bit over 50 percent of the total cost of wages, which ran about $7.3 million. By 1899, however, net profits were just about double the $10.9 million paid in wages. If, as Carnegie was fond of saying, there was truly a partnership between capital and labor, the latter group needed to call in its accountants.

Clearly, Schwab had heeded Frick and Carnegie's lessons when it came to managing labor costs. And any misgivings that Carnegie had harbored about Schwab and his role in the armor-plating crisis seemed to have vanished. In early 1898, after Schwab had paid him a call in France, Carnegie wrote Frick, "Schwab's visit has made a great impression upon me, and you are no doubt feeling as I do that a great load is off our shoulders. We have got the man, and having him, there is no reason why we should hesitate about going forward and keeping the lead."

Though Carnegie had recently expressed some second thoughts to Frick about the practice of establishing partnerships for talented young managers ("We should now go very slow about increasing interests; they grow of themselves about ten per cent every year. . . . Just look over the amounts now held by the various young partners, and see how rapidly their interests increase"), he did not doubt their investment in Schwab. A few weeks after his first communiqué on Schwab, Carnegie wrote Frick again, "I hope you feel as I do that we have got the right man in the right place, also that he relieves you from much anxiety, as he certainly does me. I never felt so happy and contented in regard to our business as at the present time." In fact, with Schwab at the helm, Carnegie felt comfortable enough to absent himself in Europe for the entire summer, until October 1898.

In addition, he had never felt closer to Frick. In March 1897, Carnegie, then sixty-one, became a father for the first time. The birth of his daughter, Margaret, became a conduit through which he and Frick—whose surviving daughter, Helen, was eight—could communicate. Here was a human dimension that had been lacking when Frick was in charge of the company.

It was in this spirit that Carnegie began writing Frick in the spring of 1898, expressing the hope that he and his family would visit him at his new Scottish Highlands home, Skibo Castle. The previous year, at the request of his wife, who wanted a permanent summer home for their new family, Carnegie had paid £85,000 (perhaps $80 million in contemporary terms) for the estate, the former residence of the Roman Catholic bishops of Caithness. Carnegie was now involved in the reconstruction of a new manor house, as well as the creation of a long-sought waterfall and any other number of improvements, and was eager to show off his new holdings to someone who could appreciate the scope of the undertaking.

"Delighted here," he told Frick, "so far beyond all expectations. Highland and lowland, grand trees equal to any in the best English park, and yet the heather hills, lochs and streams around us—never saw anything like it, climate mild and yet more bracing than Cluny. The only fear in regard to your coming here is that it would render you dissatisfied with any other life, but in case that should happen I have my eye on an adjoining estate, castle and all. . . . We have a splendid musician from Edinburgh for the season, plays the organ and the grand piano . . . so that we begin every morning with a religious service of music. . . . Come over and see for yourself, and don't you fail to read this to Mrs. Frick and Helen."

Many of his letters of the period suggested that Carnegie had finally found contentment. "Yesterday was Margaret's first birthday," Carnegie closed one letter to Frick. "Her conversation is limited yet, but she knows what is said to her and kisses papa sometimes, not always, when requested. You should see how well we all are—truly if you have sickness in the winter, this is the place."

Furthermore, Carnegie seemed sincere in his desire that Frick should join him in his happiness. If Margaret and Helen were to be seen together, Carnegie enthused, "people will vote them a prize pair." Indeed, and though Frick declined Carnegie's invitation, explaining that his wife, Adelaide, was in need of a restorative stay in warmer climes, it seemed that any acrimony that lingered from the contretemps of 1895 had disappeared.

When summer came, Frick took his family to France, installing his wife and children at the spa of Aix-les-Bains in the south, and then traveled with his old friend Andrew Mellon to Paris, where he purchased the first of four works of Jean-Baptiste-Camille Corot that he was destined to own. *Ville d'Avray*, Frick assured Carnegie, was a painting that would constitute "the gem of my collection."

That these two old warhorses from the business front should be corresponding over castle building, the winsomeness of their young daughters, and the finer points of art acquisition was a telling measure of how far their personal interests had evolved. But with Carnegie sixty-three and Frick nearing fifty, it seems only natural that they would relinquish a degree of involvement in matters that had grayed and bent them both.

Both had suffered bouts of illness that had nearly killed them, and both had endured worldwide scorn and outrage at their business dealings. But both were now wealthy beyond the reckoning of nearly all men. They had developed cultured tastes and interests, and were devoted husbands and the fathers of young children. Why on earth, with their ably tended company producing egg after golden egg, would they not seek, at last, some measure of personal harmony? "These are no Helen or Margaret *by a long sight,*" Carnegie wrote Frick, referring to Frick Coke and Carnegie Steel.

It had been rumored, in fact, that "the old man" was willing to contemplate a total withdrawal from business if only an individual or group with sufficient bidding resources could be found. Senior partners Henry Phipps and George Lauder had been ready to sell out since the days of the Homestead strike, and now Frick, too, having had a taste of the leisured life, was ready to retire to New York and devote himself almost fully to art collecting.

Frick, Phipps, and Lauder might have sold their holdings even earlier, but for the existence of one major stumbling block: the Iron Clad Agreement of 1887, which all had signed. According to its provisions, which were meant to protect the other partners in the event of Carnegie's untimely death, a partner who wished to retire could do so, but his shares would be redeemed at "book value" and the payment made in installments, the length of the period tied to the size of the interest redeemed.

Since Carnegie had always opposed periodic revaluation of the company, the book value of Carnegie Steel in 1899 remained at $50 million, even though the most conservative estimates placed its true value at between $200 and $250 million, around ten to twelve times its net earnings of $21 million. While Phipps reckoned the actual value of his 11-percent interest to be $27.5 million, the Iron Clad Agreement dictated that a sale would bring him only $5.5 million. Frick's 6 percent would bring him $3 million instead of $15 million; and Lauder's 4 percent would get him a paltry $2 million instead of $10 million. No wonder, then, that all three were now on the lookout for a potential buyer.

The impasse was finally broken in April 1899, when Frick and Phipps informed Carnegie that they had been approached by a buyer willing to meet the $250 million price. Under the proposed terms, Carnegie would receive $157 million, with $57 million in cash and $100 million in 5-percent bonds issued by the new company.

Carnegie pondered the offer only briefly. While he had always condemned the growing practice of companies overstating their value in advance of a public offering, thus allowing the principals to profit "by manufacturing nothing but stocks," he privately agreed with the $250 million valuation of Carnegie Steel and felt that continued operations would easily support his annual payments of $5 million.

After agreeing to the terms, Carnegie asked Frick and Phipps who the prospective buyers were. In Carnegie's mind, Rockefeller was one suspect, and another was J. P. Morgan, who had recently formed a $200 million consortium of Illinois, Minnesota, and Lake Erie interests into the Federal Steel Company. Or perhaps it was Andrew Mellon, whom Frick and Phipps had coaxed into the game.

But Frick and Phipps told Carnegie that they had been sworn to secrecy by this prospective suitor and that they were acting solely as intermediaries. There was one other thing as well: the buyer was asking for a ninety-day option to prepare for this sizable transaction.

Carnegie must have worked hard to conceal his incredulity. Just how naïve did his partners think he was? Yes, they were all friends and longtime associates, but this was business, and very big business at that. For all he knew, there was no buyer. Frick and Phipps could be asking him to sign an irrevocable agreement to sell at a fixed price. Once he'd put his name on the dotted line, there would be nothing to stop the pair from scurrying off with carte blanche to sell his holdings to any "Jim Crack" who fancied becoming a steel baron.

With $157 million dangling before him, a lesser man might have signed and taken his chances. But Andrew Carnegie was hardly a desperate man.

After some reflection, he told Frick and Phipps that he would go along with this proposal but would require a $2 million payment for the ninety-day option. If the offer was genuine, he reasoned, such a payment would be no obstacle. It would not indeed, said Frick and Phipps, and quickly produced a check for $1,170,000, reflecting Carnegie's 58-percent share of Carnegie Steel and its subsidiary, Frick Coke. They told Carnegie that in order to speed the process along, the other partners had agreed to forgo their own option payments.

Carnegie, who cared little whether the junior partners lacked good sense, pocketed his proceeds and, in late April, sailed off for Skibo. He had not been there long, however, when disquieting rumors reached him about the true identity of the buyers.

As it turned out, the men who intended to buy the Carnegie Steel Company were, in the eyes of its majority stockholders, common scoundrels and speculators. The principals included William H. Moore of Chicago, who, along with his brother, had formed the ill-fated Diamond Match Company consortium, the collapse of which had closed the Chicago Stock Exchange for three months in 1896. Another principal was John W. Gates, a notorious Wall Street speculator and a storied gambler who had once placed a sizable wager on which of two fat raindrops running down a windowpane would reach the sill first. When Carnegie ascertained that "Bet A Million" Gates was involved, he was mortified.

Despite Frick's best efforts, the truth had come out. On May 16, Frick, distressed at a leak of their plans, wrote an urgent letter to fellow conspirator Colonel James M. Schoonmaker: "I notice a bungling statement in the newspapers of this morning, from Chicago. I assume, of course Mr. Moore's brother is not responsible for this, but certainly has not exercised the proper care or it would not have appeared. Please say to Mr. Moore if statements of this kind appear in the press I will feel called upon to deny them . . . there was no publicity to be given this matter until we all agreed just how and when it should be done."

It was too late, however, and soon Carnegie divined the worst of it. Gates and the Moore brothers had persuaded Phipps and Frick to put forward their offer to Carnegie in return for a broker's fee of $5 million, which would be paid to them once the sale went through. Even more galling was the discovery that Frick and Phipps had put up $170,000 of the $1,170,000 paid to Carnegie to secure the option. The truth was that neither the Moores nor Gates had anything approaching the capital necessary to make the purchase. It was just what Carnegie had suspected: a despicable exercise in speculation, made all the more distasteful by the secretive and self-serving participation of his longtime partners.

Over the years, Carnegie had put up with a great deal from Frick. And he understood the Machiavellian impulse at the heart of mergers and buyouts. But the fact that Frick and Phipps had tried to dupe him and stood to profit at the expense of the other partners by the sale of their company was more than he could bear. Good old-fashioned business machinations were one thing; outright thievery was another.

In a series of letters to Schwab, Carnegie complained bitterly that Frick had utterly betrayed his trust and that his former CEO should have felt honor-bound to disclose what he knew.

But, despite his outrage, Carnegie, for the moment, had little recourse. He had taken the option, signed the agreement, and was obligated to accept the payment for his share of Carnegie Steel the moment that the Moores and "Bet A Million" Gates showed up with the cash in hand. All Carnegie could do was wait and stew . . .

. . . until fate once again saved him. A sudden downturn on Wall Street made many investors skittish, and even those with the where-withal, such as J. P. Morgan, shied away from dealing with the likes of Moore and Gates. In the end, no one stepped forward with the necessary funds.

In desperation, with time running out, the syndicate proposed the formation of a Pennsylvania corporation that would fund the purchase by issuing $250 million in stock and another $100 million in bonds. While the appearance of the scheme had changed, the essence remained the same. Frick and Phipps would receive $5 million as part of the proceeds of the sale, plus interest in the newly formed company.

This second maneuver met the same fate as the first, however. No investment house would underwrite the dubious venture, and in the end, Frick and Phipps were forced to travel to Skibo Castle and grovel for an extension of the option.

One can only imagine the satisfaction with which Carnegie listened to their pleas, and the relish with which he delivered his reply: "Not an hour!" The buyout was doomed.

It was more than an emotional disappointment to Frick and Phipps. At the time they had made the option payment, they had extracted a verbal promise from Carnegie that he would refund any part that had been put up by Carnegie Steel partners. But the Scotsman drew the line at honoring promises made to men he now considered thieves, and his refusal to return any monies to Frick and Phipps must have given him great glee.

It should also be noted that Frick would later dispute Carnegie's claim that he and Phipps would have profited at the expense of the other partners. In a letter written in 1913 to James Bridge, Frick insisted that there was never any provision for a broker's fee for him and Phipps. He suggested that Carnegie had simply lost his nerve at the prospect of stepping away from the company in which he had invested so much of his very being. And there was another possibility: perhaps the canny Scotsman had simply decided that he could find someone of the ilk of Morgan or Rockefeller able to pony up a sweeter price.

As far as Frick was concerned, his tight-fisted former partner had simply fastened upon an excuse to keep Frick's $170,000 in his pocket. This was the real perfidy.

Whatever the truth, it is said that, in later years, Carnegie would delight in taking guests on a tour of his new manor at Skibo, renovations to which had cost just a bit over $1 million. Following the inevitable burst of compliments, Carnegie would respond with an airy wave of his hand. "It's nothing," he would say. "Just a nice little present from Mr. Frick."

# 25

## PUT ASUNDER

———➤◆◄———

I N RETROSPECT, ONE WONDERS HOW MUCH of Frick's so-called villainy—actual or embellished—would have been forgiven by Carnegie had Charles Schwab not been on the scene. Frick had resigned twice before, only to be coaxed back into the fold. But now, with profits headed for an astronomical $40 million in 1900, Carnegie and those around him could afford to spurn the manager they had once touted as without peer.

In any case, the aborted sale of the company set in motion a series of cataclysmic battles between Frick and Carnegie—battles that might be understandable in hindsight, but which no one, least of all the principals, could have anticipated.

During the negotiations with the Moores, two other matters had arisen to threaten the internal unity at Carnegie Steel. One involved the normally cozy relationship between the parent company and its virtual subsidiary, the Henry Clay Frick Coke Company, which provided the former with a steady supply of fuel. Though the price charged Carnegie for this fuel was lower than for competitors, the arrangement to sell large quantities of coke on a steady basis nonetheless resulted in handsome profits for the vendor.

Late in 1898, Carnegie had taken Frick aside to discuss these prices. He later claimed that Frick had verbally agreed to sell coke to Carnegie Steel at the rate of $1.35 a ton for the next three years, some fifteen cents per ton less than the rate for other customers. Told of the deal, the always fearful Henry Phipps wondered, "But where will we be if the price for the coke drops *below* $1.35?"

The response stopped a happy Carnegie in his tracks; it was a possibility he had never considered. "Then you had better get a concession from Frick," Phipps suggested. "You had better get that promise in writing."

Though Carnegie agreed, other concerns, among them the proposed sale of the company, apparently distracted him. Meanwhile, the price for coke had actually risen dramatically, and by early 1899 Frick Coke was selling its product to competitors such as Duluth Steel and Ohio Valley Iron for as much as $3.25 a ton—a fact that distressed Frick greatly.

Responsibility for what happened next remains a matter of conjecture. Instead of the $1.35 that Carnegie assumed was fixed, Frick Coke raised its prices for product shipped to Carnegie to $1.45 for the first quarter, $1.60 for the second, and $1.75 for the remainder of 1899. Presented with these invoices, Schwab approved the payments but instructed that all remittances above the rate of $1.35 should be marked as "payments on advance accounts only."

When word of these maneuvers finally reached Carnegie, he demanded that the matter be resolved at a late-October board meeting of the HCF Coke Company. The minutes show that when confronted by members loyal to Carnegie, Frick dissembled, claiming that he had no authority to make contracts on behalf of the company and would never have suggested otherwise to Carnegie.

"Mr. Carnegie and I had considerable talk about what the price of coke should be for, as he called it, 'a permanency.' For the sake of harmony I was personally willing to agree to almost anything. I am willing to talk the matter over with Mr. Carnegie at any time," Frick insisted. But he was simply the chairman of the board of directors of HCF Coke. So far as any binding agreements went, such matters would have to be referred to Thomas Lynch, the president of the subsidiary.

George Lauder was hardly put off by such transparency. "You and Mr. Carnegie represent a vast majority of stock in the two companies, and if you cannot fix the matter it is a very strange thing."

Strange, perhaps, Frick responded. But nonetheless true. The effects of such an unfair agreement upon those who held stock only in HCF Coke and not in Carnegie Steel would have to be taken into account. Those stockholders, he argued, clearly deserved a say in any agreement that would diminish their position. With that said, Frick pushed through a motion that denied the existence of any such contract and stated that no claim against HCF Coke on the basis of an alleged verbal agreement between himself and Andrew Carnegie would be entertained.

The meeting adjourned on an acrimonious note, with an angry Lauder pointing out that Frick's coke holdings would have been nothing without the beneficence of Carnegie Steel, a point at which Frick took umbrage. Only one thing seemed certain: such an internecine dispute favored no one, and a resolution that favored either side simply moved cash from one internal account to another. It seemed that in the end only ego was at stake. But in the case of Carnegie versus Frick, that was more than enough.

There was another complicating issue taken up at the subsequent board meeting of Carnegie Steel in early November, which was attended by Carnegie himself. A short time before, Frick had acquired a tract of land downriver from Homestead, a parcel well suited for a specialized steel-tubing plant that the Carnegie partners were considering building. The property had been appraised for $4,000 an acre, but Frick offered to sell it to the company for $3,500. It seemed fair enough, and with little discussion and no dissent, the board voted to make the purchase.

In the corridors outside, however, Carnegie suddenly found a great deal to say. He reckoned that Frick, who had purchased the tract for less than $700 an acre just a few months before, would make a profit of more than $1 million, which Carnegie considered unconscionable.

Here was Frick, he muttered, the traitor, the man who had recently tried to sell them out and who had reneged on a promise to provide fuel at an agreed-upon price, once more attempting to profit immensely at the expense of his partners.

Carnegie expressed none of this directly to Frick, of course. Rather, he continued to maintain the pretense that all was well between them. Shortly after he returned to New York City, he dashed off a series of notes to Frick suggesting that their disputes were petty: "Very foolish when it's only business with nothing personal in it. Isn't it?" He urged Frick to set down in writing the terms of their agreement on coke prices, and concluded with an almost laughable observation: "We've never had friction before—it annoys me more than dollars."

When Frick did not respond to such blandishments, Carnegie wrote again, this time urging that Frick not only recognize the $1.35 agreement but acknowledge how generous it really was, and how beneficial it would be in the long run to HCF Coke. "We all have our 'crazy bones,' " Carnegie allowed, "but now all's over and you have a mighty good bargain and a big profit. . . . I believe all back things are also settled—so now all's well."

By this time, however, Frick had learned of Carnegie's backstabbing comments following the early-November board meeting, and was seething at the apparent hypocrisy. When no reply was forthcoming from Pittsburgh, Carnegie proposed yet another means of resolving the dispute: perhaps Frick would agree to a formal merger of HCF Coke with Carnegie Steel, a move that would allow Carnegie to set coke prices internally with no interference.

Frick replied through clenched teeth that he might be willing to permit a merger—provided that the newly formed company would be capitalized at no less than $150 million. Though the figure was low in comparison to what he believed the new entity would be worth, and would have netted Frick just a little more than half of an outright sale of Carnegie Steel for $250 million, Carnegie would have none of it. There would be no such revaluation of their holdings, he insisted.

Once again, matters had stalled between the two. But Frick was not about to let things rest. At a late-November board meeting, he read into the minutes a rebuke of Carnegie. "The value of our coke properties for over a year has been, at every opportunity, deprecated by Mr. Carnegie and Mr. Lauder," Frick declared, "and I submit that it is not unreasonable that I have considerable feeling on this subject."

Frick went on to say that Carnegie had threatened to buy his own coke lands and run HCF Coke out of business, and further suggested that Carnegie was less than a man for not voicing objections over the land acquisition to his face. He demanded that Carnegie apologize personally, and closed, "I have stood a great many insults from Mr. Carnegie in the past, but I will submit to no further insults in the future."

If Carnegie had entertained the slightest hopes of patching things up, Frick's latest invective dashed them completely. While he had no intention of responding to Frick's request for an apology, he had much to say to Lauder, Phipps, and Schwab. To each he offered the opinion that Frick was losing his health and his mind. He was finished with his attempts to appease the man: "It is a clear case of 'Incompatibility of Temper,' always sufficient cause for divorce," he wrote to Lauder and Phipps.

It was Carnegie's intention to abolish the office of chairman once and for all at the first board meeting in December, though he advised Schwab that it would be far preferable for Frick to withdraw and avert a public spectacle. Carnegie's hope was that Schwab would lay it all out for Frick and persuade the man to resign.

Schwab had something of a dilemma on his hands. He had seen apparently irreparable ruptures between Carnegie and Frick patched up before. And, despite all his nettlesome actions, Frick continued to hold influence with a number of the partners, including Phipps. What if Schwab attempted to intervene, then found himself trumped by Frick? Look what had become of poor John Leishman.

Following a meeting with Carnegie in New York, Schwab hit upon a plan he was comfortable with. He wrote a lengthy letter to his old patron and mentor, in which he warned Frick of Carnegie's intentions to abolish Frick's position at the next board meeting. Whatever their personal feeling, lamented Schwab, the junior partners and even Schwab himself would have no choice but to obey Carnegie's wishes. "I beg of you for myself and for all the Junior Partners, to avoid putting us in this awkward position," he wrote, in closing.

Though he intended to mail the letter to Frick, Schwab's sense of decency and long-standing obligation to the man who had brought him into the business demanded something better. And so it was that he rode out to Clayton on the eve of the December board meeting and told Frick at the door that he carried a letter that he wished very much for him to read.

It seems likely that Frick had some premonition of what was coming, but his response was hardly less than if he'd been blindsided. Schwab recalled that as he sat in the quiet drawing room, watching Frick read through his painstakingly composed letter, he had seldom seen a person so consumed by fury. Moments later, Schwab was fleeing out the door, with Frick's angry imprecations cutting the chill December air in his wake.

For all his attempts at diplomacy, it was Schwab who'd had to bear the brunt of Frick's temper. To the board itself, Frick's written response was uncharacteristically mild. When that body convened on the fifth of December, they read simply this:

Gentlemen:

I beg to present my resignation as a member of your Board.

Yours very truly,

H. C. Frick

Never had a coup d'état gone more smoothly—or so it must have seemed. With the troublesome Frick out of the way at last and the able Schwab maintaining a firm hand on the controls, Carnegie could envision only smooth sailing. But then, so did the passengers on the *Titanic*.

# 26

## DEVIL IN THE DETAILS

———◆———

THERE WERE MATTERS TO BE ATTENDED TO in the wake of Frick's ouster, of course. The question of coke prices to Carnegie Steel had not been settled, and, despite his resignation from the chairmanship at Carnegie, Frick remained the chairman of the board at HCF Coke.

Carnegie and Schwab had put a contingency plan into effect, however. At the board meeting of HCF Coke in early January of 1900, Carnegie saw to it that a new membership was elected, one that reflected his and his loyalists' controlling interest in the company. The five new Carnegie men on the seven-member board of HCF Coke got quickly down to business, abolishing the office of chairman and leaving the company in control of its president, Thomas Lynch.

The new board rammed through another motion that recognized the existence of the disputed verbal agreement between Carnegie and Frick and demanded that Frick sign off.

"I would like this agreement executed," Carnegie supporter A. M. Moreland said.

"I want some time to look into it," Frick countered.

"I would like it executed now," Moreland said. "The board has authorized you to sign it."

"It is now three o'clock," Frick said. "Can't you give me until four o'clock to sign it?"

Moreland was unfazed. "Can't you decide now as well as at four o'clock? We want it executed now."

It was the end, and Frick knew it. "The President will execute the contract as directed by the board," he said finally. "But under protest as a stockholder."

Frick, though still a member of the board, could do nothing. Deposed for a second time through the machinations of Carnegie—and now dropped from the very company he had founded—he simply walked out of the meeting in silent protest.

It was not the final indignity. On the following day, Wednesday, January 10, Frick was reading a letter from a Carnegie Steel stockholder in his office in the Carnegie Building in downtown Pittsburgh, when there was a knock at his door. Mr. Carnegie was there to see him, an assistant announced. Would it be convenient for Mr. Frick to grant an audience?

Frick allowed that it was convenient enough, and Carnegie made his way into those chambers where, eight years ago, an assassin had burst in with his weapon blazing. No pistol was in Carnegie's hand on this day. He carried an instrument far more lethal.

As Charles Schwab sat in his office next door, ear pressed to the wall, Frick stared inquiringly at Carnegie. In his typically patronizing manner, Carnegie first offered smiling assurances that he and Frick were still partners in an amazingly profitable enterprise. To ensure the continuing profitability of that venture, Carnegie continued, Frick must surely recognize that a threatened coke embargo should never take place. They should simply agree that there had been an agreement: coke at $1.35 a ton. Frick had already admitted as much to their mutual associates, had he not? Time to set aside their petty differences, Carnegie said, and get back to the business of minting money. Or words to that effect.

Frick pursed his lips thoughtfully, nodding as Carnegie sat back, his arms folded. And what did wee Andy propose if Frick did not choose to send off coke to his mills at break-the-bank prices, he wondered.

Carnegie drew a copy of a document from his coat pocket. He might have smiled—or did he wear the same expression as Alexander Berkman as he fixed the sights of his pistol between the eyes of Henry Clay Frick?

As he handed over the document, Carnegie explained that on January 8, the day before the meeting at which Frick had been deposed from his own company, there had been a special session of the Carnegie board of managers. They'd had just one piece of business, and here, said Carnegie, was its result.

What Frick read was as unmistakable as it was infuriating. As Frick had proven to be an obstruction to the continued and efficient operation of their mighty leviathan of steel, the document stated, the board had no choice but to invoke the provisions of the Iron Clad Agreement. Frick's interest in the company must forthwith be surrendered, his compensation fixed at book value and not a penny more. Frick would receive about $1.5 million for stock that was worth at least ten times as much.

Next door, Schwab might not have been able to make out the exact words the two men traded next, but he understood that the air had become plenty "thick."

Frick was on his feet by now, his chair tipping backward with a crash. "For years I have been convinced there is not an honest bone in your body," he shouted at Carnegie. "Now I know that you are a god damned thief."

He crumpled up the document and tossed it aside. "We'll have a judge and jury of Allegheny County decide what you are to pay me," he added. He spun around his desk, advancing on Carnegie with his fists raised.

Carnegie's description of what ensued next—apparently recollected, as Wordsworth was fond of saying, "in tranquillity"—seems somewhat understated: "He became wilder and I was forced to leave."

Other accounts suggest a slightly more frenzied scenario: Startled workers stared as a frightened Carnegie burst out of Frick's office, his face pale. On his heels rushed an enraged Frick, who chased him down the hallway to his office, where Carnegie barely managed to duck inside and slam the door behind him.

Whatever the precise choreography and its attendant imprecations, it was the last meeting between Andrew Carnegie and Henry Clay Frick.

◆　　　◆　　　◆

LATER THAT DAY, FRICK ENTERED THE OFFICES of his old associate John Walker, who had been a partner in the coke concern since the early days of the association between Frick and Carnegie. With Walker, Frick was uncharacteristically sheepish, allowing that he had lost his temper earlier that day. Walker thought for a moment, then replied, "Well, I always knew you had one to lose."

Their talk turned to the substance of Carnegie's visit and his threats to enforce the terms of the contract as well as the Iron Clad Agreement. Although Walker had come over from the Carnegie camp and was no fan of Frick's personal style, he agreed that Carnegie's threats were unjust in the extreme. That Walker had been an employee of Frick Coke for more than a decade, with a position of his own to protect, likely had some influence on his perspective.

Well aware that Carnegie would lose no time in moving forward, Frick and Walker quickly mapped out a strategy of their own. After a meeting with Frick's Pittsburgh attorney, D. T. Watson, the man who had drawn up the original Iron Clad Agreement, the two decided to contact Philadelphia attorney John A. Johnson, the most noted trial lawyer of his day. Frick assured Walker he would write Johnson that very afternoon, but Walker shook his head. Johnson outshone even Clarence Darrow; what if Carnegie should get to him first?

Frick nodded and picked up the telephone. It was fortunate that he did. The next day Carnegie showed up personally at Johnson's office, only to discover that the noted lawyer had already agreed to represent Frick.

Losing the race for Johnson must have galled Carnegie, but he would not let that deter him. On January 15, Francis Lovejoy appeared at Frick's office to hand over a petition signed by thirty-two of the thirty-six Carnegie Steel partners, requesting that Frick immediately relinquish his interest in the company at book value. A glum Lovejoy was one of the four partners who refused to be pressured by Carnegie into signing the petition; the others on Frick's side were Phipps, Henry Curry, and A. R. Whitney. While none of them counted Frick among their personal favorites, all agreed that Carnegie's aims were dishonorable.

As for the coke contract, Carnegie had called a meeting of the newly constituted board of Frick Coke for January 24, where a motion was quickly proposed and adopted: the new board agreed that the company would supply coke to Carnegie Steel at the price of $1.35 per ton for the next five years, retroactive to January 1, 1899. With current coke prices hovering around $3.50 a ton, the agreement would result in an annual loss to the coke company of approximately $4 million. The retroactive pricing alone would cost Frick Coke nearly $600,000 for shipments already delivered and billed.

Frick, meanwhile, had Phipps poring over the fine print of that storied Iron Clad Agreement. Since it was Phipps's brainchild in the first place, he was the logical person to discover its faults. And, soon enough, he found them.

Language in the agreement, originally drafted in 1887 and revised in 1892 and 1897, seemed to exclude certain partners from its terms. If a partner owned or had earned his shares outright, with no debt outstanding to the company, then he was exempt from the buyout clause, Phipps maintained. Phipps had also discovered that none of the partners had ever signed the 1892 version of the agreement, which might invalidate the document altogether from that date forward.

At a February board meeting, Frick lodged a formal protest, objecting that HCF Coke was being forced to sell its product for $1.35 a ton when the January market price had risen to $3.50. "These communications are simply a preliminary statement to an action at law," was board member A. M. Moreland's terse response. "It might as well come."

And come it did. On March 12, Frick filed suit, charging, among other things, that Carnegie had unjustly attempted to force him out of the company and acquire his holdings at a sum far below their value.

Most distressing to Carnegie was the fact that the details of the company's business affairs were laid out in the accompanying brief. If the suit actually went forward, the public would, for the first time, learn details of the immense profits being generated by Carnegie's enterprise.

Furthermore, Frick's attempt to force a revaluation of the company was bad enough, but if documents held by Frick were widely publicized—revealing that Carnegie had refused to renew the option for the Moore brothers' purchase unless the value of the property was raised to a more rightful (by Carnegie's own reckoning) $500 million—it would forever hamstring efforts to manipulate the value of his holdings and buy out troublesome partners for a song.

To Carnegie, that such information concerning the inner workings of the company should be made public was an affront, an embarrassment, and, most important, a disadvantage to doing business. Other prominent entrepreneurs wrote to urge him to find a way to put this airing of dirty laundry and privileged information to a speedy end.

From Washington, George Westinghouse sent a letter calling it "a calamity by reason of the fact that the private affairs of your company will undoubtedly be made public. . . . I may add that Mr. Frick has recently spoken to me in such terms that I feel there must be a way to adjust matters between you and him."

And, once again, Carnegie found himself under pressure from Republican Party leaders desperate to avoid another scandal that might sway the upcoming presidential election, as the Homestead Strike had done in 1892. William McKinley, who had been elected over William Jennings Bryan in 1896, was locked in another tight race with the Populist Party candidate for the 1900 election, and McKinley supporters were fearful that the feud between Carnegie and Frick would provide ammunition for Bryan's fervent attacks upon Big Business.

Ohio senator Mark Hanna, a wealthy ore and coal broker and shipper, urged Carnegie to settle with Frick out of court, immediately.

The "Great Egoist" Carnegie had dismissed similar pleas from party bosses eight years before, but this time he saw the writing on the wall. If he were to prove in court, for instance, that the value of Carnegie Steel was just a fraction of what Frick claimed, how on earth would he attract a buyer willing to pay what he privately knew the company was worth? On the other hand, Frick stood to lose, too. His suit demanded that, in the event that Carnegie was unwilling to value his interests fairly, the company was to be liquidated immediately and the interests of all partners settled by the proceeds. So he would be forcing a fire sale that might gain him little more than if he were forced out under the Iron Clad Agreement.

In the end, and for once, reason prevailed between the two men, and a Solomonic compromise was laid out: Carnegie Steel, to be valued at $250 million, and Henry Frick Coke, to be valued at $70 million, would be merged.

Carnegie swallowed his pride and agreed, with one stipulation. Neither he nor any of his loyal partners would attend the signing of the agreement in Atlantic City if Henry Clay Frick were allowed to be present. Frick did not attend, in fact. His interests were represented by Francis Lovejoy and Henry Phipps, who quickly dealt with the terms creating the new Carnegie Company.

As a result of the agreement, signed on March 19, 1900, Henry Clay Frick would remove himself from any role in the management of the new company. In return, he would receive about $15.5 million in stock and nearly $16 million in 5-percent first-mortgage bonds. It was a tidy sum compared to the $1.5 million pittance he would have received under the Iron Clad Agreement, and also a sight better than if the Moore deal had gone through. Incidentally, Frick also received some relief in the dispute over coke prices: the two would split the difference, with Carnegie paying HCF Coke half of its outstanding bill.

Perhaps it had cost him a job and the friendship of Andrew Carnegie. Then again, he had $31 million with which to console himself.

# MONEY, HAPPINESS

—▶◆◀—

I F THE SETTLEMENT OF 1900 MARKED the last time that the affairs of Henry Clay Frick and Andrew Carnegie would directly intersect, it was hardly the end of things between them. Though each had declared "divorce" from the other—forevermore—and though each would throw himself into the pursuit of interests that apparently diverged from the other's, it is clear now that much of what these two men undertook over the last nineteen years of their lives was profoundly influenced by the immensity of all that had passed between them since 1892.

In the aftermath of the settlement, Frick wrote to A. R. Whitney, one of the partners who stood by him, "I get what is due me. All well. I, of course, have not met this man Carnegie and never expect or want to."

Carnegie, who had received nearly $175 million as his share of the reorganized company, seemed pleased as well. He wrote Andrew Mellon that company profits for the month of March 1900 alone were more than $5 million. If the ratio of profits against capitalization were not what they were when the company was valued at $25 million, the prospect of a net of $40 million or more for the coming year was hardly "hay."

When a sniping cable arrived at Skibo that summer, saying, "You are being outgeneraled all along the line, and your management of the Company has already become the subject of jest," Carnegie dismissed it out of hand. After all, it had been signed by a disgruntled former employee, some forgotten fellow named Frick. As Carnegie blithely pointed out in a letter written to his cousin Dod, "Isn't it wonderful we are to have such a good year."

In truth, Carnegie was facing a serious challenge. Those combines created by the Moores and others that he had once sneered at—along with J. P. Morgan's Federal Steel, which he had lampooned as "the greatest concern the world ever saw for manufacturing stock certificates"—had introduced a new wrinkle into the competitive mix. Instead of being content to purchase from Carnegie the raw steel from which they made such finished products as wire and nails and tubes and tin plate, they had begun to produce steel billets themselves, pioneering the concept of vertical integration.

Carnegie had not been blind to such possibilities himself, and had authorized the purchase of those disputed lands along the Monongehela from Frick to build a tubing plant. But he faced opposition concerning these and other undertakings from partners who balked at the cost of retooling for the manufacture of additional finished products. Many of the senior partners were getting on; they wanted to increase dividends and enjoy the fruits of their investments, not tie up capital in projects that might not come to fruition until well after they were in the grave.

The emergence of these new vertical entities caused Carnegie and Schwab to reevaluate the situation. When American Steel and Wire, American Hoop, and National Tube threatened to cancel orders from Carnegie unless their terms were met, Schwab estimated that it would cost them about 40,000 tons of production. He suggested to Carnegie that they immediately invest $1.4 million to build plants that would produce their own steel rods, nails, and wire. Carnegie agreed. "Only one policy open," he wrote from Scotland, "start at once hoop, rod, wire, nail mills, no half way about . . . have no fear as to result, victory certain. Spend freely for finishing mills, railroads, boat lines. Continue to advise."

He was nearing the age of sixty-five, but Carnegie's competitive instincts were as keen as ever. When Schwab reported that his careful analysis convinced him that they could build a new steel tube-making plant on property the company owned at Conneaut, Ohio, on Lake Erie, and beat the price of J. P. Morgan's National Tube by ten dollars a ton, Carnegie didn't hesitate. Carnegie Steel would never kowtow to such craven manipulators as the Moore brothers and "Bet A Million" Gates. Instead they would compete head-to-head.

"Go ahead and build the plant," he told Schwab.

Another advantage to the plan was the fact that Carnegie Steel could use its own rail line to carry coke from Pittsburgh to Conneaut to fuel the furnaces, then use the same cars to return to Pittsburgh with Minnesota iron ore offloaded at the Conneaut docks. Thus they could transport the raw materials for virtually nothing.

The news was disheartening to the likes of J. P. Morgan, to say the least. Morgan understood the folly of a long-term battle with the Carnegie Company, a firm that controlled its own sources of raw materials, transport, and manufacture, and that was far more deeply capitalized than his or any other of the upstarts. They might stay in the game for a while, and they might put a dent in Carnegie's armor, but in the end, Carnegie would run them into the ground, every one.

In Morgan's mind there was only one course of action, and he did not hesitate. Key to his plan was Carnegie's alter ego, Charles Schwab.

On the night of December 12, 1900, Schwab attended a testimonial dinner in his honor, given by a group of bankers at New York's University Club. When it came time for Schwab to speak, he rose to deliver an oration that described an industrial future for steelmaking and fabrication the likes of which no one had ever heard. Listening raptly to this picture of the perfectly organized vertical institution, which would banish forever the need for wasteful competition and ensure monumental profits produced at prices that would bankrupt any foolhardy interlopers, was none other than J. P. Morgan, who had been seated at Schwab's right hand.

Following the address, Morgan leaned over to Schwab and suggested that the two of them had much to discuss. A delighted Schwab agreed. A few weeks later he returned to New York for a meeting with Morgan, Gates, and Morgan's partner, Robert Bacon.

It took the whole of the night, but in the end this group gave to Schwab's utopian concepts a habitation and a name. The United States Steel Corporation would be the embodiment of all that Schwab had envisioned. Only one question remained:

How much would it take to get Andrew Carnegie to sell?

◆　　◆　　◆

WITHIN A WEEK SCHWAB HAD RETURNED to New York, though his first visit was not to Carnegie, but to Carnegie's wife, Louise. He confirmed to her the rumors that had been swirling around the city since that clandestine meeting of steel's new supermen, and then sought Louise's advice about how best to approach her husband on the matter.

Louise Carnegie, who at the time was immersed in plans for building their grand new home at 91st Street and Fifth Avenue, expressed pleasure at the prospect of a sale and of her husband finally severing his ties with the all-consuming world of business. She suggested that Schwab arrange a golf date with Carnegie for the following day. Carnegie, who had taken up the game at the age of sixty-three, had become obsessed with it. He told Louise that virtually nothing else had such a therapeutic effect on his spirits.

Schwab arranged the game—at Westchester County's St. Andrew's Club—and amazingly enough, Carnegie found himself the winner. Over lunch, Schwab may not have admitted throwing the golf match, but he made a clean breast of his intentions. He was sitting across from Carnegie with what was essentially a blank check. What figure did Carnegie want him to insert?

Carnegie was hardly surprised by Schwab's recital, but he was thoughtful just the same. He would sleep on it, he said, and they would meet the following morning.

We cannot know what went through Carnegie's mind during those twenty-four hours, but it is easy enough to speculate. He was sixty-five, and yet a new father and husband to a young and vital wife. There were good years to be lived and a chance to step away from the strife that had consumed him—even at a distance—for a dozen years or more. Best of all was the prospect of stepping away on his own terms:

"Name your price, Andy. Just name your price." Schwab's words echoed in his mind.

And that was exactly what he did. When Schwab returned the next morning, Carnegie ushered him into his study, where they sat on either side of a handsome, burled desk. Carnegie produced a sheet of paper and moistened the tip of a pencil with his tongue.

Schwab watched, intrigued, as Carnegie quickly scrawled his notes. When he was finished, Carnegie handed the sheet over and waited as Schwab read what was written:

Capitalization of Carnegie Company:
$160,000,000 bonds to be exchanged
at par for bonds in new company                    $160,000,000

$160,000,000 stock to be exchanged
at rate of $1,000 share of stock
in Carnegie Company exchanged
for $1,500 share of stock in new
company                                            $240,000,000

Profit of past year and estimated
profit for coming year                             $80,000,000

Total price for Carnegie Company
and all its holdings                               $480,000,000

There was but one further stipulation: his own shares as well as those of his cousin George Lauder and his brother Tom's widow would have to be paid in the form of 5-percent bonds. Carnegie wanted no part of being a shareholder in the new company.

Schwab glanced at the document only briefly. Carnegie had named his price. The next step was to go to Morgan.

When Morgan examined this penciled document, he glanced casually up at Schwab and said, simply, "I accept this price." With that, one of the most storied deals in the history of American business had been done.

A few days later Morgan phoned Carnegie and invited him down to his Wall Street offices to shake hands on the agreement. Carnegie said he reckoned it no farther from Morgan's office to his home on West 51st Street than the other way around.

Morgan was not about to stand on ceremony. In short order he arrived at Carnegie's home, where the two met briefly to confirm the terms of the agreement. As he was leaving, Morgan took Carnegie's hand and said, "Mr. Carnegie, I want to congratulate you on being the richest man in the world."

Whether that was an overstatement is difficult to say. But Carnegie's share—about $225 million—did represent the largest liquid fortune in the world at the time. His bonds, along with Dod's and those of brother Tom's widow, Lucy, totaling nearly $300 million, were deposited directly into a specially built vault at the Hudson Trust Company of Hoboken.

To Dod he wrote, "All seems right about Steel matter—no hitch—so be it." A rather terse summary for the end of the most successful business career in history.

# 28

# IN THE WINGS

———▶◆◀———

CARNEGIE, COUSIN GEORGE LAUDER, and his sister-in-law were not the only ones to become rich from that momentous transaction. Henry Phipps saw his share in the new company suddenly transformed into $50 million. Told of the news on his sickbed during a bout of bronchitis, Phipps managed to respond, "Ain't Andy wonderful."

And another beneficiary was one Henry Clay Frick. His interest in the newly formed United States Steel Corporation was $61.4 million, a sizable stake even in a firm capitalized at $1.1 billion (the first ever to break the billion-dollar barrier).

If Carnegie relished the prospect of retirement, Frick evidently did not. While it would be taxing for a man of fifty-one to be the chief executive officer of a concern as vast as the new United States Steel, he made it known he would be willing to consider the possibility. Carnegie lobbied hard against that possibility, however, and it is likely that others among the old guard also let their feelings be known. In the end, Charles Schwab was elected president of the new company, though Frick was voted onto the board of directors.

The arrangement did not last long. Less than two years into his tenure, often at odds with the "outsiders" who had purchased the Carnegie Company, and piqued by Frick's continuing influence on the board, Schwab resigned, to be replaced by Elbert H. Gary, one of the firm's original architects. Gary remained at the helm of U.S. Steel for more than twenty-six years, until his death in 1927. And for more than fifteen of those years, he counted on the advice of his partner and senior board member, Henry Clay Frick.

Although Frick would remain active in the affairs of U.S. Steel until nearly his dying day, his attitudes and assumptions began to change, if for no other reason than a need to accommodate himself to an entirely new group of associates who owed him little. Interviewed by a reporter for the *New York World* in 1905, Frick made what for him was a momentous concession. No longer could any company find its way by running roughshod over its competition, Frick said. "Gradually the whole fabric of American industry, commerce, and finance has grown into intersupporting relationships, the result of a sensible understanding of the present and the future."

It is debatable whether the man who had once thrown a striking miner into a creek had altogether lost the desire to grind the competition into dust. But he had at least learned to pay lip service to the concept of mutual dependency.

THERE IS LITTLE TO INDICATE whether Frick's softened stance on competition extended to labor relations, for his days in active management were well behind him. In addition to his membership on the board of U.S. Steel, Frick ventured into banking, helping to found the Union Trust Company along with his old friend, Andrew Mellon, and joining the board of the Mellon National Bank when it was incorporated in 1902. In subsequent years he would become a board member of several other banking and insurance companies and serve as the secretary-treasurer of the Diamond Light and Power Company.

His longtime interest in rail led him to sizable investment in and board membership on the Reading Railroad, the Chicago and North-western, the Union Pacific, the Atchison, Topeka and Santa Fe, the Baltimore & Ohio, and the Norfolk & Western. With the acquisition of 168,000 shares of Pennsylvania Railroad stock, he ascended in 1906 to the directorate of Carnegie's old employer and his former freight-rate nemesis. By that time Frick had become the largest individual owner of railway stock in the United States, a distinction that helped lead to the passage of the Clayton Act of 1914, which put an end to interlocked railroad boards and the rate- and price-fixing activities that such corporate incest encouraged.

Frick also became more active in politics, and backed former Carnegie Steel legal adviser Philander C. Knox as attorney general during William McKinley's second term. In 1904 Knox attempted to return the favor by offering to have Frick appointed as Pennsylvania senator to replace Matthew Quay. But Frick declined that post and others, among them offers to become secretary of the treasury under both McKinley and Theodore Roosevelt.

Roosevelt also attempted to entice Frick to chair the committee on the feasibility of the Panama Canal, but once again Frick declined. He was by no means averse to wielding political influence or seeking its favors, but devoting his own time to the duties of a bureaucrat seemed out of the question.

One of Frick's principal occupations during the years following the sale of the Carnegie Company to Morgan was the acquisition of real estate in and around Pittsburgh, which he continued assiduously until 1904, by which time he had become the largest single owner of property in the city. Real-estate speculation, he knew, was a profitable undertaking, but one of his acquisitions suggests that there were other motivations as well.

In 1900, despite the laments of citizens and editorial writers, the attractive St. Peter's Episcopal Church at the corner of Grant and Diamond Streets in downtown Pittsburgh had been sold to developers. When Frick learned that the property was available, he bought it for

$180,000 and commissioned the noted Chicago architect Daniel Burnham, who had led the architectural design of the Chicago World's Fair and designed Washington, D.C.'s Union Station, to draw up plans for the Frick Building. Burnham, a Beaux Arts devotee, created a twenty-story office tower of white granite-encased steel, in the classical Greek style, with a soaring lobby and stained-glass windows by La Farge.

The building, named a national historic landmark in 1978, might have been an unalloyed source of pride for the city were it not for a curious coincidence: it was built immediately east of the fifteen-story (and far more modest) Carnegie Building. As one newsman aptly (if somewhat inaccurately) editorialized, "To build a 14 storey [sic] building and then to have your former chum build a 22 storey building to shut out its light is not much different from the temper displayed when one boy, building a sand mound, finds that his former chum is undermining it to build another beside it."

Frick would have probably denied the charge, but E. R. Graham, a partner in the firm of Burnham and Company who knew both Carnegie and Frick well, told *Wall Street Journal* editor Clarence Barron that, in his opinion, Frick had "poisoned himself with hatred for Carnegie." And indeed, in the aftermath of Carnegie's testimony before the 1912 Stanley commission, which sought to dissolve U.S. Steel, Frick wrote his former partner a letter suggesting that little had changed since the day he had gone after Carnegie with fists flying.

"The result [of the aborted Moore brothers sale and matters before the committee] is that there is now in the public archives a permanent record of charges against Messrs. Frick and Phipps of untruthfulness, chicanery, dishonesty, infidelity to associates, avarice and double-dealing; and these perjured records are backed by the name of a man whose public gifts may hereafter erroneously be supposed to represent his private virtues." Twelve years after the incidents, Frick was still thundering his outrage. "This is an intolerable condition and must be relieved," he concluded.

It was at about the same time that James Bridge, who had collaborated with both men on matters literary, took it upon himself to try to rectify a situation in which (as he wrote to a mutual friend vacationing in Egypt with Frick) two of the most prominent figures in the history of American industry were "now linked only in antagonistic memory."

Upon Frick's return from Egypt, Bridge had the friend arrange a meeting in Frick's office; he was sure that, after all these years, they could find a way to bring reason to bear. The moment that Frick discovered the true purpose of Bridge's visit, the former King of Coke blew up. Bridge hurried from the meeting, his ears still ringing from Frick's outburst, which he described as an out-and-out "denunciation of the man with whom he shared so much of success and fortune. I had never suspected such . . . in this usually quiet and undemonstrative man."

Others might not have agreed with Bridge's characterization of Frick as "usually quiet and undemonstrative." But no one could dispute that this undying bitterness directed at Carnegie pervaded every aspect of Frick's existence, extending to matters far beyond the business arena.

◆　　◆　　◆

DESPITE HIS CONTINUED INVOLVEMENT WITH U.S. Steel, Frick realized, along with many prominent businessmen of the day, that a seriously expansive place in commerce required a base of operations in New York, at least for a significant part of the year.

From 1902 until 1905, then, Frick rented an apartment suite in a Manhattan hotel. In 1905 he took the rather momentous step of leasing the fabulous Vanderbilt "chateau" at 52nd Street and Fifth Avenue. Though the architect and critic Louis Sullivan had once dismissed the elaborate fifteenth-century, French-styled palace as "a characteristically New York absurdity," it must have given Frick a jolt of pride to inhabit the grandiose home where he had first been introduced to New York "society" during a trip with Andrew Mellon nearly twenty-five years earlier.

In 1880, during a stopover on their way to Europe, the two young men had gawked from the sidewalk at the Vanderbilt compound. Frick, still a bachelor, mused that the cost of maintaining such a place—never mind buying it—would be as much as $300,000 a year. Mellon said that sounded about right. At 6-percent interest, it would take about $5 million in the bank, Frick continued. Once again, Mellon nodded. "That is all I shall ever want," Frick replied, and they walked on.

By 1905, Frick had acquired his five million and twenty times more. That a lowly store clerk could have somehow come to have such a fortune and inhabit the New York mansion of William Henry Vanderbilt—it must have seemed the very incarnation of all those Horatio Alger–like dreams. At any rate, Frick and Adelaide would make this monument their home until 1914, when he was ready to make his final move.

This time Frick would inhabit a palace of his own making on Millionaires' Row, where he intended to move the bulk of his ever-growing art collection—even then said to be worth as much as $50 million—from the smoky, acid-laden air of Pittsburgh to quarters more properly suited to its display. With this in mind, he had in 1906 acquired the much-admired Lenox Library, a private facility that occupied most of a city block at Fifth Avenue and 70th Street. Frick commissioned first Daniel Burnham, then the firm of Carrère and Hastings (responsible for the New York Public Library), to design a structure on the library site that could not only serve as a comfortable home for Adelaide and himself, but that could be readily converted, upon their deaths, into a full-fledged museum.

Once again, though, what might have been an undertaking of philanthropic—even visionary—character took on unfortunate overtones. Mindful of an outcry over the Lenox Library's demolition, Frick offered to pay for its reconstruction at any suitable site in the city. But when no such site was offered, Frick decided that it was his property, in fact, and in 1911 he ordered the library demolished and his own sixty-room palace erected in its place.

Even that action—the replacement of a private library with an even lovelier gallery-to-be, housing one of the world's great private collections of art—could have been defended were it not for comments that Frick made during construction. Carnegie's mansion up the street had cost only $1 million, Frick was quick to say. His home would set him back much more than that, and part of the reason was simple: Frick had never found the humor in Carnegie's clever remarks concerning the source of funds for the purchase and renovation of Skibo, a bon mot Carnegie recycled with visitors to his impressive New York home—"just a little gift from Mr. Frick . . ." "I'm going to make Carnegie's place look like a miner's shack," Frick famously told friends, and he spent as much as $5.4 million attempting to do just that.

Construction at One East Seventieth Street began in early 1913 and continued for more than a year and a half, the pace intensifying in early 1914, when George Vanderbilt, Frick's landlord, died, and heirs Cornelius and Grace Vanderbilt announced plans to move into their newly inherited property.

Frick had been a taskmaster with architect Thomas Hastings from the beginning. As Hastings told James Bridge, a meeting with Frick never failed to exhaust him of "all nervous energy," and as the October 1, 1914, deadline for Frick's move neared, Frick became even more contentious.

Frick had hired two different interior designers to work on the home that he privately confided would be his "monument." The first was Britain's Sir Charles Allom, who had recently redone Buckingham Palace and had worked in the United States for the likes of William Randolph Hearst. While Allom had responsibility for all the rooms on the first floor, along with the breakfast room and Frick's sitting room on the second, Frick hired Elsie de Wolfe, a former actress who had proclaimed herself America's first professional interior decorator, to be in charge of most of the rest.

While he seemed happy with the work of all three, Frick could be maddening. To Allom, Frick wrote, "From what I see Mr. Hastings is favoring too much carving. Please impress upon him my earnest desire to avoid anything elaborate."

With De Wolfe, the issue was often money. While he was happy with most of her choices, he complained that she was over budget in her choice of furnishings: "I should also think you might secure better prices. Take your time—you know time is money!" Frick told her. A better capacity to bargain, he wrote, was all she lacked "to make you perfect."

In September of 1914, Frick was stricken with another bout of rheumatism, which confined him to his bed. From that vantage point, Frick fired off a series of angry notes to his architects and decorators. "You are very much behind on all contracts with me," he wrote Allom. "What are you going to do about it?"

When Allom replied that England was now engaged in a war that had diverted any number of craftsmen and their sources of supplies, Frick was scarcely mollified. "Simply outrageous unbusinesslike your dilatory manner completing contracts with me," he shot back. "War excuse absurd."

Finally, however, the bulk of the work was completed. On December 16, despite the absence of locks on a number of doors and other minor oversights that Frick found deplorable, he and Adelaide moved into their new home—one that included a main gallery nearly one hundred feet long and thirty-five feet wide, with twenty-six-foot-high ceilings. In typical fashion, Frick wrote to Hastings to let him know that, while the house had ended up costing far more than anticipated, "All the same we are enjoying it, and there are many features for which we are indebted to you."

Not so bad, if only Frick had stopped there. Alas, he went on, "I think it is a great monument to you, but it is only because I restrained you from excess ornamentation."

While Frick was on shaky ground in his claim to have mentored one of the world's great architects, there is little doubt he understood which works of art would suit his home-cum-gallery. As Charles Schwab put it, "Frick knew art."

Much of his appreciation came from travels through Europe, where it was said that he would often knock on the doors of prestigious estates to ask if the owners would like to sell some of their paintings. An equal amount came via his association with art dealers of the highest caliber, including Joseph Duveen, whose work with King George V at Buckingham Palace would lead to a knighthood, and Roland Knoedler. Even though it meant that his newly constructed drawing room would have to be remodeled to accommodate them, in 1915 Frick paid Duveen $1.25 million to acquire the series of huge, ten-by-seven-foot Fragonard oils collectively titled *The Progress of Love* from the estate of J. P. Morgan.

In addition to the Fragonards, Frick's collection included works by Rubens, Raphael, Bellini, Corot, Manet, Verrocchio, Turner, Constable, Piero della Francesca, Degas, Van Eyck, Goya, Gainsborough, Millet, El Greco, Hals, Hogarth, Van Dyck, Vermeer, Titian, Murillo, Rembrandt, Monet, Renoir, Rousseau, Whistler, Sir Joshua Reynolds, and many, many more. In June of 1915, Frick finally drew up his will, formalizing his intention to have his home and art collection opened to the public following the death of his wife, Adelaide. He added an endowment of $15 million for its maintenance and continued acquisitions.

If the name Carnegie is commonly associated with libraries, the name Frick has an analogous association with art, as in "The Frick" (which is how his art collection and museum are commonly known). Always a reader and a proponent of education as a means of self-betterment, Carnegie's prodigious endowment of libraries seems a natural choice. But why did Frick go to such lengths to align himself with art?

Certainly, Frick had seen other men of means point with pride to their fine-art holdings, and understood that an appreciation of such work was the mark, if not the obligation, of the cultured soul. But the

degree to which Frick devoted himself to the enterprise went far beyond mere obligation or ostentation.

Martha Sanger proposes that many of Frick's acquisitions were
prompted by a deep-seated urge to find earthly objects that would, in
their beauty and inspirational nature, compensate for the loss of his
two beloved children. But the truth is that Frick ("a little too enthusiastic about pictures" from his first days in coke) had demonstrated an
interest in art long before either of his children were born.

Another theory is that Frick experienced his vast and impressive
collection as a kind of microcosm of the world—a world, moreover,
that was firmly under his control.

Whatever the reason, after Adelaide's death in 1931 there began
a four-year process of renovation on One East 70th Street, during
which the furnishings, paintings, and various *objets* were wrapped
and stored in a sealed vault, while architect John Russell Pope converted the home into a museum. In 1935, at the height of the Great
Depression, the Frick Collection was opened to an appreciative public and has remained so since, its creator's initial endowment having
grown to upward of $300 million and its holdings having increased
by more than a third.

Collecting art was one of the few endeavors in Frick's later life
that seemed entirely unconnected to his old nemesis, Carnegie. Although Carnegie possessed no small amount of art, he had never been
especially passionate about acquiring it, and Frick had never been
heard to brag of putting Carnegie to shame in this regard. (Ironically,
Carnegie's 91st Street mansion has become a museum as well, housing the Smithsonian Institution's Cooper Hewitt National Design
Museum, a transformation that took place in 1976, long after its former inhabitant had anything to say about it.)

Nor did Carnegie seem consumed by thoughts of Frick. If he
rankled at Frick's building of a Pittsburgh office tower to dwarf his
own and cast it in eternal gloom, he made no public comment. And
he had no retort to Frick's boast that One East 70th Street would

make the Carnegie mansion look like a hovel. (He did admit to friends that Charles Schwab's new "chateau" at 72nd Street and Riverside Drive—four stories, ninety bedrooms, a sixty-foot pool, a bowling alley, and an on-site power plant—put his own home to shame: "Mine is a cottage by comparison," Carnegie was reported to have said.)

And though Frick's continued role in the affairs of the mighty corporation that had once been *his* must have rankled Carnegie, he did his best to ignore past slights. By all appearances, the principal occupation of "the richest man in the world" from the moment of his retirement was giving all his money away.

While he had long been building libraries around the nation and the world, and had, as early as 1892, provided $2 million to build Carnegie Hall (originally named the New York City Music Hall), the "wee Andra" now threw himself into philanthropic activity with a zeal that had never before been witnessed among mighty American industrialists. Although entire volumes have been written on Carnegie's philanthropy and on individual Carnegie foundations, a thumbnail overview might convey just how much $327 million can accomplish:

The endowment of nearly three thousand public library buildings around the world accounted for some $60 million of his total giving. While some communities were put off by Carnegie's failure to provide stipends for books, and others were hard pressed to come up with funds to maintain the facilities, few acts of philanthropy have enjoyed such universal, enduring recognition; nearly a thousand of the buildings are still in use as libraries to this day, more than thirty in the boroughs of New York City alone.

Some cities, particularly those seen as strongholds of labor, were not pleased at the prospect of a Carnegie library, though there is no truth to the rumor that Carnegie insisted on a consistency of design or that his name adorn the buildings. The objections ran deeper than that.

Carnegie might have explained that he was only trying to live up to one of his more famous dicta: "The man who dies rich, dies disgraced." But as one spokesman put it when the city of Detroit turned down the offer of a library in 1902, "Carnegie ought to have distributed his money among his employees while he was making it." And Detroit was not the only community to remember Homestead, where workers had grumbled, "What good is a book to a man who works twelve hours a day?"

Even more ubiquitous than his libraries were the organs he had given to churches. This was a program that had begun almost by accident, after Carnegie gave an organ to a church in Allegheny City, his first American home. Before it was over, Carnegie, an agnostic who said he continued the practice because it "lessened the pain of the sermons," had given away nearly eight thousand organs, at a cost of over $6 million.

Though Carnegie was highly sought after as a donor by institutions of higher learning, he resisted most such requests, quite possibly because he had never attended one himself. In 1902, he did donate $32 million to endow the Carnegie Institution of Washington, a still-extant think tank for advanced research in the sciences. At about the same time, he established the Carnegie Trust for the Universities of Scotland with a gift of $10 million, something of a slap at the superior attitude manifested by their cousin institutions at Oxford and Cambridge.

In 1895, Carnegie dedicated the Carnegie Library of Pittsburgh, an imposing, 300-foot-long structure made possible by a grant of $1 million. By the turn of the twentieth century, the library had become the centerpiece of the still-standing Carnegie Institute, a monument to culture that included art and science museums and a concert hall. Ultimately, Carnegie's original $1 million investment would grow to more than $25 million.

At a Pittsburgh dinner in late 1900, Carnegie announced that he was offering the city a $1 million endowment to build a technical school as an adjunct to the Institute. He would later add another

$6.5 million. First called the Carnegie Technical Schools, then the Carnegie Institute of Technology, it was merged in 1967 with the Mellon Institute of Industrial Research (founded by Andrew Mellon in 1913) and is known today as Carnegie Mellon University. (Noting that all the broad hallways in Carnegie Mellon's original "old main" slope steeply from one end to another gives modern-day visitors to the campus first-hand exposure to Carnegie's ever pragmatic mindset. Just in case the college notion didn't work out, it is said, Carnegie had the building designed for quick conversion to a foundry where hand cars could zip easily down the stations of a production line.)

Another major gift to education came in 1905, when Carnegie, prompted by a visit to Skibo from Henry Pritchett, the president of MIT, gave $15 million to create the Carnegie Foundation for the Advancement of Teaching. The foundation went on to found such programs as the Teachers Insurance and Annuity Association and the Educational Testing Service. It still operates worldwide.

In 1911, somewhat overwhelmed by the task of giving away money, he made his single greatest gift, endowing the Carnegie Corporation of New York, formed for "the advancement and diffusion of knowledge," with $125 million. The corporation was to oversee many of the projects already undertaken, as well as to create a board of trustees that would assume the burden of determining worthy recipients for the remainder of Carnegie's fortune, which totaled about $180 million. Today the Carnegie Corporation's endowment is valued at about $1.8 billion and continues its work in teacher education, urban school development, the improvement of the economy, and increased participation of the citizenry in the political process.

Carnegie's gifts supported a wide range of projects, many still in operation, including the Carnegie Hero Fund ($5 million), designed in 1904 to recognize extraordinary acts of peacetime bravery and compensate those injured while performing those acts of heroism. While such creations as the Hero Fund continue to affect the lives of citizens worldwide (the fund made a significant number of awards in

the wake of the September 11 tragedy), some of Carnegie's other undertakings were less well conceived.

In 1906 he came up with the notion of a Simplified Spelling
Board, charged with promulgating the use of a phonetic version of
English, including such variants as *thru, tho, prolog,* and *dropt.*
Though the project was widely ridiculed—the *New York Times* suggested that "the Bored of Speling" begin the project by revising the
spellings of all members' names, starting with "Androo Karnege"—
Carnegie stuck with it doggedly for nearly ten years, until one day in
1915, when he wrote that he had finally "had enuf." He had better
uses for $25,000 a year, he declared, casting much of the blame for
the project's failure on an ineffectual board of trustees. "A more use-
less body of men never came into association," he wrote to the publisher Henry Holt.

In all his record of giving, however, nothing came to engage
Carnegie more deeply than his quest to put an end to war between
nations. Though it may be commonplace today for a schoolchild to
begin an essay positing a heartfelt desire "to achieve world peace,"
for Carnegie, it was no mere wish upon a star.

Distressed by U.S. actions in the Spanish-American War and the
deaths of some 200,000 Filipinos during the ensuing clash, and dismayed by the comportment of the British during the Boer War and
the subsequent uprising in Somalia, Carnegie delivered a blistering
speech early in the century at New York's Metropolitan Club, where
he denounced war as "the foulest blot upon humanity today." He
questioned just how far civilization could be said to have progressed,
"as long as we can find no better substitute for the settling of international disputes than the brutal murder of one another."

One of the immediate results was the endowment of an international law library and center for the arbitration of disputes between
nations at The Hague, site of an 1899 conference on world peace.
Though he was at first hesitant about usurping the business of nations, Carnegie ultimately gave $1.5 million for the construction of

the International Peace Palace and the establishment of the Permanent Court of Arbitration.

In 1910, heartened by President Taft's resolve to ensure his own legacy as a peacemaker among nations, and disturbed by growing tensions in Europe, Carnegie approached Taft with the idea of endowing a private organization to support the president's agenda. After consulting with Taft and his secretary of state (and former Carnegie Company attorney), Philander C. Knox, Carnegie made his proposal. In return for Taft's efforts to secure a network of peace treaties between the United States and other major powers, Carnegie would contribute $10 million to endow the Carnegie Endowment for International Peace, "to promote a thorough and scientific investigation and study of the causes of war and of the practical methods to prevent and avoid it."

While Taft did succeed in reaching agreement with Britain and France, various political blunders resulted in the failure to have those agreements ratified by the U.S. Senate. It was a bitter blow to Carnegie, and the outbreak of hostilities in Europe affected him even more deeply. Informed by Louise in August 1914 of Britain's declaration of war on Germany, Carnegie collapsed into a chair. "All my aircastles have fallen about me like a house of cards," he muttered, presaging an emotional decline that would continue to the end of his days.

Following the disclosure that Germany had proposed an alliance with Mexico, promising the return of Texas, New Mexico, and Arizona in exchange for a broadening of the war against the United States, then-President Woodrow Wilson led the United States to join the war on April 6, 1917. Though he deplored the action, Carnegie had come to believe that only such a proclamation by the United States would persuade the Germans to negotiate a peace. Carnegie cabled Wilson to congratulate him on the decision.

Still, America's joining of the fray affected Carnegie profoundly, and this time the effects were physical as well as emotional. He suffered a severe attack of influenza that confined him to his bed for several days and weakened him so greatly that nurses would care for him in his New York home from that point forward.

When a starving Russian populace revolted and forced out Czar Nicholas, and the Bolshevik leaders Lenin and Trotsky agreed to terms with the Germans in March of 1918, Carnegie's hopes dimmed for a speedy resolution to the war. The development might have spelled disaster altogether but for the arrival of American soldiers to reinforce the Western Front. By early November the German lines had been overrun by American and British forces, and Kaiser Wilhelm had fled to the Netherlands. On November 11, the war officially ended.

The end of "the war to end all wars" renewed Carnegie's sense of hope, for he saw in the aftermath the possibility of effecting treaties among nations that had been derailed just a few years before. During a January 1918 speech to Congress, Wilson had enumerated his famous "Fourteen Points," in which he outlined the essential aspects of a postwar existence. The final point called for "a general association of nations" to be fashioned for the purposes of "affording mutual guarantees of political independence and territorial integrity to great and small states alike."

Wilson was actually able to include in the Treaty of Versailles, signed on June 28, 1919, a provision ensuring Germany's participation in this "League of Nations." At last, it seemed that a semblance of Carnegie's dream was about to come true.

Ironically, Wilson's efforts would only set the stage for the final collision of Andrew Carnegie and Henry Clay Frick, possessors of the two strongest wills in American industry.

◆　◆　◆

THERE HAD ALWAYS BEEN GREAT RESISTANCE in the United States to the notion of a League of Nations. Some of it was motivated by general opposition to suspicious-sounding mutual defense agreements, as well as to the concept of America forming alliances with weaker partners. Let other nations fend for themselves, went such thinking. Still other opponents to the League were eager to attack Wilson for reasons of political partisanship.

Chief among Wilson's foes was Massachusetts senator Henry Cabot Lodge, a staunch "big-stick" Republican in the mold of Teddy Roosevelt, and chairman of the powerful Senate Foreign Relations Committee. Lodge saw no reason to extend the resources of the United States to lesser nations, and the idea that the country would be on remotely equal footing with the likes of Germany was appalling to him and fellow conservatives, who had dubbed themselves "the Irreconcilables." Lodge vowed to fight Wilson to the end, and predicted that the Treaty of Versailles would never achieve the necessary two-thirds vote of the Senate for ratification.

Initially, Wilson and his supporters, including a fair number of Republicans led by former President Taft, seemed to have the better of it. But the longer the fight stretched out, the more chances opponents had to sway public opinion.

One of the Irreconcilables was General Leonard Wood, an associate of Theodore Roosevelt and a potential Republican candidate for the presidency in 1920. Wood was an arch-conservative who was convinced that the Bolsheviks' next target was the United States, a prospect that in his eyes required an immediate military buildup and a concerted rooting out of the "Reds" in America's midst. His forceful views on the rights of industrialists to protect their property from Bolshevik-influenced strikers had of course endeared the general to Henry Frick, still a powerful member of the board of United States Steel. So, on an evening in May 1919, Frick agreed to host a dinner at his New York home on behalf of the aspiring candidate Wood.

Previously, Frick had had little to say about the proposed League of Nations, but during the dinner he became intrigued by the general's fervent denunciation of the prospect. Biographer Harvey writes that Frick approached General Wood with a summation of ideas that he had gleaned during dinner:

"As I understand it, then, the proposition is to pledge the United States, now the richest and most powerful nation in the world, to pool its resources with other countries, which are largely its debtors, and to agree in advance to abide by the policies and practices adopted by a majority or two-thirds of its associates; that is, to surrender its right of independence of action upon any specific question whenever such a question may arise."

Wood nodded, assuring Frick that he had pretty much hit the nail on the head.

"Well, I am opposed to that," Frick countered, not surprisingly. "Of course I am. I don't see how any experienced businessman could fail to be. Why, it seems to me a crazy thing to do."

He agreed to join the Irreconcilable cause on the spot, and soon helped to secure the support of Andrew Mellon. Together they raised considerable monies to support a massive public awareness campaign against the League of Nations, one meant both to defeat the proposal and to ruin its chief proponent, Woodrow Wilson.

◆　　◆　　◆

EVEN TO THE END, THEN, the two titans remained locked in combat.

Though confined to a sickbed and apparently willing to let bygones be bygones when it came to the business battles of the past, the eighty-four-year-old Carnegie could not shake his dream of a world without war.

Frick would have none of it. Though he would turn seventy in a few short months, he was still aghast at the notion of aligning oneself with the weaker or less fortunate, and bent on forging alliances with like-minded men of fiber. (Later in 1919, General Wood would lead a military contingent against striking steelworkers in Gary, Indiana.) Frick remained the living exemplar of the credo that had made him who and what he was: one of the fittest, a survivor.

There would be no caving in for Frick, not to weak sister nations, and not to sniveling entreaties from a former business partner whose storied acts of philanthropy amounted in his eyes to a bald-faced attempt to buy one's way into heaven. Because Carnegie's autobiography would not be published until 1920, Frick could not have known of his former partner's summary reflection on the lessons of Homestead: "Nothing I have ever had to meet in all my life . . . wounded me so deeply. No pangs remain of any wound . . . save that of Homestead."

Had Frick read the passage, he would have scoffed at Carnegie's hypocrisy. He might also have pointed to Carnegie's subsequent lines, which put his claim of eternal suffering into perspective:

"It was so unnecessary. The men were outrageously wrong. The strikers, with the new machinery, would have made . . . thirty percent more than they were. . . . While in Scotland I received the following cable from the officers of the union of our workmen: 'Kind master, tell us what you wish us to do and we shall do it for you.' . . . [M]ost touching, but, alas, too late. The mischief was done, the works were in the hands of the Governor; it was too late."

In context, then, this reflection on an incident that had supposedly wounded Carnegie deeply comes off as a complaint rather than a confession. If he had only been in Pittsburgh to oversee the situation, Carnegie would have his audience believe, the entire tragedy might have been averted!

Given all that he had seen in his long association with Carnegie, it is little wonder that Frick reacted as he did when he read the letter handed to him by James Bridge on that spring day in 1919.

No surprise, really, that he wadded up Carnegie's plea for peace. They'd have an eternity to go over all that they had done, and there would a well-lit place to hold the discussion. One wag later observed that the closest Frick ever came to a blast furnace was on the day he died.

◆    ◆    ◆

CARNEGIE WAS DISHEARTENED BY FRICK'S REBUFF, of course, and was made even more dour by the prospects for U.S. ratification of the Treaty of Versailles. It had become increasingly clear that Lodge and the rest of the Irreconcilables would have their way. There might be peace in Europe, but there would be none between Carnegie and Frick, and there would be no League of Nations.

If Carnegie had other reasons to keep up the fight, they did not endure. He died on August 11, 1919, at Shadowbrook, a fifty-four-room estate in the Berkshire Mountains of Massachusetts, the second-largest private home in the United States (after the Vanderbilts' Biltmore in North Carolina), a place that Louise had purchased in 1916 for its many similarities to Carnegie's beloved Scotland retreat.

Louise describes Carnegie's passing in a simple but poignant entry in her diary: "I was called at 6 AM, and remained with my darling husband, giving him oxygen until he gradually fell asleep, at 7:14. I am left alone."

◆　　◆　　◆

NOR WOULD FRICK LONG SURVIVE HIM. On election day of 1919, Tuesday, November 4, already suffering from a cold he had caught while golfing, he was diagnosed with ptomaine poisoning attributed to a lobster he'd enjoyed at a celebratory lunch with one of the Irreconcilable leaders, James A. Reed. The cold, combined with the food poisoning, escalated into an inflammatory rheumatism, which put him in bed for more than two weeks. Typically undaunted, he had the November 7 board meeting of U.S. Steel moved to his home.

On November 19 he finally felt strong enough to rise from his bed and make his way downstairs at One East 70th Street for one of his "little visits" with his beloved pictures. That communion seemed to revive him, and soon afterward he insisted on being driven out to Long Island, where one of his surviving sons, Childs, lived with his family.

The excursion was ill-conceived, and Frick was soon confined to his chambers once again. On December 1, James Bridge found Frick revived a bit, sitting in his bed, surrounded by newspapers, eager to hear who Bridge felt was going to win next year's presidential election. Bridge refrained from asking whether Frick had read accounts of the recent memorial service held in Pittsburgh on what would have been Andrew Carnegie's eighty-fourth birthday, but he was heartened by Frick's improved appearance.

On the following morning, December 2, Frick awoke and asked his butler to bring him a glass of water. He drank it down and then announced, "I think I will go to sleep."

With that, he closed his eyes and, moments later, died. Though some accounts attributed his death to ptomaine, his doctor's statement set the record straight. Frick's heart, weakened by recurring bouts of inflammatory rheumatism, had simply given out. He was three weeks shy of his seventieth birthday.

# 29

# EARTHLY GOODS

———▶◆◀———

**N**O NOVELIST COULD HAVE CHOREOGRAPHED it more neatly. In the end, partners turned nemeses Andrew Carnegie and Henry Clay Frick, born fourteen years apart, died within mere weeks of each other. Who of any imagination wouldn't wonder whether Frick had taken up Carnegie on his offer of a meeting after all?

There were holdings to be disposed of in the immediate wake of each man's passing. Though the tally of Carnegie's giving had risen above $350 million by the time of his death, more than $25 million of that damnably sticky money remained. Having long ago provided amply for his wife and daughter, Carnegie made no further bequest to either in his will. Rather, that instrument sent the bulk of what he had left, $20 million, to the Carnegie Corporation, and another $4 million to a special fund that would provide annual pensions of $5,000 to $10,000 for a diverse group of individuals, including relatives, old friends from Dunfermline, British prime minister David Lloyd George, former president Taft, and the widows of Theodore Roosevelt and Grover Cleveland, there being no pension funds for such notable public servants at the time. Another $1 million was divided among the Hampton Institute, the University of Pittsburgh, the Stevens Institute, the Cooper Union, and the St. Andrews Society.

Of Frick's $145 million estate, $117 million was given to various public entities. He left his collection of art, valued at $50 million, to the city of New York, along with a $15 million endowment for its maintenance. As mentioned earlier, his home on Fifth Avenue would go to the city following the death of his wife, Adelaide, when funds from the endowment would provide for its conversion into a public museum.

He also left gifts of $15 million to Princeton University, where his son Childs was an alumnus, $5 million to Harvard, $5 million to MIT, and another $5 million to the Educational Commission of Pittsburgh, which he had established in 1909 to assist in the training of public-school teachers.

To the city of Pittsburgh he also left a 150-acre parcel of land, along with a $2 million endowment to establish what is now the sprawling Frick Nature Preserve. Another $7 million went to various institutions and charities in the Pittsburgh area, including $1.5 million to Mercy Hospital, where he had finally consented to receive medical treatment following Alexander Berkman's attempt on his life.

To his daughter, Helen, then thirty-one, he left $6.5 million for her to disperse among whatever charities she saw fit. The $25 million that remained was divided among his wife, his daughter, his son Childs and grandson Henry Clay II, three other grandchildren, and various other relatives and associates.

ALTHOUGH NO VANDERBILT- OR ROCKEFELLER-LIKE dynasty would follow from either Frick or Carnegie, their descendants were many and did not lack entirely for accomplishment. Carnegie's daughter, Margaret, married and had four children; by the 1990s, a great-granddaughter, Margaret Carnegie Miller Thompson, had made her way back to the country of her forefather's youth. She lived not far from Skibo Castle and was willing to make an appearance now and then for visitors at her great-grandfather's former manor, converted to an exclusive private club and hostelry. (Pop star Madonna married Guy Ritchie there in 2000—rooms are $2,000 and up.)

There was, in fact, an Andrew Carnegie II, though he was actually the son of Carnegie's brother, Tom. Another of Tom Carnegie's nine children, daughter Nancy, married a grand nephew of John D. Rockefeller Sr.—her first son was named Andrew Carnegie Rockefeller, a name to live up to if there ever was one.

The Carnegie descendant who achieved perhaps the greatest notoriety, however, was in fact no descendant at all. A small-time criminal and confidence woman named Elizabeth Bigley, born to Canadian parents on October 10, 1857, had, after a checkered career that included stints in fortune-telling and forgery, moved to New York City in the latter years of the nineteenth century. Living under an assumed name, she met and married a physician named Chadwick. In short order, "Cassie Chadwick" divulged a dark secret to the wives of her new husband's acquaintances: they were to tell no one, but she was Andrew Carnegie's illegitimate daughter.

The "secret" was dutifully circulated among New York City's elite, many of whom delighted in such "proof" that the sanctimonious Carnegie was no saint. At the same time, the rumors proved to be no obstacle to the new Mrs. Chadwick, who, over the ensuing eight years, secured more than $20 million in credit from various lending institutions, sometimes forging Carnegie's name as co-signer. She was eventually caught in 1906 and was sent to prison, where she died the following year.

Frick's son, Childs, took advantage of his position to further an interest in paleontology; if he remained an amateur, he was an avid one, donating some 250,000 specimens to the American Museum of Natural History when he died in 1964. Henry Clay Frick II, Frick's grandson, lived a productive if quiet life as a physician and surgeon. One of Childs's grandchildren, John Fife Symington, became governor of Arizona, only to be shamed by accusations of bank fraud during the savings-and-loan scandals of the early 1990s.

Perhaps best known and most successful of the Frick heirs was his daughter, Helen. At the time of Frick's death, estimates of the value of her inheritance were as high as $38 million. By the time she died, in 1984, *Forbes* magazine reported the value of her estate at more than $150 million.

A noted philanthropist in her own right, Helen Clay Frick, who never married, held convictions scarcely less rigid than her father's. Having developed a near-pathological antipathy toward things German as a result of that country's actions in two world wars, she always insisted that the Fricks were Swiss, not German, and even tried to reclaim a building she'd donated to the University of Pittsburgh when that institution persisted in hiring professors with German-sounding names and including modern art in its collections.

One of her most notable actions—aside from the formation of the Frick Art Reference Library, adjunct to the Frick Collection in New York, and the endowment that would develop her childhood home of Clayton into a formidable art and historical museum (including that "lesser," two-ton, twelve-foot high, still-functioning Orchestrion)—was the filing of a lawsuit in 1965 against the historian Sylvester K. Stevens, who had made the mistake of including a few brief, if mildly derogatory, remarks concerning her father's personal style and relations with labor in a volume with the decidedly uninflammatory title *Pennsylvania: Birthplace of a Nation.*

Though the suit, directed at both Stevens and his publisher, Random House, was dismissed after more than two years of wrangling, it represented an unprecedented attack on the academic and publishing establishments, which discovered just how difficult and expensive it could be to prove that the dead could not be defamed, especially by the facts. Said the judge in rendering his opinion: "Miss Frick might as well try to enjoin publication of the Holy Bible, because, being a descendant of Eve, she does not believe that Eve gave Adam the forbidden fruit . . . and her senses are offended by such a statement."

◆     ◆     ◆

THAT HELEN FRICK WAS SUFFICIENTLY OUTRAGED by reference to her father as "stern, brusque, [and] autocratic" to spend a significant sum attempting to expunge such language from a mild-mannered volume of history should be no surprise, for passions have always run hot in the vicinity of Frick. After the final resolution of the strike of 1892, the *New York Times* carried the story of a cook at the Homestead works who had confessed to poisoning the food of the hated scabs whom Frick had installed at the factory. Six men were reported dead, and scores more were hospitalized. Even the comfortable quarters Frick had created for his imported labor behind the walls of his "fort" could not insulate them from the rancor of the displaced men.

Likewise, there remain to this day Monongahela Valley establishments where a Frick or Carnegie might be unwise to dine, and many households where the thought of stepping foot inside a Carnegie library would be an act of heresy against every workingman ever born or yet to be—and this more than one hundred years in the lee of the Battle of Homestead. Tour guides leading groups from buses to a lovingly restored Clayton in Pittsburgh's east end have witnessed men and women turn on their heels the moment it was revealed that the beautiful Victorian mansion the group was about to enter had once been the home of Henry Clay Frick.

Meanwhile, the seeds of dissension that gave rise to the Battle of Homestead continue to fuel debate in the nation's every nook and cranny—*especially* in its nooks and crannies.

Some will say that in this country the likes of Frick and Carnegie can still rise from nothing, just as a peanut farmer from Georgia can become president. But others will ask how much room there truly is at the top of the pyramid. And while every American loves a bargain, how many profit when a national retail behemoth purveying hardware, clothing, groceries, and more comes to Everytown and annihilates the local mom-and-pop establishments with rock-bottom pricing, all the while paying the minimum wage and actively opposing unionization—just like Carnegie and Frick?

Unions in general continue their struggle to achieve that vaunted commonality of interests that Carnegie was quick to invoke. At the turn of the twentieth century, the time of the formation of U.S. Steel, about 13 percent of nonagricultural workers in the U.S. were unionized. The figure rose to about 40 percent by 1950, but then both industrialization and unionization began a steady and intertwined decline. In 2000 the percentage of unionized workers had sunk to 13.5 percent—just where it was when Carnegie and Frick held sway over the new steel industry.

In the middle of the twentieth century, nearly half of American workers were employed in manufacturing. By 2000, the figure had diminished to less than 15 percent.

Whatever one's position on the rights of industrial workers to organize and strike, the issue may soon be hypothetical in the United States, where a 1992 third-party presidential candidate claimed to hear a "giant sucking sound" as jobs poured out of the country. Euphemistically termed "outsourcing" these days, the practice is as common in the steel industry as in any other.

While steel is still produced in Pittsburgh and elsewhere in the United States, production is down from more than half of the world's total to about 12 percent. Though a modernized and much diminished Edgar Thomson Works still operates in Braddock, local observers point out that few of its employees are drawn from the surrounding community. The streets of the nearby Braddock business district, if one can call it that, are a bleak warren of boarded-over shops and businesses shuttered for decades.

Open-hearth and blast furnaces are a thing of the past in the United States, where most steel is produced in non-union or "mini" mills devoted to the recycling of scrap iron or the making of highly specialized, technologically dependent alloys in smaller (if significantly cleaner) electric-powered furnaces. The total number of steelworkers, which rose to a historic peak of 650,000 in 1953, declined to about 120,000 by 1990 and to 80,000 at the turn of the twenty-first century, a trend that reflects the deployment of the American workforce in general.

According to a recent report by the Department of Labor, 308,000 new jobs were opened to American workers in March 2004. About 70,000 of those were in construction, almost 50,000 in retail, 40,000 in professional and business services, another 40,000 in health and education, 30,000 in tourism and hospitality, and 30,000 in the government sector. The number of new jobs in manufacturing? Not one.

Surveys showed that workers' wages rose all of 0.6 percent in 2003; during the same period, the average CEO received a 16-percent salary increase and a 20-percent hike in bonus pay—hardly reflective of Carnegie's insistence that the interests of capital and labor are one. In another study, by Northeastern University, researchers showed that while the economy was indeed on the rise once more at the beginning of the twenty-first century, American workers received their lowest share of the nation's income growth since the days of World War II.

A RECITATION OF SUCH STATISTICS and a tour through the streets of the former bustling steel towns on the Monongahela suggest that history has traveled in one great circle in the century since Carnegie and Frick brought their enterprise to the apex of the Western world. Carnegie finally built a library for the workers of Homestead in 1898, an even grander sandstone monument than its counterpart across the river in Braddock. The building, complete with pool, auditorium, and lofty reading rooms, still stands, not far from where General Snowden's troops once camped, keeping a watchful eye over the nearby town. And it is likely that the number of workingmen and -women from Homestead and Munhall who find the time to take some pleasure there is about the same as it was a century ago.

For all that, if an outsider were to saunter into a Pittsburgh tavern today and utter a few salient criticisms of capitalism or the American Way, it would be an invitation to a brawl. Although hard-liners remain who would never set foot inside a Carnegie building, those libraries in Braddock and Homestead are well used. Afternoons and evenings find them full of schoolchildren pulling down books from shelves, navigating the Internet at computer banks, and hard at work at school projects on venerable wooden tables that sit beneath lofty ceilings that "wee Andra" built.

Furthermore, most of the children in those rooms are convinced they have a shot at a good life—a job, a healthy family, and a home, at the very least. Some dream that the sky is the limit, and it is difficult to imagine a parent who'd look them in the eye and say the least bit different.

◆　　◆　　◆

ONE OF CARNEGIE'S LIBRARIES WENT UP in the blue-collar hill town of Cambridge, Ohio, shortly after the turn of the century. It wasn't on the scale of those virtual palaces in Braddock and Homestead; the library grants were tied to the size of the population, and Cambridge was an unprepossessing town of a few thousand souls. It remained pretty much that way into the 1950s, when I got my first library card there.

To me, however, the building seemed grand. The staircases were broad and made of marble, the ceilings were high, the walls paneled in wood, and everyone inside moved carefully and spoke softly, the way they did in church. Certainly, the books I read there opened onto grand and boundless vistas. It is even possible that I read of the amazing rags-to-riches rise of the Scottish immigrant Andrew Carnegie.

What I do remember reading there is a series of letters from a distant pen pal. It was something my sixth-grade teacher had inveigled us into—a flurry of correspondence between boys and girls in Cambridge and their counterparts in various foreign places. Our teacher was the nexus, dealing out letters from the front of the classroom every couple of weeks like an army noncom at mail call.

My pen pal happened to be a young woman named Joyce Scott, who lived in Edinburgh, Scotland, about fifteen miles southeast (as the crow flies) from a place called Dunfermline. Joyce sent me a grainy black-and-white picture once, which showed her in a knee-length coat and scarf, atop a wind-whipped hillside overlooking an enormous body of water called the Firth of Forth. She might as well have told me she was on the surface of the moon.

I would read and reread Joyce's letters between homework stints in the library, where I spent my after-school hours while my mother finished up her shift at Champion Spark Plug and my father his at Continental Can. I recall the letters being mostly filled with descriptions of everyday life in Scotland, but it all sounded pretty exotic compared to mine.

One letter, one of the last I received, stunned me. Joyce was about fourteen, three years older than I, and she wrote that she had made an important choice at school. Next year she'd go into training for the trades—a curriculum designed for a career as a secretary or stenographer. That was the way things worked over there, she wrote. One didn't later decide to go to college. She had chosen. She was fourteen and now she knew what she would be, presumably forever.

When my mother picked me up at the library that evening, I thrust the letter at her and demanded an explanation. How could you be forced to make a decision like that at such an age? How could it work that way anywhere?

My mother glanced up from the letter and shook her head. The letter must have seemed as strange to her as to me; despite the fact that she had worked the assembly line all her adult life, she saw no reason why her son would have to. "I don't know," she said, finally. "I really don't know."

◆　　　◆　　　◆

IT WAS THE DREAM OF ALCHEMISTS to transform base metal into gold, and it could be argued that by combining iron ore and coke to create the richest and most powerful manufacturing entity on earth, Andrew Carnegie and Henry Clay Frick succeeded in doing just that. It cannot be overlooked, however, that they accomplished this at the expense of thousands who labored more arduously and at greater peril than anyone should ever have to.

Henry Frick never expressed a shred of public doubt about what happened at Homestead. And while Carnegie danced around the matter, he was never quite able to admit his own culpability, either.

Freud reminds us that there will always be a contest between the hairy, insatiable id and the colorless and repressive counter-self. The goal is not to choose one or the other, we are told, but to properly integrate the two. When we look at Frick and Carnegie, then, perhaps what we see are two men unable to choose—men at war with themselves. Men who reflect the wars within ourselves.

But whether one views Frick and Carnegie as rags-to-riches heroes, greed-mongers, or something in between, their contributions to the emergence of the United States as the economic leader of the world are undeniable. Over the half-century or so of their combined business careers, they saw—and in large part saw to—the transformation of an undeveloped and rawboned United States, divided by geography and any number of provincial interests, into the most powerful nation in the world. That much is a legacy to stand in awe of, even if their methods were sometimes faulty and even if the full promise of that legacy remains to be achieved.

That would seem to leave the matter up to those of us who follow in the footsteps of the guilt-ridden champion of capitalism and his unrepentant shadow self. Otherwise we are sentenced to roll that Sisyphean boulder of accomplishment up its steep slope and then watch it, always, roll back down again.

Not capital or labor, then. Not capitalism or something else.

Balance. Here. Where we live and work and strive for something better. Every day.

# SELECT BIBLIOGRAPHY

———◆—◆—

A LIST OF ALL THE SOURCES containing information that bears upon the lives and times of Andrew Carnegie and Henry Clay Frick, the development of the steel industry, and that industry's impact upon the economic development of the United States would be virtually endless. The principal repository for the personal papers of Andrew Carnegie is found at the Library of Congress in Washington, D.C. Considerable correspondence and other archival materials, especially that pertaining to the business dealings of Henry Clay Frick and Andrew Carnegie, reside in the archives of the University of Pittsburgh's Hillman Library. The main repository for the personal papers of Henry Clay Frick, particularly those materials bearing upon his formidable collection, is found at the Frick Art and Reference Library in New York City.

For the reader interested in delving deeper into the subjects and events touched upon in this book, I have listed some of the principal titles and their authors. I am greatly indebted to them all.

Berkman, Alexander. *Prison Memoirs of an Anarchist.* New York: Schocken, 1970.

Bridge, James Howard. *The Inside History of the Carnegie Steel Company: A Romance of Millions.* Pittsburgh: University of Pittsburgh Press, 1991 (reprint).

Carnegie, Andrew. *The Autobiography of Andrew Carnegie*. Boston: Northeastern University Press, 1986.

———. *The Gospel of Wealth and Other Timely Essays*. New York: Century, 1900.

Demarest, David P., Jr., ed. *The River Ran Red: Homestead 1892*. Pittsburgh: University of Pittsburgh Press, 1992.

Fabian, Larry L. *Andrew Carnegie's Peace Endowment: The Tycoon, the President, and Their Bargain of 1910*. Washington, D.C.: Carnegie Endowment for International Peace, 1985.

Garland, Hamlin. "Homestead and Its Perilous Trades," *McClure's*, June 1894.

Goldman, Emma. *Living My Life*. New York: Dover, 1970.

Harvey, George. *Henry Clay Frick: The Man*. Private edition, 1936 (reprint).

Hendrick, Burton J. *The Life of Andrew Carnegie*. New York: Doubleday, 1932.

Hessen, Robert. *Steel Titan: The Life of Charles M. Schwab*. New York: Oxford University Press, 1975.

Ingham, John N. *The Iron Barons: A Social Analysis of an American Urban Elite, 1874–1965*. Westport, CT: Greenwood, 1978.

Krass, Peter. *Carnegie*. New York: Wiley, 2002.

Krause, Paul. *The Battle for Homestead, 1880–1892: Politics, Culture, and Steel*. Pittsburgh: University of Pittsburgh Press, 1992.

Livesay, Harold C. *Andrew Carnegie and the Rise of Big Business*. New York: Longman, 2000.

McCullough, David. *The Johnstown Flood*. New York: Simon & Schuster, 1968.

Sanger, Martha Frick Symington. *Henry Clay Frick: An Intimate Portrait*. New York: Abbeville, 1998.

———. *The Henry Clay Frick Houses: Architecture, Interiors, Landscapes in the Golden Era*. New York: Monacelli Press, 2001.

Schreiner, Samuel A., Jr. *Henry Clay Frick: The Gospel of Greed*. New York: St. Martin's, 1995.

Tedlow, Richard S. *Giants of Enterprise: Seven Business Innovators and the Empires They Built.* New York: HarperCollins, 2001.

Wall, Joseph Frazier. *Andrew Carnegie.* New York: Oxford University Press, 1970.

Warren, Kenneth. *Triumphant Capitalism: Henry Clay Frick and the Industrial Transformation of America.* Pittsburgh: University of Pittsburgh Press, 1996.

Weber, Max. *Economy and Society.* Edited by Guenther Roth and Claus Wittick. New York: Bedminster Press, 1968.

Weingartner, Frannia, ed. *Clayton: The Pittsburgh Home of Henry Clay Frick.* Pittsburgh: Helen Clay Frick Foundation, 1988.

# INDEX

# ABOUT THE AUTHOR

**Les Standiford** is the bestselling author of fourteen books, including the novels *Bone Key* and *Havana Run* and the critically acclaimed work of nonfiction *Last Train to Paradise: Henry Flagler and the Spectacular Rise and Fall of the Railroad That Crossed an Ocean*. He has received the Barnes & Noble Discover Great New Writers Award, the Frank O'Connor Award for Short Fiction, and fellowships from the National Endowment for the Arts and the National Endowment for the Humanities. A native Ohioan, he is a graduate of Muskingum College and holds an M.A. and a Ph.D. from the University of Utah. He is Professor of English and Director of the Creative Writing Program at Florida International University in Miami, where he lives with his wife, Kimberly, a psychotherapist, and their three children, Jeremy, Hannah, and Alexander. Visit his website at www.les-standiford.com.